Dav...

Young Students Encyclopedia

19

Tornado

Westward Movement

Funk & Wagnalls, Inc.
New York, N.Y.

Library of Congress Catalog No. 76-179290
Printed in U.S.A.

Acknowledgements

All photographs supplied by Armando Curcio Editore, SpA, except the following:

Federal Bureau of Investigation–page 2843.

Philip Grushkin–pages 2876 (Hawaii), 2940 top.

The Joseph Mordecai Hirschmann Collection, courtesy of Leah Read Barkowitz–page 2891.

Russell F. Hogeland–pages 2857 bottom, 2935 bottom, 2938 bottom.

Iowa Development Commission–pages 2834, 2876 (farm).

Library of Congress–pages 2852, 2859 bottom, 2865 top, 2927 bottom, 2954.

Mack Trucks, Inc.–pages 2847 bottom, 2848 bottom.

Maine Dept. of Economic Development–pages 2816 top, 2817 top left.

Michigan Tourist Council–page 2816 bottom.

Charlotte M. Mitchell–page 2896 top, 2896 bottom.

NASA–pages 2922 left, 2922 right, 2955 bottom.

National Galley of Art, Washington, D.C.–page 2934.

National Historical Wax Museum, Washington, D.C.–page 2947 top.

National Park Service–page 2837 top (by Cecil W. Stroughton), 2921.

Nebraska Game and Parks Commission–pages 2832, 2942.

New Hampshire State Division of Economic Development–page 2876 (skier).

New Mexico State Tourist Bureau–page 2879 bottom left.

New York State Dept. of Commerce–page 2880 bottom.

Daniel Ocko–page 2829 right.

Oregon State Highway Photo–pages 2876 (Portland), 2878 left.

San Francisco Convention and Visitors Bureau–page 2879 bottom right.

State of North Carolina Dept. of Natural and Economic Resources–page 2878 right.

Trans World Airlines Photo–page 2815 bottom.

United Air Lines–pages 2831 bottom, 2833.

United Press International Photo–pages 2819 bottom, 2838 top, 2842, 2849 bottom, 2853 top, 2869 bottom.

U. S. Air Force Photo–pages 2882, 2951 top.

USDA Photo–pages 2813 top, 2871, 2950, 2957 bottom (SCS Photo by Erwin W. Cole).

U. S. Naval Observatory–page 2876 (telescope).

U. S. Navy Official Photograph–pages 2881 right, 2908, 2951 bottom.

U. S. Virgin Islands Government Information Center–pages 2818 bottom, 2961 top.

Utah Travel Council–pages 2875 top, 2887 bottom, 2940 bottom.

Vermont Development Dept. Photo–pages 2837 bottom, 2876 (church), 2901, 2903 top, 2903 bottom.

Virginia State Travel Service–pages 2836, 2876 (cannon), 2914 bottom, 2915 top, 2915 bottom.

Harold Wang–page 2817 center.

Washington State Dept. of Commerce and Economic Development–pages 2930 top, 2930 bottom, 2931 top.

West Virginia Dept. of Commerce–pages 2964 bottom, 2966 top left, 2966 top right.

T. C. Young–pages 2846 top, 2945 top.

Maps from the Pictograph Corporation.

Children and adults alike can enjoy the hundreds of beaches in the United States. Those who do not live near the ocean can often find a nearby lake beach such as this one in Michigan. (See UNITED STATES OF AMERICA.*)*

TORNADO A tornado is one of the most violent and destructive of all storms. A tornado is a storm in which winds whirl around at speeds of 600 miles an hour or more. A tornado may be only 100 feet wide and is seldom wider than a mile. Its path may be only 10 miles long and rarely is more than 100 miles.

Tornadoes start in muggy thunderstorm weather, usually in late spring and summer. Hot, moist air begins to rise rapidly from the ground. Temperature conditions higher up cause the rising air to begin to whirl. The whirling air may spin at speeds of 100 to 600 miles an hour. This forms a long, funnel-shaped cloud that reaches from low-hanging clouds to the ground. Within the funnel, the rising air reaches speeds of 200 miles an hour. This updraft picks up much dust. The dust and water droplets in the tornado cloud give the tornado its dark appearance. The lower end of the tornado funnel may rise from the ground and descend again several times before it finally disappears upward into the clouds.

The great speed and force of tornado winds can pick up things as heavy as automobiles and hurl them hundreds of yards. The updraft causes a very low air pressure within the funnel. If the funnel passes over a building, air pressure outside the building is suddenly lower than inside. As a result, the building may explode outward.

There are 150 to 200 tornadoes in the United States every year. Most are in the Midwest, but tornadoes also occur as far north and east as New England. Australia and the Soviet Union also have tornadoes. *Waterspouts* are tornadoes over the ocean. Tornadoes cause millions of dollars in damage and sometimes kill many people.

ALSO READ: AIR PRESSURE, CLOUD, HUMIDITY, HURRICANE, LIGHTNING AND THUNDER.

▲*The funnel-shaped cloud of a tornado twists its destructive path through a Kansas town.*

TOTEM A totem is an animal, plant, or object in nature that a particular group or clan holds in high regard. People who revere totems often believe that they are descended from the totem. They may use its name to designate their clan or use a symbol of the totem to decorate their property. They may also have rules against killing the totem creature or eating it.

Totems are revered in Australia, Africa, Asia, and North and South America. Indians in the Pacific Northwest carved and painted the images of their totems on totem poles. The poles told the history of a family or clan. They were erected in front of the owner's house or over the grave of a dead ancestor.

These huge poles represent some of the most accomplished art of the American Indian. Some of them soar 30 feet in the air. The entire pole reflected both the totem of its owner and the achievements of his life.

ALSO READ: INDIANS, AMERICAN; RELIGION.

▼*Totem poles highlight an exhibit of Northwest Coast Indian art.*

TOUCH Touch, or feeling, is one of the five senses. The organs that register touch are nerve endings in the cells of the skin. The nerve endings, or *end organs,* are found in the *dermis,* the bottom layer of skin. They are not distributed evenly throughout the body. The fingertips and tongue have the most end organs. These parts of the body are the most sensitive to touch. The back has the fewest end organs, so it is the least sensitive.

Blindfold yourself with a handkerchief. Ask a friend to press a pencil point lightly on the top of a finger of your upturned hand. Have him repeat this action, using two pencil points held about a quarter of an inch apart. Let your friend continue to press the pencil points on your fingertips, sometimes using one point and sometimes two. You probably will have no trouble telling whether he is using one or two. Have him repeat this action on the skin of your back, between your shoulder blades. Now, you probably will not be able to tell how many pencil points are being used. Touch the back of your hand with the point of a pencil. At some points the pencil will feel cold. Do you know why?

Touch is usually thought of as a single sense, but the sensation of touch is really a combination of five different kinds of feelings—pressure, pain, contact, heat, and cold. The different kinds of end organs for pressure, pain, contact, heat, and cold are distributed unevenly over the body. Because of this, some areas of the body may be more sensitive to a particular kind of feeling, such as heat, than others.

ALSO READ: NERVOUS SYSTEM, SENSE ORGAN, SKIN.

▼*A painting of Jane Avril by Henri de Toulouse-Lautrec.*

TOULOUSE-LAUTREC, HENRI DE (1864–1901) Henri de Toulouse-Lautrec was the son of a French count. At the age of 13, Toulouse-Lautrec slipped on a hardwood floor and broke one leg. The next year he fell into a dry creek bed and broke the other one. Neither break mended properly, and his legs stopped growing.

In his early years, Toulouse-Lautrec studied painting with various well-known teachers. His family was wealthy, so he did not have to depend on painting for a living.

He was fascinated by the world of nightclubs, cafés, and dance halls. Lautrec spent long hours in Paris nightclubs sketching the people and trying to capture the drama of their lives on paper. This lonely little man loved the company of these colorful people—the singers, dancers, and other performers. Lautrec could put a sense of "right now" in his work, and from his pictures we get a glimpse of the night life in Paris during the late 1800s.

Look at Lautrec's oil painting (shown here) of a dancer named Jane Avril. His skillful brushwork captures a feeling of movement and action. Yet Lautrec also tries to show the pert dancer's character. This is not a picture of just anyone dancing. This is Jane Avril—a very definite, frail, elegant person.

Toulouse-Lautrec also created beautiful advertising posters. He and a few other artists of his time made the printed poster a new art form. He used a Japanese style—simple lines and flat colors to create a strong feeling. The one here advertises dancer Jane Arvil, at the Jardin de Paris. Compare the painting and poster, both showing her.

In spite of the greatness of his art Lautrec remained a lonely man. He thought everyone laughed at his short, crippled body, and he felt left out of the world of normal people. He eventually became an alcoholic. His death at age 37 cut short the life and career of a kind, gentle man and a great artist.

ALSO READ: DEGAS, EDGAR; MODERN ART; PAINTING.

▲*A poster of Jane Avril by Henri de Toulouse-Lautrec.*

TOURISM see TRAVEL.

TOWER OF LONDON The Tower of London is an ancient fortress in the heart of London, England. It was first built by King William I, "the Conqueror." The Tower was a royal palace during the Middle Ages. After about 1450, it was used as a prison by the kings and queens of England. Today, the crown jewels of the royal family are kept in the Tower. The guards at the Tower are called "beefeaters." They still wear the colorful uniforms of the 1500s.

The oldest part of the Tower is the massive White Tower at the center. This is surrounded by two walls and a *moat,* or ditch. Several smaller towers were added later. Tower Bridge, built in the 1800s, leads across the Thames River to the Tower.

▼*The Tower of London (left background) stands in the city's East End. The Tower Bridge (right) crosses the Thames River.*

Many prisoners were brought to the Tower by river. They entered through the gloomy Traitor's Gate. The torture chambers in the White Tower can still be seen. Prisoners were executed either within the Tower or outside the walls on Tower Hill. Many were buried in the Tower chapel.

During the 1500s, the Tudor monarchs sent a great number of important people to the Tower. Princess Elizabeth (later Queen Elizabeth I) was imprisoned there for a short time. The statesman Sir Thomas More and two wives of King Henry VIII were executed in the Tower. Sir Walter Raleigh was imprisoned there for 13 years before he was beheaded.

ALSO READ: CROWN JEWELS, ENGLISH HISTORY, LONDON.

TOYS Dolls, wagons, balls, toy soldiers, puppets, and miniature objects have been favorite playthings of children for thousands of years. Toys may be very simple (like a rattle or a game of marbles) or very complex (like a model ship or a chemistry set). Many toys, such as cards, dice, board games, and electric train sets are enjoyed by adults as well as children. Some people

▲*Playing in the sand with a variety of beach toys can be great fun.*

keep their teddy bears for years after the usual teddy bear age. Toys are any playthings that give fun and amusement to the people who use them.

Toys and Children

The simplest toys are made for babies and very young children. Rattles, pull toys, stuffed animals, and blocks have few or no moving parts, are usually unbreakable, and give small children practice in learning to handle objects with skill. Stuffed toys and dolls are soft and cuddly, and children often become very attached to them. Children give these stuffed toys names, talk to them, take care of them as if they were alive, and play all sorts of imaginary games with them,

As a child grows older, he is able to handle and take care of more complex toys with more parts and pieces. Children push their dolls in baby carriages. They build things with sets of blocks, logs, metal girders, and Tinker Toys. They create things with clay, paint, and crayons. They can put jigsaw puzzles together and use sports equipment such as baseballs and bats.

Older children enjoy doing scientific experiments, learning to cook and sew, constructing furniture and other objects with carpenter's tools, building model airplanes, cars, and ships, plus many other things. As a child grows up, his toys become more and more the objects and tools he will use as an adult.

▼*Children have been fascinated by toy boats for almost as long as sailing vessels have cruised the oceans.*

History of Toys

Early man probably had few real toys. His whole life was taken up with getting food and protecting himself. Small children may have played with gourd rattles or toy hunting tools. But in a nomadic hunting tribe, people had little time to make toys and even less time to play with them.

Some simple toys were made as long as 6,000 years ago. Archeologists have found rough-hewn, flute-like musical instruments and balls made from animal skins and stuffed with dried reeds. Children in ancient Egypt, Greece, and Rome pulled little wheeled carts and also played games using wooden balls. They played with dolls that had movable arms and legs and with toy animals whose jaws could open and close. Puppets, toy chariots, little metal soldiers, and miniature weapons were all toys from ancient civilizations. All over the world, children and adults have played early versions of dice, jacks, marbles, chess, and other types of board games. In Asia, people have enjoyed flying kites for thousands of years. In Alexandria, Egypt, about 100 B.C., a scientist named Hero was creating very complicated *animated toys* (toys that can be made to move when wound up or cranked).

Toys have often been miniature copies of things used by adults. For this reason, toys provide a miniature record of man's

◀ *Dolls' beds are toys that can be conveniently made at home. These homemade dolls' beds were Christmas gifts.*

civilization. Just as Roman children played with chariots, children of the European Middle Ages played with tiny horses, knights in armor, toy lances, spears, and bows and arrows. Dolls were dressed in long, flowing robes in the same styles as adult clothing of those times. Toy making became a skilled profession, and craftsmen traveled from town to town selling their toys.

In the early 1900s, the United States, Great Britain, and Japan began making toys for export all over the world. Many old-style toys were made with wind-up mechanisms and electrical motors inside to make them move. New inventions, such as airplanes, submarines, automobiles, trucks, space vehicles, military tanks, and weapons, began to be copied in toys.

Today, with the exception of a few special, handmade toys, almost all toys are produced in factories. Toys are made from a wide variety of materials—wood, rubber, metal, cloth, paper, and plastics. By walking through a toy store, you can see the objects of today's world in miniature.

▲ *A hobbyist put together these toy soldiers and a model train to show in miniature a daring raid during the Civil War.*

Toy Safety

The U.S. government, toy companies, and many parents' organizations have become interested in the safety of toys. The Product Safety Division of the Food and Drug Administration sets up rules for toy manufacture. Electrical toys must have safe wiring. Toys cannot be made of materials that burn or break easily. Toys must be non-poisonous.

Parents' organizations investigate new toys, checking them for all possible safety hazards. They test toys to make sure they are well designed and sturdily built. These parent groups send their suggestions to the toy manufacturers who usually cooperate in altering toys that may be unsafe.

▼ *This toy power shovel is a model of a real one.*

A Toy You Can Make

Toys do not have to be expensive to be fun. Some of the best toys are the ones you make yourself. Any kind of sturdy fabric can be used to make a beanbag or stuffed toy. First decide what shape you want your beanbag to be and draw the outline

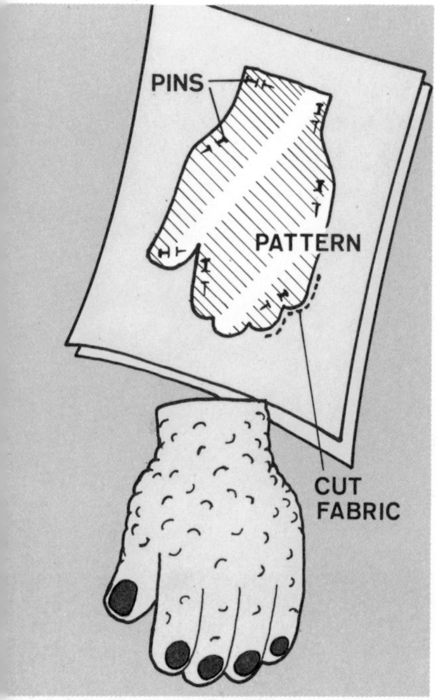

on a piece of newspaper. A turtle pattern is easy to draw, or perhaps you prefer a bear, a horse, a giraffe, or an elephant. Funny beanbags can be made by using your own or someone else's hand or foot as the pattern. Be sure to make the pattern fairly large.

Once your pattern is drawn, cut it out and pin it to a double layer of fabric. Then cut the fabric along the edges of your pattern. You should now have two pieces of fabric the same shape as the pattern. Put the two pieces together evenly so that the surfaces you will want on the outside are facing each other. Sew the beanbag tightly all around the edges, leaving an opening. Turn the beanbag inside out so your stitching will be on the inside. Now stuff your beanbag. You can use dried lima beans (from the grocery) or small pebbles. If you are making a stuffed toy, use cotton or old rags that have been cut into small pieces. After you have sewn up the opening, decide how you want to decorate your beanbag. Buttons make good eyes and yarn makes good hair. If your beanbag is a hand or a foot, you can make fingernails and toenails from pieces of red cloth.

ALSO READ: DOLL.

TRACK AND FIELD The athletic events that include running races, jumping contests, and weight-throwing contests are called track and field sports.

Races are run on an oval-shaped track. Outdoor tracks are usually made of earth with a hard-packed cinder surface. Indoor tracks are made of wood. An outdoor track is a quarter of a mile, or 440 yards, around. To run a mile you would have to go around the track four times. An indoor track is usually much smaller.

Jumping and weight-throwing contests are held on the field inside the oval track. That is why they are called field events. Sometimes the weight-throwing events are held on fields away from the track to avoid the danger of runners and jumpers being hit by the weights being thrown.

▼*Three young sprinters dash toward the finish line during a school track meet in the Virgin Islands.*

Track events are timed for speed and field events are measured for distance. The fastest times and the greatest distances are called *records.* There are world records, Olympic records, records for each country, intercollegiate records, interscholastic records, meet records, and records for each school and college. Perhaps your school has a set of track records.

The great Jesse Owens set three world records in a college meet in 1935. The records were for the 220-yard dash, the 220-yard low hurdles, and the broad jump (now called the *long jump*). Owens's record for the broad jump–26 feet, 8¼ inches –remained unbroken until 1968. In that year, at the Olympic Games in Mexico, Robert Beamon of the U.S. broke Owen's record with an incredible jump of 29 feet, 2½ inches.

All international track and field events are measured by the metric system. Races are held at 100 meters, 200 meters, and so on. In the United States, Canada, and Great Britain, the events are usually measured in yards.

Track Events

DASHES. The shortest and swiftest running events are called "dashes," or "sprints." Indoor dashes are run over distances of 40, 50, or 60 yards. Outdoors, the distances are 100 yards or 100 meters, and 220 yards or 200 meters. In running the dashes, the athlete crouches at the starting line with his feet placed in special starting blocks. At the crack of the starter's pistol, the runner pushes off from the blocks, straightens up, and runs at full speed to the finish line. The first runner to break the tape stretched across the finish line is the winner of the race.

▲*A group of cross-country runners are still closely bunched just after the start of a race. After a few miles, they will be strung out over a distance.*

MIDDLE DISTANCES. Races ranging from 440 yards to two miles are called middle-distance races. They include the 880-yard and one-mile races, the 400, 800, 1,500, and 3,000 meter races. The 440-yard and 400-meter races are run as dashes almost all the way. In these events, the runners go at top speed for about 200 yards, then "coast," or relax a bit for 150 yards, and finish the race with final bursts of speed. Champions run these distances in less than 46 seconds. In the other middle-distance races, the runners do not go at top speed until they are about 150 yards from the finish line. The mile run is one of the most popular track events. For many years the world record for this race was over four minutes. In 1954, Roger Bannister of England ran the mile in 3 minutes, 59.4 seconds. Since that time, the record has been broken many times. In 1967, Jim Ryun of the U.S. set a record of 3 minutes, 51.1 seconds.

DISTANCE RUNS. Races longer than two miles are considered distance events. They include three-mile, six-mile, 5,000-meter and 10,000-meter runs. All of these races are held on a track. Some races are called cross-country races, and they are run over fields and hills for a distance of six miles. The longest race is the *marathon,* which is usually run on roads. The marathon distance is 26 miles, 385 yards. This is the distance a Greek messenger is supposed to have run in bringing the news of a Greek victory from the battlefield of Marathon to Athens.

▼*The woman at the right has almost cleared a hurdle as her opponent just starts her long leap over the high barrier.*

HURDLES. Hurdling events are races in which the runner must jump over a series of wooden fences called hurdles. The hurdles are evenly spaced between the start and finish of a race. Indoors, races are run at 50, 60, and 70 yard distances over high hurdles. High hurdles stand at 3 feet, 6 inches from the ground. Outdoor high-hurdle races are held at 120 yards or 110 meters. Races at 220 yards or 200 meters are over low hurdles which stand at 2 feet, 6 inches from the ground. The 440-yard or 400-meter races are run over intermediate hurdles which are 3

▲*A runner finishes his lap of a relay race and passes the baton to his teammate.*

feet high. In all hurdle races a runner must clear the hurdles without breaking the rhythm of his stride. The runner must have the speed of a sprinter plus excellent coordination and timing. A longer type of hurdle race is called the *steeplechase.* This event is run over a 3,000-meter course in which the runners must jump over hurdles, hedges, and pools of water.

RELAY RACES. Team events in track are called relay races. In these events, teams of four runners compete against other teams. Each man runs a given distance, called a *leg,* then passes a *baton* (stick) to the next man. The most popular relay races are at 440 yards, 880 yards, and one mile. Metric relay races are at 400, 800, and 1,500 meters.

WALKING RACES. The walking events in a track meet are held at various distances from one mile or 1,500 meters to as long as 25 miles or 50,000 meters. Walking races are fun to watch because the contestants seem to shuffle along in an awkward manner. The rules state that the heel of a walker's forward foot must touch the ground before the toe of his rear foot leaves the ground. Try walking in this way and see how different it is from your normal way of walking!

Field Events

The distances in the field events are measured either in feet and inches or in the metric system (meters and centimeters). Each contestant in these events gets three tries. Jumpers need speed, springy legs, and good muscular coordination. Weight throwers must be heavy and powerful.

LONG JUMP. In the long jump (formerly called the broad jump), the contestant dashes along a marked path, springs into the air from a take-off board, and tries to jump as far as he can. While still in the air, the jumper does a bicycle kick and then tries to stretch his legs out in front of him without losing his balance. The jump is no good if he falls backward after landing.

TRIPLE JUMP. This event was once called the *hop, step, and jump.* The jumper dashes down the path as he would for a long jump. He hops into the air from the take-off board and comes down on his take-off foot. He then steps or "springs" forward on that foot, lands on the other foot, jumps into the air once more, and lands in the sawdust pit as a long jumper does.

▼*A high jumper is about to clear the bar using the belly roll.*

HIGH JUMP. In this jump, a contestant has to leap over a crossbar resting on two upright supports that stand about 12 feet apart. There are several jumping styles, such as the *Western roll,* the *belly roll,* and the *dive.* In the Western roll, the jumper "rolls" across the bar with his back to it. In the belly roll, he clears the bar face down. In the dive, he dives across the bar head first. All high jumpers run toward the bar from about a 45-degree angle, spring upward from the take-off foot, and kick powerfully with the other foot. The jumpers land in a pit covered with sawdust or plastic cushions. A high jump of over seven feet is considered excellent.

THE VAULT. In the pole vault, the crossbar is set in the same way as it is for the high jump, but at much greater heights. The vaulter holds the pole, with one hand a few feet from the top of the pole and his other hand a few feet lower down. He races down the runway, digs the tip of the pole into a slot in the ground, and swings upward toward the bar. As his feet near the bar, the vaulter is almost doing a handstand on the pole. He pushes the pole away from him and drops feet first over the bar into a padded pit. His body may just graze the bar, but if he knocks the bar off the uprights, the vault is no good. A vaulter must have speed, powerful arm and shoulder muscles, and acrobatic ability. Until about 30 years ago, bamboo poles were used and the best vaulters cleared the bar at about 13 feet. Then aluminum poles were used, and vaulters were able to go over 15 feet. Recently, fiber glass poles were introduced. These poles bend and "whip" the vaulter much higher than the old poles. With fiber glass poles, vaulters now clear 18 feet.

▲*High in the sky, a vaulter pushes away from his pole and hopes that his body will not knock the bar down.*

SHOT PUT. In this weight-throwing event, a round metal ball (called a *shot*) is used. The standard shot weighs 16 pounds. The one used in high school events weighs 12 pounds, and an 8-pound shot may be used by younger athletes and women. The shot putter stands at the back of a seven-foot circle. He holds the shot in the palm and fingers of his throwing hand and rests the hand against his shoulder. He then hops across the circle in a half-crouch. When he reaches the front edge of the circle he straightens up suddenly and pushes the shot away from his shoulder. His whole body acts like a coiled spring to release the shot. Shot puts are measured from the front edge of the circle to the point where the shot hits the ground.

▼*A discus thrower puts all his muscular power behind the swing of his arm as he throws the discus.*

DISCUS THROW. A discus is a metal-rimmed wooden platter. Some are made entirely of metal. If you put two Frisbees together, you would have an object that looks like a discus. The standard discus weighs 4 pounds, 6⅔ ounces and measures about 8½ inches across. The discus thrower stands at the back of a circle about 8 feet across. He holds the discus flat against his palm and wrist, whirls rapidly around, reaches the front of the circle, and hurls the discus forward with a whipping motion of his arm. A throw is measured from the front edge of the circle to the point where the discus lands on the ground. Championship discus throwers may hurl the platter over 210 feet.

HAMMER THROW. In the hammer throw, a contestant hurls a metal ball attached to a wire which has a triangular metal handle. The ball, wire, and handle weigh 16 pounds and form a unit that is 4 feet long. The thrower stands at the back of a seven-foot circle, grips the handle with both hands, and starts whirling the hammer around his head. He then spins around three times, reaches the front edge of the circle, and releases his grip on the handle. The hammer flies outward and upward. The best throws may be over 225 feet. A variation of the hammer throw is the weight throw in which the handle is attached directly to the ball without a wire in between. The weight may be either 35 pounds or 56 pounds. The throw with the weight is made in the same way as the hammer. Because of the increased heaviness, these weights are not thrown nearly so far as the hammer.

DECATHLON. The decathlon is a two-day contest in which each contestant competes in ten events. Five events are held on one day and the other five on the next day. The events are the 100-meter dash, long jump, shot put, high jump, 400-meter run, 110-meter high hurdles, discus throw, pole vault, javelin throw, and 1,500-meter run. An athlete's score in each event is rated against an ideal score of 1,000. The ideal score for all 10 events is 10,000 points. Nobody has yet scored 10,000 points in the decathlon. The best scores are over 8,000 points. A decathlon contestant must be big and husky. He must have speed, and above all he must have strength and stamina (endurance). A shorter form of the decathlon is the *pentathlon* which has only five events.

ALSO READ: BANNISTER, ROGER; JAVELIN; OLYMPIC GAMES; OWENS, JESSE; SPORTS.

TRADE Long before man learned to write, he was taking part in trade. Perhaps a tribe heard of a land where a strong, gray-black stone for axes could be found. The tribe had an abundant supply of furs, so they loaded the furs on their backs, and set off for the distant land where people had the gray-black stone (which we call flint). The people with the flint were happy to exchange some of the stones for furs. This kind of action was the beginning of commerce–trade with distant lands. The tribe with their new supply of flint returned to their own country the same way they had come. They remembered the mountains they had crossed, and the rivers they had gone through so they could use the same path again to go back for more flint. That may have been the way trade routes started.

▼*Camel caravans have been carrying merchandise on desert trade routes for centuries. This caravan is about to start out across the Nigerian desert.*

Old Trade Routes

In many parts of the world, archeologists have found evidence of trade routes that go back thousands of years. Some early routes dealt in gemstones. On one early route, a black stone called *obsidian* was carried from central Europe to Africa.

The Phoenicians on the eastern shore of the Mediterranean Sea were the first people to develop seaborne trade routes that connected with overland routes. They became great sailors and traded all around the Mediterranean Sea and along the Atlantic

Coast up to the British Isles. There they headed for the shore of Cornwall on Great Britain's southwest tip to the ancient tin mines. These enterprising traders needed tin for mixing with copper to make the alloy bronze.

The ancient Greeks introduced the use of money into commerce. Before this, trade was conducted by barter (exchange of goods). When Rome became a great city, much commerce was needed to keep it supplied with food.

Following the decline of Rome, Constantinople became the chief trade center of the Mediterranean world. Constantinople had a good money and banking system. It manufactured textiles, armor, leatherwork, metalware, and pottery. Its imports consisted of grain and raw materials for its industries. Goods came in from all directions. One trade route ran from the Black Sea up the Dneiper River into Russia, with goods being shipped overland at Novgorod into the Scandinavian territory. The furs and hides of the Scandinavians were desired by the Byzantines at Constantinople, while the Vikings took in trade the gold and silver of the Byzantines.

THE MIDDLE AGES. Little international trade took place during the European Middle Ages until the Crusades (around the 1100s). The Italian town of Venice on the Adriatic Sea built up trade with the Byzantine city of Constantinople in the east. This trade made Venice a rich city-state by the year 1200 A.D.

▲ *Roman sailing vessels carried trade goods across the Mediterranean Sea about 2,000 years ago.*

The wondrous tales told by Marco Polo, the Italian traveler to China, and reports from thousands of Europeans who went to the Holy Land on Crusades created a great desire for the silks, spices, well-made steel, and other fine things from the rich cultures of the East.

During the 1300s and 1400s, trade kept increasing in northern Europe as nations developed. Trade spurred the growth of towns such as Amsterdam, Hamburg, London, Antwerp, and Cologne. Every year fleets of galleys from the Mediterranean loaded with silks and spices sailed up the Atlantic coast to Bruges, Flanders (now Belgium) and then to London. The ships came back loaded with wool, hides, and metals.

Trade in silks and spices was cut off from northern Europe when the Ottoman Turks conquered Constantinople in 1453. Venice and Genoa then became the trade centers of Europe. Many traders and sailors began searching for new trade routes to the East. With the invention of the astrolabe and the compass, navigators no longer needed to stay within sight of land. The age of discovery had begun. The Portuguese gradually worked their way down the west coast of Africa and sailed around the Cape of Good Hope. Christopher Columbus headed westward in search of new trade routes to India, and ran into the Americas instead. Magellan's voyage around the world brought a whole new view of the globe.

►*Goods flowing in and out of New Orleans have made the city an important port and trade center. This scene shows bales of cotton and other merchandise on the docks in the late 1860s.*

The Beginning of Modern Trade

A great increase in world trade took place in the 1800s. Trade changed because of great inventions–steam vessels, railroads, telegraph, and telephone. Thousands of people migrated from Europe to new homes all over the world. Commerce increased, supplying new settlers all over the world with the European goods they were used to. Another new factor in the growth of world trade was investment of money by nations in foreign lands. With this investment, underdeveloped countries could provide more raw materials for trade.

TRADE CHANGES AFTER WORLD WAR II. World War II affected world trade in many ways. Before the war, the British, French, Germans, Japanese, and Americans had dominated world trade. After the war, Germany, Italy, and Japan were out of the trading markets for several years because their factories were shattered by the fighting. The United States replaced Britain as the leader in world trade. However, Japan and Germany gradually came back to strong trading positions in the world.

Look at a globe of the world and pick a very large city at random. Study its location, looking for rivers, harbors, nearby seas, and oceans. Where would the trade routes be? You can easily see why trade centers become large cities. They are connected with trade routes and have become places where goods from all over the world are imported and distributed.

ALSO READ: COLONY; COLUMBUS, CHRISTOPHER; EAST INDIA COMPANY; ECONOMICS; EXPLORATION; INDUSTRIAL REVOLUTION; INTERNATIONAL TRADE; MAGELLAN, FERDINAND; MONEY; PHOENICIA; TRANSPORTATION.

TRAFFIC PLANNING If you have ever been caught in a traffic jam, you know what a maddening experience it is. Cars and trucks stand bumper-to-bumper. Drivers lose their tempers, engines overheat, and the whole situation becomes very dangerous. It is especially dangerous in large cities that have become polluted and strangled by the flood of motor vehicles and pedestrians on the streets.

Traffic is especially bad during certain peak periods—at *rush hours* (from about 7:00 to 9:00 AM and 4:00 to 7:00 PM) when people are going to and from work, and on *holidays* when many people "take to the road" on trips. The growth of the suburbs has also added to city traffic problems. Suburbanites by the thousands drive every day to their jobs in the city. Most city streets are not designed to handle such large numbers of vehicles.

City planners and traffic experts are trying to find ways to ease the traffic problem. One of the best solutions is to establish inexpensive but efficient means of rapid public transportation, both within the city and from the city to the suburbs. But until such systems can be built, traffic planners must try to ease the present congestion on the streets. To do this, planners have set up combinations of regulation, routing, and physical and mechanical devices.

Regulation is the job of traffic policemen. It involves strict enforcement of traffic laws. If traffic laws (such as no double parking, no blocking of intersections, and so on) are not enforced, then traffic jams will result no matter what else is done. Pedestrian laws must also be enforced to keep people on foot from blocking traffic at intersections.

Routing involves a number of things. A road may be made into a permanent one-way street when traffic on it is always heavy in one direction. A street may be one-way into the center of the city in the morning, and one-way going out of the city in the evening. Some cities are considering banning all auto traffic from downtown areas. Suggestions have even been made to route all auto traffic onto underground streets, leaving the surface for pedestrians and delivery trucks.

Physical and mechanical ways of controlling traffic involve everything from new road construction to better traffic lights. Most traffic planners have concluded that building bigger and wider roads does not solve traffic problems. When a bigger road is built, more cars start coming into the city. The new roads soon become as badly congested as the old narrow streets.

Various systems of traffic lights have been tried. One is called the *synchronized block system,* in which all traffic lights on one street turn red at the same time, while the signals for the cross streets turn green. All traffic on a street is halted, which leads to congestion and delay. The *progressive light system* is somewhat better. Lights at intersections along the street turn green at certain intervals one after the other. This permits a vehicle moving at about 25 miles per hour to proceed along the street without a stop. But in heavily jammed traffic, this system rarely works.

Traffic signs are another device for regulating traffic. The United States is gradually beginning to use the international traffic signs found in Europe and other parts of the world. These signs give the driver information about highway regula-

▼*Good traffic planning involves, in part, trying to separate local traffic from through traffic. This model of a downtown expressway network shows how this might be done in a section of one city.*

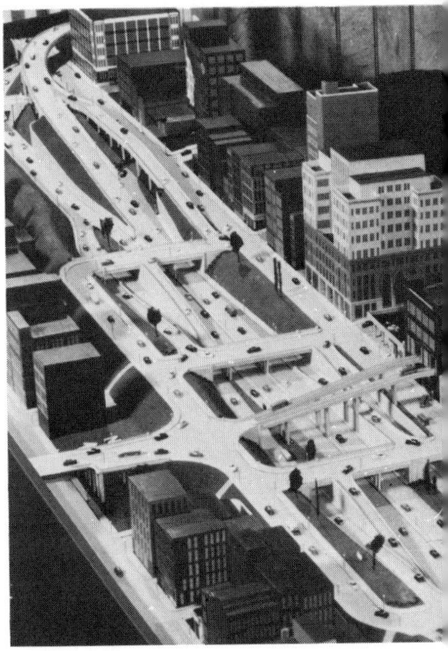

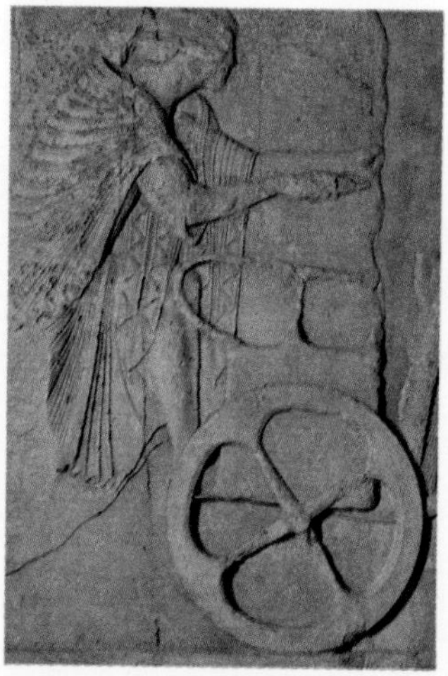

▲ *The ancient Greeks were among the first people to use the chariot for transportation. This low-relief sculpture was made over 2,500 years ago.*

tions and conditions through pictures using various colors and designs. With these picture signs, you can drive in almost any country of the world without having to know the language.

ALSO READ: AUTOMOBILE, CITY, POLICE, STREETS AND ROADS, SUBURB, TRANSPORTATION.

TRAIN see RAILROAD.

TRANSISTOR see ELECTRONICS.

TRANSPORTATION For thousands of years, man has moved from one place to another. He has traveled on foot, on the backs of animals, and in various mechanical vehicles. He has transported himself and his goods over land, on the water, through the air, under the ground, under water, and even into outer space. Whether carrying something on foot to a neighboring village or rocketing to the moon, man uses transportation.

Uses of Transportation

People have traveled and used transportation for a wide variety of reasons. The earliest and most basic reason was for survival. Primitive man hunted for his food. When food ran out in a certain area, he picked up his belongings and moved to a location where food was plentiful. Survival also meant moving to escape dangers, such as enemy attacks, floods, and fires.

People use transportation in order to trade and do business with one another. Thousands of years ago in the Middle East, long trade and caravan routes were already being used by men to carry goods over great distances. Today, man still transports goods and produce to places where they will be sold.

Transportation has always been the main tool of exploration. Marco Polo traveled by ship and overland by caravan from Italy to China in the 1200s A.D. Columbus and later explorers sailed across the Atlantic to investigate the New World. Modern-day explorers set out in spacecraft to explore the moon.

Man uses transportation for purposes of communication. In ancient times, there was no way to talk to an individual except by being in his presence. This might involve going on a long journey or sending a communication by messenger. Postal systems later developed as a means of transporting messages. Communications transport is still used in modern-day postal systems and messenger services. But the actual carrying of messages has been eliminated in such communications devices as the telephone, telegraph, radio, and television.

Today, one of the greatest uses of transportation is for pleasure. More people than ever before are traveling just to see new things and gain new experiences. At vacation times, people "hit the road," moving by car, train, plane, and ship to places of interest and relaxation. The tourist industry—businesses that cater to pleasure travelers—is one of the biggest in the world.

TRANSPORTATION THROUGH THE AGES
LAND TRANSPORTATION
Prehistory
Man pulled burdens on a sledge, tamed animals, and invented the wheel
1800s
The steam locomotive brought the railroad era
1900s
The automobile meant cheaper transportation
WATER TRANSPORTATION
Prehistory
With simple rafts man first moved over water
1200s
With the compass man sailed out of sight of land
1900s
The submarine became important in the world's navies
Prehistory
The sail was invented and man set out to sea
1800s Canal-building era brought new waterways
1900s
Huge tankers and big ocean liners revolutionized cargo and ship travel
1800s The steamship made faster travel possible
AIR TRANSPORTATION
1800s
Balloons first took man aloft
1950s
The Space Age began
1969
U.S. Astronauts landed on the moon
1930s
Airships flew briefly
1903
Wright brothers flew first airplane
1920s
Air pioneers explored in monoplanes
1970s
Supersonic airplanes crossed oceans in 2 hours
1950s
Jet aircraft made world wide air travel cheap and easy

▲*Pedicabs and bicycles, shown here on a street in Cambodia, are familiar forms of transportation in the Far East. The pedicab is pedaled just like a bicycle, but it has a passenger seat in front.*

Kinds of Transportation

Various kinds of transportation have developed with man's need to travel longer distances in shorter lengths of time. A person living in India 8,000 years ago didn't need to travel to England in a few hours. His whole life was taken up with farming and the problems of survival. He had no time and no reason to travel halfway around the globe as many people regularly do today.

WALKING. Man's built-in means of transportation is his own two feet. When you walk to school or to a friend's house, you are transporting yourself. Walking was the first transportation. A person who walks from place to place must carry his belongings with him. Man has used his hands, shoulder slings, backpacks, and even his head to transport things on his person. Then man discovered that he could move more weight if he dragged it rather than carried it.

BEASTS OF BURDEN. As people began to domesticate animals, they trained them to pull the litters and sledges. Animals used as beasts of burden are stronger than men and can pull heavier loads longer distances. Dogs were probably first used, then oxen. Throughout the world, animals such as the water buffalo, elephant, camel, llama, donkey or burro, mule, reindeer, and yak are still used to transport people and goods.

THE WHEEL. Logs used as rollers were probably forerunners of the wheel. Man discovered that a very heavy load could be transported by rolling it over a series of logs. As the load was rolled along, the last logs were pulled out and placed at the front of the load. This process was repeated over and over until the load reached its destination.

True wheels were first used about 5,000 years ago in the Middle East. Wheeled vehicles were never used in the Americas until Europeans brought them. The earliest wheels were solid sections of tree trunks firmly attached to each end of a longer and thinner piece of trunk. Over time, wheels became less cumbersome and more efficient. Ancient Middle Eastern chariots

▶*The stagecoach was a popular form of transportation in the 1700s and 1800s. This one carried passengers between Rome and Brindisi, Italy.*

had four wheels and could move quite fast. Improvements in the wheel led to all kinds of vehicles—carts, wagons, coaches, gigs, traps, cabriolets, bicycles, and automobiles.

As wheeled transportation became more and more common, more and better roads were needed. The ancient Romans constructed the first lengthy network of roads paved with stone. The Incas of South America also built a complex and well-constructed road system.

Roman roads fell into disrepair and disuse during the Middle Ages when the primary means of long-distance transportation were walking, horseback riding, or ox riding. Heavy farm carts were used, but mostly for hauling things short distances. In the 1500s and 1600s, with the development of faster coaches and gigs, new road systems were established. The development of the automobile has brought road construction to the quality it has reached today.

◀ *The first railroad trains were not much faster than horse-drawn vehicles, but they could carry much heavier loads and many more passengers. This 1832 model even hauled a carriage on a flatcar.*

Rails. In 1825, a British engineer named George Stephenson designed the first steam-powered locomotive. Railroads developed rapidly. The first U.S. transcontinental railroad was completed in 1869. Rail transportation was the first great advance in land transportation since the development of the wheel. For the first time, man could travel at significantly greater speeds and could haul many tons of goods over great distances. The Industrial Revolution, which began in the early 1800s, was given a tremendous boost by the new railroads. Manufacturers had a fast way to transport their products to distant places.

On the Water. Water transportation developed much faster than land transportation. People have been using dugouts, canoes, and rafts since earliest times. Early civilizations developed along rivers and other larger waterways. The water was used not only for irrigation of the land, but also as a means of transportation to distant places. Boats and ships were built for use in commerce, warfare, and exploration. Ships were first propelled by sails, oars, or combinations of both. With improvements in shipbuilding and rigging, and with the invention of the directional compass, seamen could travel out into the

▼ *A form of double transportation is shown here. Passenger buses are carried across a Norwegian fiord by a sturdy little ferryboat.*

open ocean, out of sight of land. By the 1600s, man could transport himself and his goods almost anywhere in the world by ship. Shipping brought about the use of maps, and the whole globe eventually became charted and explored.

The world's first successful steamboat, the *Clermont,* was built in 1807 by the American inventor Robert Fulton. As engines improved, so did the speed and capacity of the ships. Metal ships were in operation by the end of the 1800s. The construction of the Suez and Panama canals shortened considerably the routes from the Atlantic to the Indian and Pacific Oceans. Shipping is now and always has been man's quickest way of transporting gigantic tons of cargo from place to place.

IN THE AIR. In 1903, Orville and Wilbur Wright made the first successful powered airplane flight. Even though air travel is man's newest form of transportation, it enables man to travel longer distances at greater speeds than he ever dreamed possible. From propellers to jet propulsion to rocketry, men are now walking in outer space and exploring the surface of the moon.

Transportation for Tomorrow

Modern transportation is separated into four categories—shipping, railroads, motor carriers, and air carriers. The transport of people is called *passenger service,* and the transport of goods is called *freight service.*

SHIPPING. In the future, more and more ships will be nuclear powered—cargo ships as well as military vessels. *Containerization* is used for both railroad and water transport. All goods to be shipped are packed in large metal containers of a standard size. These are transported by specially built trucks or railroad cars to the dock where the containers are tightly packed in the ship's hold. Shipping is also being increased by the use of gigantic tankers to carry liquid cargo, such as oil. The Japanese have plans to set afloat a 500,000-ton tanker. The largest one now afloat weighs 209,000 tons.

The *hydrofoil* ship will be in common use for future passenger service on water. The hydrofoil, once it reaches a certain speed, raises above the water on narrow, ski-like projections. Hydrofoils are now being used by the U.S. Navy and for ferry service in the United States and Europe. The *hovercraft,* another future passenger ship, travels above the water on a cushion of air, reaching speeds of 100 miles per hour and more.

▼*A modern monorail, which carries passengers at high speed for short distances.*

RAILROADS. Railroads, too, will become automated. Trains will be dispatched and eventually even run by computer. Containerization, like that used on ships, is now used by railroads.

At present, trains have very little passenger service. People prefer cars and airplanes for traveling. But auto traffic has become too great in the cities, and airlines will not be able to handle enough of the future short-distance passenger transport.

Experiments are being done in high-speed rail travel for trips of less than 200 to 400 miles. Gas-turbine and jet engines have been successfully tested. *Monorails,* that ride passenger vehicles on one rail, are now being tested for commercial use in the U.S. Another future project is the *aerotrain* that has no wheels and travels over 250 miles per hour. It will be supported over a single track on a cushion of air.

Plans are being made to combine auto and rail transport. One plan involves giant magnets that would clamp to the roofs of cars. The cars, with people in them, would be raised to elevated tracks and whisked away to their destinations. A fantastically fast subway is also being designed. Air forced through an underground tube would propel 100 passengers in a capsule at speeds ranging from 500 to 2,000 miles per hour.

MOTOR CARRIERS. Motor carriers are primarily automobiles and trucks. New and better safety devices for autos are constantly being developed—air bags to protect passengers in a crash, seat harnesses, no-glare windshields, auto bodies that can absorb the force of a crash, and so on.

In the future, privately owned cars will probably not be allowed on the streets of crowded cities. Commuter transportation may be by small vehicles attached to conveyor belts. A passenger could drive one of these vehicles from his house to a station where the vehicle would be attached to a belt and transported into the city. The passenger would then leave the vehicle at the station. When ready to go home, the passenger would get on another vehicle. The conveyor belt would whisk him to his home station, where he would then drive the vehicle to his house.

AIR CARRIERS. Future air transportation offers many possibilities. One of the most interesting is individual rocket packs that people would wear on their backs and with which they could travel through the air to their destinations. Experimenters have already flown at speeds of 40 miles per hour.

New kinds of helicopters, or vertical take-off and landing (VTOL) craft, are also being tested. One VTOL craft can move straight up like a helicopter and then fly like a regular plane for faster and longer trips. Huge supersonic transport planes will carry an enormous quantity of goods and passengers over ever longer distances in shorter amounts of time. Nuclear-powered freight and passenger airplanes are another possibility for the future, as are nuclear-powered, helium-filled dirigibles.

OUTER SPACE. Travel in outer space will become more and more common in the future. Many kinds of vehicles (from large tractors to buses) are being designed to transport men and equipment on the moon and on the other planets of the solar system. Larger and more powerful spacecraft will come into use, some of which will be able to land at airports on Earth.

▲*In the early days of air transportation, the passengers rode in the open* (above). *Passengers in a huge, modern Boeing 747 enjoy quiet comfort and excellent service* (below).▼

Manned and unmanned space stations will be built, where scientists can set up observatories and conduct experiments in outer space. Space ships will stop at space stations for fuel, supplies, and repairs. The problem of weightlessness in space means that travelers will have to learn a whole new way of living to adapt to the weightless condition.

For further information on:

Land Transportation by Wheel, *see* AMBULANCE, AUTOMOBILE, BICYCLE, BRIDGE, BUS, CABLE CAR, CARRIAGE, CHARIOT, DRIVING, HOTELS AND MOTELS, MOTORCYCLE, RAILROAD, SOAP BOX DERBY, STREETS AND ROADS, SUBWAY, TIRE, TRAFFIC PLANNING, TRUCKS AND TRUCKING, TUNNEL.

Other Land Transportation, *see* CAMEL, DONKEY, ELEPHANT, ELEVATORS AND ESCALATORS, HORSE, HORSEBACK RIDING, PONY EXPRESS, SKIING, SLEDDING, SNOWMOBILE.

Power Sources and Instruments, *see* COMPASS, DIESEL ENGINE, ENGINE, FUEL, GAS, GASOLINE, HORSEPOWER, JET PROPULSION, MAP, MOTION, NUCLEAR ENERGY, RADAR, ROCKET, SIMPLE MACHINE, WIND.

Transportation by Air, *see* AIR-CUSHION VEHICLE, AIRLINE, AIRPLANE, AIRSHIP, AIR TRAFFIC CONTROL, AVIATION, BALLOON, GLIDER, PARACHUTE, SPACE TRAVEL.

Transportation by Water, *see* BOATS AND BOATING, CANAL, HARBORS AND PORTS, LIGHTHOUSE, MERCHANT MARINE, NAVIGATION, OCEAN LINER, SAILING, SHIPS AND SHIPPING, SUBMARINE.

Transportation Pioneers, *see* BOWDITCH, NATHANIEL; DURYEA, CHARLES AND FRANK; FORD, HENRY; FULTON, ROBERT; GAGARIN, YURI; GODDARD, ROBERT H.; LEONARDO DA VINCI; MAURY, MATTHEW; STEPHENSON, GEORGE; VON BRAUN, WERNHER; WATT, JAMES; WRIGHT BROTHERS.

Uses of Transportation, *see* COMMUNICATION, EXPLORATION, TRADE, TRAVEL.

▼Backpacking is a most healthful way to travel. It also affords plenty of opportunity to enjoy the scene.

TRAVEL Every year, thousands of Americans travel to different parts of the United States and Canada or to other countries. They use airplanes, trains, automobiles, ships, and bikes. Airplanes carry most of the long-distance travelers. Buses and automobiles keep highways busy with short-distance passengers. Young people in recent years have begun to tour on foot with packs on their backs.

Why Do People Travel?

Until quite recently, most people stayed close to home for much of their lives. Those who lived near a lake or seashore made short trips to these places at holiday times. But few Americans saw both East and West coasts of the United States during their lifetime. People began to travel more after the first railroads were built. Automobiles gave travelers even greater independence. The bus companies followed, improving their services all the time. Airplanes made travel anywhere quick and easy.

Today, many people travel away from home for a holiday during the year. Airports, railroad stations, roads, and hotels are most crowded during June, July, and August. Families with children take their holidays during these months, when schools are closed. More and more people are also planning winter vacations during Christmas holidays. They go south in search of warm sun. They go to the mountains to ski.

▲ *Air transport is the fastest form of travel over long distances. Here, an airline official explains a schedule to some passengers.*

The Travel Industry

Travelers need meals, places to sleep, and other services. A whole new industry has grown up to provide these facilities. Hotels, motels, and restaurants earn millions of dollars every year through *tourism,* the business of serving travelers. People often travel to distant places after reading about them in *travel magazines.* When people travel, they shop for *souvenirs,* or things to remind them of their trip. They also take pictures of the places they have visited. Shopkeepers expect brisk business wherever travelers come and go.

Some people have their trips planned by *travel agents,* who give out information about traveling. The agents talk with their clients, find out how they like to travel, what kinds of places they like to visit, and how much they plan to spend. They suggest places to stay and things to see and do. The agent will buy the necessary tickets and make reservations. This service is free to the traveler. The agent receives a commission, or fee, from the companies with whom he does business.

People on the Move

Many families travel on holidays in the United States, Canada, and elsewhere by automobile. This type of travel is inexpensive. Passengers can see more of the countryside, and children feel more at home in the family car. Families can obtain information about interesting sites to visit by writing ahead to the Visitors Bureau or the Chamber of Commerce in the different cities and states. Road maps, which are provided free at most service stations, help the driver to plan the trip. Major hotel and motel companies provide folders about their inns in the area the family will visit. Some families pack tents and sleeping bags and stop overnight at campgrounds. Other people tow trailers, or mobile homes, behind their automobiles. These provide comfortable sleeping quarters.

Passenger ships are used today mainly to take people on *cruises,* or shipboard holidays. In the wintertime, many cruise ships steam down to the warm Caribbean Sea. The passengers can usually land at various ports for shopping and sightseeing.

▶*An economical way to travel is by camper-truck. No hotels or restaurants are needed.*

People such as businessmen, who want to travel quickly, usually go by airplane. Many people fly abroad for their holidays. A person who travels to a foreign country usually carries a *passport,* issued by his own government, to prove who he is. Many countries require travelers to obtain *visas,* or special entry permits. Travelers must often have *vaccinations* to prevent them from spreading certain diseases.

Students used to learn about distant places mostly from books. Today, they can travel to another city or country and learn for themselves. A traveler will meet people with a different way of life from his own. If the people he meets speak a different language, he will probably pick up a few words and phrases quite quickly. This will help him to travel around more easily and get to know the people. He will learn about their history and art by visiting museums, art galleries, and historical sites. Many places have special music and drama festivals at certain times of the year. The traveler will taste new types of food, see new plants and animals, and even enjoy a different climate.

There are few things more exciting than entering a tropical rain forest for the first time, or standing in the clear, pure air of a mountain region. The traveler will return with snapshots, souvenirs, and a much greater understanding and appreciation of other people in the world.

ALSO READ: AIRLINE, AIRPLANE, AIRPORT, AUTOMOBILE, BUS, CAMPING, HOLIDAY, PASSPORTS AND VISAS, RAILROAD, SHIPS AND SHIPPING, TRANSPORTATION.

TREASON A person who deliberately endangers the safety of his own country is usually said to have committed the crime of treason. The laws of some nations have ruled that any act of disloyalty to the government is treason. Other nations have allowed their people more freedom and have stated that only certain acts should be called treason. A person who commits treason is called a *traitor.*

In most democratic countries today, people are allowed to speak out and demonstrate peacefully against their government. If people riot to protest government policies, this is not usually considered treason. People are free to support a political leader who wishes to defeat the government in an election. According to the Constitution of the United States, "Treason against the United States shall consist only in levying war against them or in adhering to (joining with) their enemies, giving them aid and comfort." The first Americans convicted of treason were Julius and Ethel Rosenberg, in 1953. They gave atomic secrets to a Soviet spy.

One of the best-known treason cases in U.S. history was that of Benedict Arnold, an American general in the Revolutionary War. In 1780, Arnold made plans to surrender the fort at West Point, New York, to the British. He was discovered, but he escaped and became a general in the British army. During World War II, a Norwegian political leader named Vidkun Quisling encouraged the German dictator Adolf Hitler to invade Norway. Quisling then became leader of a Norwegian government completely controlled by the Germans. After the war, Quisling was convicted of treason and shot.

In nations ruled by a monarch or an emperor, treason is usually any act that would harm the ruler or the heir to the throne. In the past, some kings and queens of England have accused anyone who disagreed with them of treason. Among the best-known treason cases in English history were those of statesman Sir Thomas More, adventurer Sir Walter Raleigh, and Mary, Queen of Scots. In a nation ruled by a dictator, any criticism of the government is often considered to be treason.

ALSO READ: CRIME; DEMOCRACY; DICTATOR; MARY, QUEEN OF SCOTS; MORE, SIR THOMAS; RALEIGH, SIR WALTER; SPY; STALIN, JOSEPH.

Accused of treason during World War II were three radio broadcasters who urged Allied troops to surrender. "Lord Haw-Haw" (Englishman William Joyce) was hanged by the British after the war. "Axis Sally" (Mildred Gillars of Oregon) served a prison sentence. "Tokyo Rose" (Iva Toguri of California) was also imprisoned.

TREASURE HUNT If you're having a birthday party soon, you may want to plan a Treasure Hunt for your guests. Hide a treasure (such as a bag of candy) in a secret place. Then write down a number of clues on pieces of paper that will lead the guests step by step to the treasure. You may want to make your clues rhyme, as in "One, two, three, four–take a look behind the door!" Then hide all the clues except the first one. Give that to the guests and let them find their way, clue by clue, to the treasure. You can join them, but don't give out any hints!

TREATY Treaties are agreements made between the governments of two or more nations. One of the marks of an independent nation is its ability to make treaties with other nations. The state of California, for example, is not an independent nation. California cannot make treaties with any foreign government.

Treaties are the result of negotiations in which representatives of each government discuss their needs and come to an agreement. The agreements are written down and copies prepared for each of the negotiators to sign. The treaty does not go into effect, however, until it has been *ratified* (accepted), usually by the chief lawmaking body of each participating nation. In the United States, the President ratifies a treaty with the consent of two-thirds of the senate.

There are three main categories of treaties. *Political* treaties may deal with the terms of peace after a war. Political treaties establish military and political alliances, such as treaties that formed the North Atlantic Treaty Organization (NATO), the Southeast Asia Treaty Organization (SEATO), and the Warsaw Pact (alliance of Communist nations in eastern Europe with the Soviet Union). *Commercial* treaties set up rules for a nation's foreign trade and deal with fishing rights, tariffs, and other economic concerns. *Legal* treaties deal with agreements on copyrights and patents. A legal treaty may also be an agreement to help return criminals who have fled to other countries.

Treaties end in many ways. Some include an expiration date. Some are ended by general agreement of the signers. Others are ended because nations violate them.

ALSO READ: INTERNATIONAL LAW, INTERNATIONAL RELATIONS, NORTH ATLANTIC TREATY ORGANIZATION, WARSAW PACT.

TREE The largest living thing on Earth is a tree—a California sequoia called "General Sherman," 272 feet tall with a trunk 32 feet thick. The oldest living thing is also a tree—a scrubby bristlecone pine 4,900 years old, growing on the cold, bare side of a Nevada mountain.

A tree is a tall, woody plant that usually has one main stem, or trunk. Trees can be divided into two groups by the shapes of their leaves.

►*Many old trees are historic. This 300-year-old osage orange tree stands in front of Patrick Henry's home near Brookneal, Virginia. The American patriot once played the violin for his grandchildren in the shade of this great tree.*

The *needle-leaf trees* include pines, spruces, firs, hemlocks, and cedars. These trees are also called *conifers* because they bear cones. The cones produce the seeds. The seeds are "naked," or unprotected by a seed coat, so these trees are given the scientific name *gymnosperm,* meaning "naked seed." Most gymnosperms are evergreen. Their leaves stay green all year round and don't fall off in the winter.

The *broad-leaf trees* are members of a large group of flowering plants called *angiosperms,* meaning "covered seed." These include the oaks, elms, maples, birches, beeches, hickories, sycamores, and almost all trees with fairly wide, flat leaves. All of these trees, like all angiosperms, bear fruits and flowers, though the flowers of some trees are too small to see and the fruit may not look much like fruit. The acorn is the fruit of an oak, and the small-winged seed casing is the fruit of a maple. Most angiosperms are *deciduous*—their leaves fall off in the winter and grow back in the spring.

When used as lumber, the conifers are often called "softwood" and the broad-leaf trees "hardwood." But this is not always accurate. Some conifers have harder wood than some broad-leaf trees.

▲*Redwoods and sequoias are the giants of the tree world. This sequoia in Yosemite Park in California is over 300 feet tall.*

The Growth and Anatomy of a Tree

A tree grows from a seed. If you were to break open the seed, you would find inside, in miniature, all the parts that will later grow to make the tree.

The seeds normally drop from trees in winter. A seed may be carried for some distance by the wind, a bird, or an animal. With luck, it falls on fertile ground.

The seed lies dormant through the winter. In the warmth and wetness of spring it begins to sprout. The root emerges first, poking through the seed coat and digging down into the soil. Then the first shoot appears, pushing up into the air and sun.

The taproot grows straight down to anchor the tree and reach for deep water. Others roots grow outward in search of surface water. At the same time, the shoot develops into the stem, branches, and leaves. The roots and the leaves must grow at about the same rate. The leaves, through a chemical process called *photosynthesis,* make food so the tree can live and grow. The roots provide the water needed to make the food.

▼*Each tree has a different kind of bark. The thin, delicate bark of the white birch is a familiar sight in many parts of the United States and Canada.*

The flow of food and water between the roots and leaves is accomplished by layers of cells formed by the *cambium.* The cambium lies between the wood and the bark. As the cells of the cambium divide, they form an inner layer of tube-like cells called the *xylem* and an outer tube-like layer called the *phloem.* The xylem carries water from the roots to the leaves, and the phloem carries food from the leaves back down to the roots. As the phloem and xylem age, they harden and die. The dead xy-

▲*The divi-divi trees, on the island of Aruba in the Netherlands West Indies, are shaped by trade winds which blow constantly from the northeast.*

▼*Trees grow in all kinds of climates. The Joshua tree is adapted to the hot, dry conditions of the Mohave Desert in California.*

lem forms the wood of the tree. The dead phloem forms the protective bark. The cambium produces new layers of xylem and phloem to carry on the flow of fluids and the growth of the tree.

Forest Regions

The trees growing in a particular place vary with the soil and the *climate*—the temperature, sunlight, wind, and rain. North America, with its wide range of climate and soil, is especially rich in trees, having more than 800 different species (kinds). Almost as many different species of trees grow in the Smoky Mountains of Tennessee as in all of Europe.

The United States can be divided into six forest regions—Northern, Central, Southern, Pacific, Rocky Mountain, and Tropical.

The Northern forest runs across New England and the Great Lakes from Maine to Minnesota. A thin finger of this forest follows the ridges of the Appalachian Mountains down into Georgia. The Northern forest is a mixture of conifers and broad-leaf trees. The conifers include pine, fir, cedar, hemlock, and spruce. The most common broad-leaf trees are the yellow birch and the sugar maple.

The Central forest stretches across the middle of the Eastern United States from Cape Cod to Texas. This is the largest forest region, and it includes mostly broad-leaf trees—oaks, ashes, poplars, gums, beeches, and walnuts.

The Southern region runs from Virginia across the coastal southern states to Texas. The most important trees are pines—loblolly, slash, and longleaf. But broad-leaf trees also grow here—oaks, cypresses, elms, red maples, and cottonwoods.

The three eastern forest regions are separated from the two western regions by the vast, almost treeless plains of the Midwest. Beyond the plains lies the Rocky Mountain region, an area with scattered forests of tall conifers—ponderosa pine, lodgepole pine, Douglas fir, and others.

West of the Rockies is the Pacific region, the home of the largest trees in the world—sequoias, redwoods, Douglas firs, and other great conifers. This lush strip of land, running from Canada to Mexico, provides one-third of America's lumber.

Small tropical forests are located at the southern tips of Florida and Texas. Mahogany and bay trees grow there.

Over half the forest land in North America is located in Canada. In the East, along the Great Lakes and the St. Lawrence River, the forest is a mixture of conifers and broad-leaf trees. To the north and west are almost all conifers—great stands of fir, pine, spruce, and hemlock stretching to the treeless tundra of the Arctic. Canada's forests provide the pulpwood used to make over half the newsprint in the world.

Trees and Men

Trees have long been useful to men. Early men used wood to make tools and build fires. Later, they cut trees to build shelters. They probably never thought about protecting trees because the supply seemed to be endless. But they were wrong. There are now deserts where there were once thick forests.

Today millions of acres of trees are grown for lumber. Houses and furniture are built of wood. The paper in this book is a product of trees. We eat the fruits and nuts from trees. Birds and wildlife need trees for food and shelter. The changing beauty of trees delights us. Trees flower in spring. Their summer green provides welcome shade. Autumn brings glorious color to trees, and in winter their bare branches are like lace against the sky.

Ecology is the relationship among plants, animals (including man), and the rest of the environment. Trees are an irreplaceable part of the Earth's ecology. The oxygen we breathe is produced by plants through photosynthesis. Trees are the largest plants, so they make the most oxygen. When trees are cut down and more roads are built, fewer and fewer trees are left to make oxygen. More roads carry more cars, buses, and trucks. The exhaust from these vehicles pollutes the air. Many varieties of trees cannot live in heavily polluted air. They sicken and die. Sycamores and ginkgo trees are often planted on city streets and in parks, because they are sturdy enough to grow in the unfavorable environment.

Trees also absorb sound and control noise pollution. Trees keep moisture in the ground by holding the soil in place to prevent erosion.

▲*The lovely blossoms of cherry trees frame a view of Mount Fuji in Japan as they herald the arrival of spring.*

Tree Identification

How can you tell one kind of tree from another? The first step is to decide whether the tree is a conifer or a broad-leaf tree.

Look at the leaves. Are they thin, like needles? If they are, you are looking at a conifer. Each needle is a separate leaf. Each scale of the cone has a flat seed at its base. These seeds are not covered.

If the needles are long and arranged in small bundles, the tree is probably a pine. If the needles are short and grow on all sides of a twig, the tree may be a spruce. If the needles are short and flat and grow side by side on opposite sides of the twig, the tree may be a balsam fir or a hemlock. Most conifers have a single trunk.

Suppose the tree has a broad leaf. How can you tell what kind of broad-leaf tree it is? There are almost 700 kinds of broad-leaf trees, so this is a little harder than separating the varieties of conifer. You will want to narrow the selection. First, see if the leaf is *simple* or *compound.* A simple leaf is one leaf growing alone on a stem. Oak and maple leaves are simple. A compound leaf has many leaflets growing on one stem. Hickory and walnut leaves are compound. Some compound leaves are confusing because their leaflets may be as large as simple leaves. There is an easy way to decide which one you are looking at. A simple leaf usually has a bud growing on the twig right under the stem. The leaflet of a compound leaf does not.

The next clue you will need for identification is the shape of the leaf and the leaf edges. Leaves may be almost round, heart-shaped, or long and narrow. The edges may be smooth, lobed, or toothed. A maple leaf is lobed, which means that the edges are deeply divided into sections. Toothed edges have many small points. Leaves can be both lobed and toothed. One large group of trees, the oaks, includes smooth, lobed, and toothed leaves. But oaks are not hard to identify, because they all bear acorns.

Leaves are usually the easiest way to identify a tree. But perhaps you have looked carefully at the leaves of a tree, and you are still not sure what kind it is. You may have decided, for example, that it is a maple. But which maple is it? Silver maple? Norway maple? Sugar maple? If you are just beginning, it may be enough simply to say, "It is a maple tree." As you become more familiar with trees, you will want to be more specific. You will learn how to look for the identifying leaf scars on winter twigs. Buds have distinctive shapes, too. Tree bark is as individual as skin. Oaks and elms have thick, rough bark. Beeches have smooth, gray bark that looks like stretched metal. Many birches have bark that peels off like paper.

You can often tell the kind of tree by the shape of its bare branches. Some trees can be identified by their fruit. Some trees bear nuts that are easy to identify. Nuts are tree seeds enclosed in a shell.

When you are able to identify trees, you can begin to observe how and where different trees grow. What trees grow in wet areas? In dry areas? You may notice that certain trees usually grow in groups, while others, such as the tulip tree, usually grow alone. Which trees grow fast and which grow slowly? If you find a cut stump, you can count the rings to see how old the tree was when cut down. Most trees add one growth ring a year.

For further information on:

Ecology and Forestry, *see* ECOLOGY, EVOLUTION, FOREST FIRE, FORESTRY, PLANTS OF THE PAST.

Kinds of Trees, *see* CONIFER, EVERGREEN, FRUIT, PALM.

Tree Anatomy and Growth, *see* BARK, BUD, CELL, FLOWER, GROWTH, LEAF, PLANT, PLANT BREEDING, SEEDS AND FRUITS, SHRUB.

Tree Products, *see* CITRUS FRUIT, LUMBER AND LUMBERING, NUT, PLANT PRODUCTS, WOOD.

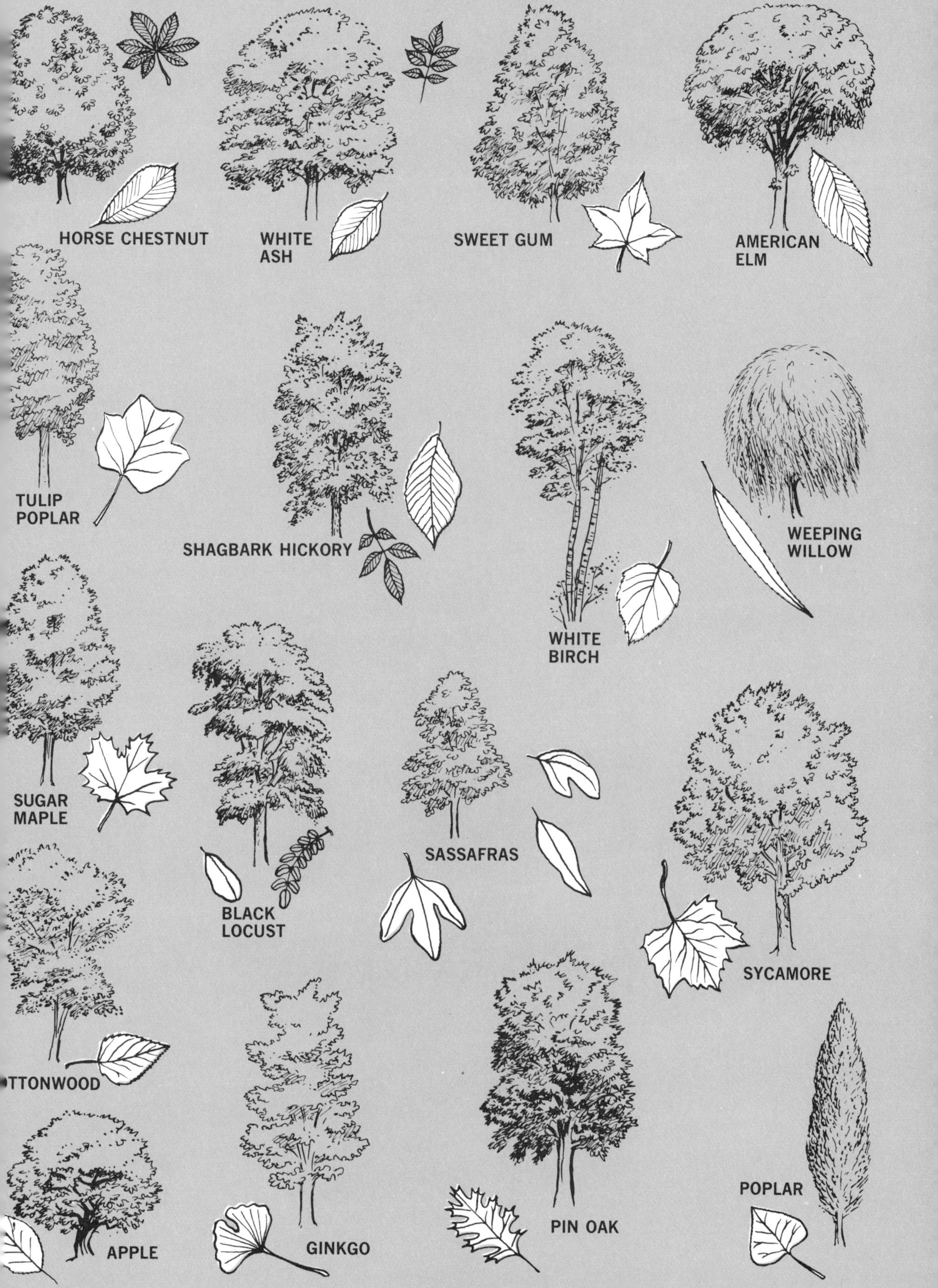
HORSE CHESTNUT
WHITE ASH
SWEET GUM
AMERICAN ELM
TULIP POPLAR
SHAGBARK HICKORY
WHITE BIRCH
WEEPING WILLOW
SUGAR MAPLE
BLACK LOCUST
SASSAFRAS
SYCAMORE
TTONWOOD
APPLE
GINKGO
PIN OAK
POPLAR

▶*People who give evidence at a trial must take an oath to tell the truth before they testify. The members of the jury are seated* (right background).

TRIAL A trial is a legal procedure that gives people a chance to go to a court and present facts before a judge or jury in order to seek justice in a dispute. A dispute brought before a court is called a *case.*

Cases brought before a court are of two types–civil and criminal. A *civil case* is any legal dispute between two private individuals or between two states, organizations, or businesses. Divorce cases, cases concerning property or business disputes, and many others are civil cases.

A *criminal case* is a dispute between the state and a private individual, business, or other organization. The individual or organization is accused of having broken the criminal laws of the state. The state tries to prove the individual guilty of having committed a crime (of having broken the criminal laws of the state). Murder, drunk or reckless driving, theft, kidnapping, and illegal business practices are a few examples of criminal cases.

Bringing a Case to Trial

In a civil case, one party (the plaintiff) files charges with the court against another party (the defendant). The charges are a written document outlining the matter in dispute and the accusations of wrongdoing against the defendant. The charges also list any civil laws the defendant is accused of breaking. The case is entered in the court *docket* (schedule) and a date set for trial.

Bringing a criminal case to trial is more complicated. The state must file charges against an individual or group suspected of committing a crime. In the case of felonies (very serious crimes), the state's attorneys must submit evidence of a crime to a *grand jury,* made up of between 6 and 23 people. If the jury decides that the evidence against a suspect is sufficient, it hands down an *indictment.* An indictment is a written statement charging an individual with committing a crime. The indictment is filed with the court, and the accused person is *arraigned*–summoned before a judge to answer the charges in the indictment.

At arraignment, the accused usually pleads *guilty* or *not guilty.* If he pleads "guilty," no trial is held because there is nothing to argue over. The judge merely *declares sentence* (decides the punishment that the person must undergo). If the accused pleads "not guilty," a trial must be held. The case is entered on the docket, and a trial date is set.

Trial Procedure

For a civil or criminal jury trial, people eligible for jury duty are summoned to the court. In the United States, any citizen between the ages of 18 or 21 and 70 able to read and write is eligible for jury duty. The first 12 persons accepted as satisfactory by lawyers for both sides are sworn in as jurors.

The trial begins with the attorneys' opening remarks to the jury. The plaintiff or prosecution then sets out to prove the charges made against the defendant. Witnesses are called by the prosecution and by the defense and questioned by attorneys from both sides.

After *direct examination* of a witness by the attorney who called him, opposing counsel may choose to *cross-examine* the witness. In cross-examination, the opposing attorney tries to discredit the witness's testimony or prove that the witness's evidence is inadequate.

At the conclusion of the defendant's case, both attorneys make closing remarks to the jury. They try to show the jury how the testimony and evidence does or does not prove the guilt of the defendant. After the closing remarks, the judge explains to the jury the laws that apply to the particular case.

The jury then leaves the court to decide on a *verdict* (a decision as to whether or not the charges against the defendant have been proved). Throughout the trial, jurors are not allowed to discuss the case with anyone. In reaching a verdict, they must talk about the trial with each other, but they are not allowed to have contact with anyone but the bailiff (the official who keeps order in a court) or his guards.

If the jury reaches a verdict of "not guilty," the defendant is *acquitted* (allowed to go free with the charges dropped). If the verdict is "guilty," the defendant is *convicted* and the judge hands down a sentence within the limits set by law. If the jury cannot reach a verdict, it is called a *hung jury*. The case must then be tried again with a new jury and judge. In civil cases, the jury decides who is at fault and what damages (usually money) shall be paid to the plaintiff. All verdicts are read in court by the *foreman* of the jury, who in some states is selected by his fellow jurors. In trials conducted before a judge only, the judge decides both the verdict and the sentence.

If a defendant and his attorneys feel that the verdict is wrong or in some way unfair, they may *appeal* their case to a higher court. Appeal procedures are very complicated and usually take a long time, but they are one way of making sure justice is done by giving suspects a second chance for acquittal.

▼An FBI technician prepares a scale model of the locale in which a crime was committed. The model will help the judge and the jury in a trial to understand the facts surrounding the case.

▲*Anne Hutchinson was put on trial in Massachusetts in 1637 for speaking out against officials of the church. She was found guilty and banished from the colony.*

Throughout a jury trial, the judge acts as an umpire. The rules for conduct of a trial are very strict. The judge must enforce those rules and make sure the trial is completely fair to both sides. If a judge fails, even in the smallest way, to enforce the trial rules or to keep the trial fair, defendant's attorneys can try to force a *mistrial.* The case must then be retried with an entirely new jury and judge.

Many civil cases are heard in *closed court.* The general public is not allowed to be present. Criminal cases are almost always conducted in *open court,* where spectators are allowed to watch the proceedings. During all trials, a *court stenographer* takes down the entire proceedings word for word. All participants in the trial receive written copies of the proceedings.

ALSO READ: COURT SYSTEM, CRIME, JUVENILE DELINQUENCY, LAW, LAWYERS AND JUDGES, POLICE, PRISON, SUPREME COURT.

TRINIDAD AND TOBAGO see WEST INDIES.

TROJAN WAR The legends of ancient Greece tell of a ten-year war between the Greeks and the Trojans. The Trojans lived in a city called Troy, located in Asia Minor (now Turkey). Homer tells of the Trojan War in his story-poem *The Iliad.* (*Ilium* was the Greek name for Troy.) The area that has traditionally been considered the site of Troy was actually the location of several ancient cities. Archeologists have unearthed several cities, built one atop the ruins of another, dating back to about 3000 B.C. The Troy of legend probably existed in the 1200s B.C. Historians believe that the Greeks may have attacked Troy for its goods or to destroy its power.

According to legend, the Trojan War began when three goddesses, Hera, Athena, and Aphrodite, all wanted a golden apple that was to be given to the most beautiful of the three. Paris, son of King Priam of Troy, was chosen to judge their beauty. He awarded the apple to Aphrodite, who promised to give him the most beautiful woman in the world. She presented him with Helen, wife of King Menelaus of Sparta, Greece. Paris and Helen ran off to Troy together. All the Greek princes, heroes, and kings gathered in anger and sailed for Troy to bring Helen back. The Greek armies surrounded the city of Troy for nine years, but the Trojans would not surrender.

During the war, the bravest Greek warrior, Achilles, killed the Trojan leader Hector. Achilles was later killed by Paris. In the tenth year of the war, the Greek hero Odysseus thought of a masterful trick. He had the Greeks build an enormous hollow wooden horse, fill it with soldiers, and leave it outside the city gates. The Trojans thought the horse was a gift and dragged it into the city. That night, the Greek soldiers climbed out of the horse and opened the city gates, letting in the army.

ALSO READ: GREECE, ANCIENT; HOMER.

▼*Greek soldiers enter the wooden horse which the Trojans later pulled inside the gates of their city. According to legend, the Greek soldiers climbed out of the horse during the night, opened the gates of Troy, and allowed the Greek army to enter the city and conquer the Trojans.*

◀ *The Sumatran barb lives in the rivers and streams of Sumatra and Borneo.*

TROPICAL FISH Tropical fish are small, brightly colored fish that come from the warm waters of the tropics. Some of these fish live in fresh water, and some live in salt water. The freshwater fish are popular as pets.

Tropical fish can be divided into two groups–those that give birth to live young and those that lay eggs. The live bearers include guppies, mollies, and swordtails. Egg layers include angelfish, tetras, Siamese fighting fish, and gouramis.

Live bearers are easier to care for and breed than egg layers. If a male and a female guppy are kept in the same aquarium, the female will almost certainly become pregnant in a short time. She should then be moved to a separate aquarium that is full of plants. Fish often eat their offspring, and the plants will provide hiding places for the young. After she has given birth, the mother should be returned to her original tank.

Egg-laying fish are more finicky breeders. If the water and the food are not just right, they are unlikely to produce offspring. Each fish has its own special requirements.

Tropical fish are of many different shapes, colors, and personalities. The guppy is probably the most popular tropical fish. It is a small, colorful, peaceful fish. It will eat almost any food, and it can live in water at temperatures from 60 to 90 degrees. Mollies, moonfish, and zebra fish are also peaceful and easy to care for. These fish can live happily with other fish.

Some fish need a special diet, or can only live in water at a certain temperature, or are dangerous to other fish. The kissing gourami is a fairly large tropical fish from Asia. Kissing gouramis kiss each other, but they attack and eat smaller fish. Kissing gouramis should be kept alone or with fish of their own size, in a tank with a water temperature of 75 to 80 degrees.

Tropical fish are easy to care for and interesting to watch. The only real danger to them is overeating. They should be fed only enough to keep them healthy, because they will literally eat themselves to death.

ALSO READ: AQUARIUM, FISH, PET.

▼ *The angelfish is at home in the coral reefs of the Caribbean Sea.*

TRUCK FARMING Truck farming is growing fruits and vegetables for market–to sell to individuals or to supermarkets and grocery stores. The term "truck farming" originated when growers began transporting their produce by truck to cities and other places to be sold. Truck farming grew up as cities grew.

▲ *A truck farmer prepares to make a sale in his roadside vegetable market.*

(When most people lived in rural areas, they could grow the vegetables they needed. But city residents must buy the food they need.) Until railroad lines were built, most truck farms were located near large cities. Now many truck farms are located far from any of their markets, but railroads, trucks, and airplanes, using refrigeration, can get produce to market while it is still fresh.

Several kinds of vegetables can be grown on a single truck farm. Farmers often plant and harvest several crops from a given area during one year. For example, they may harvest an early crop of radishes and later plant carrots or beans. Truck farmers water, fertilize, and spray their crops to kill insects so that their land will produce as many vegetables as possible.

Truck farms vary in size from large gardens to farms of several hundred acres. Small truck farms are usually located near cities. These farmers raise many kinds of fruits and vegetables —cabbage, lettuce, squash, carrots, celery, radishes, peaches, strawberries, blueberries, mushrooms, and many others. They may set up roadside stands to sell their crops or take them into the city to sell to stores. Larger truck farms usually specialize in growing one or two crops. Many of the largest farms quick-freeze their crops, package them, and send them to market.

Harvesting is done by machine as frequently as possible. But many crops, such as tomatoes, lettuce, and cabbage, would be damaged by harvesting machines and must be picked by hand. Since they need extra "hands" at harvesting time, farmers hire migrant workers, people who travel around the country working on truck farms. Migrant workers are often poorly paid and housed, but they have recently begun forming unions to force improvements in their salaries and living conditions.

Small farmers often join together in *cooperatives* to market their crops. In a cooperative, participating farmers ship their crops together so that they can take advantage of the reduced freight prices on large shipments.

ALSO READ: AGRICULTURE, FRUIT, RAILROAD, TRUCKS AND TRUCKING, VEGETABLES.

TRUCKS AND TRUCKING Whether moving furniture to a new house or hauling giant logs to a lumber mill, trucks are an essential part of a nation's economy. Trucks are motor vehicles that transport freight and sometimes people. They carry raw materials to factories. They carry goods from factories to stores. And they deliver products from stores to homes. Trucks are used to haul cargo to and from other forms of transport, such as trains, planes, and ships. Trucks are used in the construction of new buildings and roads. And trucks are used in performing important community services, such as park maintenance, garbage pickup, and fire fighting.

Trucks are much more versatile than airplanes, trains, and ships. Trains and ships can travel only on rails and water. Planes, trains, and ships can do most of their loading and unloading only at airports, rail terminals, and docks. Cargo carried by these forms of transport almost always has to be taken to its final destination by truck. Trucks can pick up and deliver cargo right to the doors of factories, stores, and homes.

▲ *A sanitation truck dumps its load of garbage and refuse at a waste disposal plant. The truck body is tilted by hydraulic pistons.*

Kinds of Trucks

Trucks come in a great variety of sizes, shapes, and weights and are designed for many different uses. Trucks are usually classified according to weight—light, medium, light-heavy, and heavyweight. A truck's weight includes the weight of the truck itself plus the weight of the maximum load it can carry. Most modern truck bodies are made of strong, lightweight metals such as aluminum. The less the truck itself weighs, the more cargo it can carry, if the truck is constructed of strong materials.

Lightweight and mediumweight trucks are usually of the *single-unit* type. In single-unit trucks, the driver's cab and the cargo-carrying space are both built on the same *chassis,* or body frame. They generally have two axles and four to six wheels. The familiar pickup, panel, and delivery trucks are examples of single-unit vehicles. These have been adapted for many different uses, such as bookmobiles and campers.

The big heavyweight trucks are usually of the *combination* type, made up of tractors and trailers. The *tractor* houses the driver's cab and the engine. The *trailer* is the large cargo-carrying part which is hooked onto and pulled by the tractor. A combination truck in which the trailer has one or more forward axles is called a *full trailer* or *tractor-trailer.* Many combination trucks have trailers with no forward axles. These are called *semi-trailers.* When not attached to a tractor, the semi-trailer's front end is supported by metal struts and wheels, called *dollies.* When being pulled, the trailer's front end is coupled to a disk at the back of the tractor. Beneath the disk, the tractor has a number of wheels that act as the semi-trailer's front axle. A full trailer, with wheels at both ends, is often coupled to the end of a semi-trailer. The tractor can then pull two loads of cargo. This largest type of truck is a *double bottom.*

▼ *A truck tractor with a powerful diesel engine hauls an aluminum-bodied trailer.*

All trucks, even the single-unit, lightweight ones, are more ruggedly built than automobiles. Their engines are more powerful and most operate on diesel or very low-octane fuels, rather than on standard-octane gasoline. Most trucks have four-wheel drive. The engine is connected to all four wheels. In an automobile, the engine is connected only to the rear wheels or, in a few models, only to the front wheels.

Truck bodies have to withstand extremely heavy loads. For this reason, most trucks have more than 4 wheels. The big-

►*A special truck is used to service the engines of a jet airplane. Other trucks are used to carry luggage and food to the airplane and to pump fuel into its tanks.*

gest ones have as many as five axles carrying 10 to 18 wheels. Double wheels are located under the areas of greatest weight. Truck tires are made of very strong, thick, reinforced nylon and rubber. They are much bigger than automobile tires. The wheels are attached to the axle so that flat tires can be changed very quickly.

Driving Trucks

Engines of heavyweight trucks have up to 12 forward gears. Automobiles have only three or four gears. The first gear is slowest but most powerful. It is used to move out from a dead stop and to climb steep hills. The twelfth gear is for cruising on flat, open highway. A truck's gears are usually shifted by hand, but automatic transmissions are being used more and more.

There are always two drivers for cross-country hauls of longer than ten hours. No driver is allowed to operate his truck for more than ten hours at a time. When one driver tires, the other takes over. Cabs are often equipped with bedding, located behind the driver's seat, so one man can rest while the other one drives. Some very modern trucks are equipped with refrigerators, showers, and all the conveniences of a tiny apartment.

In order to drive a truck in the United States, a person must pass a series of very difficult tests. He must demonstrate his ability to handle the type of truck he wants to drive. All states require truck drivers to obtain a special license, called a *chauffeur's license.*

Trucks in Use Today

A large variety of trucks is now in use for all kinds of special jobs. You have probably seen many of them yourself. *Tanker trucks* are rounded, completely enclosed tanks for carrying oil, milk, or any other kind of liquid cargo. *Cement-mixers* transport, churn, and dump cement at construction sites. *Flat-bed trucks* are open on three sides and are used for hauling logs, steel girders, bulldozers, or anything large, solid, and carried in one piece. *Dump trucks* are used to haul coal, dirt, or anything spillable. Their carrying space raises up at the front on pneumatic lifts so the load can be dumped out through the tailgate at the back. *Auto haulers* are large trailers that can carry up to six cars. *Mobile homes* are trucks whose carrying space in the back has been made into living quarters with rooms, furniture, appli-

▼*A heavy-duty flatbed truck hauls huge logs over a mountain road.*

ances, and all the comforts of home. *Tow-trucks* have equipment, such as jacks and hoists, with which they can lift and pull disabled cars and trucks. The cargo space in *refrigerator trucks* is a gigantic freezer that hauls frozen fruit, vegetables, and meat from packagers to stores.

An unusual new truck that will be used in the future is the *walking truck.* It has several legs, each with three joints. The driver controls the legs by means of cables and hydraulic fluid, much as the arms of cranes and steam shovels work. The truck can walk over exceedingly rough terrain where wheeled vehicles cannot go.

ALSO READ: AUTOMOBILE, CONSTRUCTION, DIESEL ENGINE, DRIVING, ENGINE, FARM MACHINERY, GEAR, HORSEPOWER, STREETS AND ROADS, TIRE, TRADE, TRANSPORTATION.

▲*An important industrial truck is the portable cement mixer. The striped tank revolves and mixes the cement while the truck is traveling to the construction site where the mixture will be used.*

TRUDEAU, PIERRE (born 1919) Pierre Elliott Trudeau became prime minister of Canada in 1968. He was born in Montreal, Quebec. His mother was of British descent and his father was French Canadian. Trudeau studied law at the University of Montreal and later attended Harvard University. As a student, he traveled around the world by hitchhiking and by riding a motorbike. On his return to Canada, he became a lawyer in Montreal.

During the early 1960s, when French Canadians in Quebec were demanding a separate state, Trudeau refused to support them. Instead, he spoke out for a united Canada and a "just society" for all Canadians. In 1965, he joined the Federal Liberal Party and became a member of parliament. Two years later, he was made minister of justice. Prime Minister Lester Pearson resigned in 1968, and Trudeau was elected to succeed him. In 1969, the Trudeau government passed the Official Language Act, which made French equal to English as an official language of Canada. Through his leadership, Trudeau has shown that Canada can be a strong and independent nation.

ALSO READ: CANADA; PEARSON, LESTER.

▼*Prime Minister Trudeau meets President Nixon on the U.S.-Canadian border in June of 1969.*

TRUMAN, HARRY S (born 1884) Harry S Truman served as Vice President during the three months of President Franklin Roosevelt's fourth term. Truman was called on to fill the place of one of the best-known leaders in the world when President Roosevelt died in 1945.

Harry S Truman was born in Lamar, Missouri, on May 8, 1884, and grew up near Independence, Missouri. His parents could not decide on a middle name, so they gave him just a middle initial, S. His father could not afford to send him to college, but Truman educated himself by reading widely.

During World War I, Harry Truman served in the United States Army and was promoted to the rank of major. Truman

THIRTY-THIRD PRESIDENT APRIL 12, 1945—JANUARY 20, 1953

HARRY S TRUMAN

Born: May 8, 1884, Lamar, Missouri
Parents: John Anderson and Martha Young Truman
Education: Kansas City Law School
Religion: Baptist
Occupation: Bank clerk, farmer, merchant, government official
Political Party: Democratic
State Represented: Missouri
Married: 1919 to Elizabeth Virginia Wallace (born 1885)
Children: One daughter
Died: December 26, 1972, Kansas City, Missouri
Buried: Truman Library grounds, Independence, Missouri

and the unit he commanded fought bravely in France. After the war he and a friend managed a clothing store for a few years, but the business failed. Truman held several public offices in Missouri and attended the Kansas City Law School. Truman was elected to the U.S. Senate in 1934.

During Truman's three months as Vice President (January 20–April 12, 1945), President Roosevelt was out of the country for part of the time. Not until Truman himself became the chief executive did he learn about the existence of the atomic bomb. Leading scientists, working for the American government, had been experimenting on a new kind of weapon. Early in August, Truman was told that tests on the atomic bomb, the most destructive weapon ever invented until that time, had been successful. The President made the decision to use the atomic bomb in order to end the war in the Far East as soon as possible. Two atomic bombs, three days apart, were dropped over two Japanese cities, Hiroshima and Nagasaki. The destruction was so terrible that Japan surrendered on August 15, 1945, and World War II was over.

The end of the war did not bring real peace. A non-violent conflict known as "the Cold War" developed with a former ally, the Soviet Union. During the war, Nazi forces had been driven out of several countries in eastern Europe by Soviet armies. But Soviet leaders, instead of permitting free elections as they had agreed, set up Communist governments backed by Soviet arms in those countries. In addition, armed pressure was used in Greece and Turkey to try to establish Communism there.

In response to this challenge, the President announced the Truman Doctrine–official U.S. foreign policy that gave support to "free peoples who are resisting attempted subjugation by armed minorities or by outside pressures." Congress then voted to send financial aid and military advisers to Greece and Turkey

The *Chicago Daily Tribune* was so certain that Harry Truman would lose the election of 1948 to Thomas Dewey that an edition with the headline "Dewey Defeats Truman" was actually printed before all the votes had been counted.

to enable them to keep their independence. Among other measures supported by the President to aid foreign countries was the European Recovery Program, or Marshall Plan, suggested by Secretary of State George C. Marshall. With the aid of money and materials voted by the American Congress, 16 countries in Europe rebuilt the factories, railroads, and docks which had been bombed during the war. Millions of Europeans were given work, and their countries began to prosper.

Truman was less successful with domestic issues. He tried to extend Roosevelt's New Deal with his own Fair Deal. Truman asked Congress for increased Social Security benefits, national health insurance, and public housing, among other things. Truman also wanted to establish a commission to help black people gain fairer treatment. But a conservative Congress refused to cooperate with most of his plans.

In the Presidential election of 1948, most people expected Truman to be beaten by the Republican nominee, Thomas E. Dewey. The split within the Democratic Party was so great that a group of southern Democrats broke away and formed their own party. In addition, Henry Wallace, who was Vice President before Truman, ran on the Progressive ticket. Truman surprised nearly everyone by winning the election. After the election, Congress passed Truman's programs for Social Security and public housing, but did not approve his ideas on civil rights.

In 1950, Communist North Koreans supplied with Russian weapons invaded the Republic of Korea to the south. The President ordered U.S. military forces to go to the aid of South Koreans.

In 1950, Senator Joseph McCarthy began a search for Communists in government and elsewhere in the country. This wave of "Communist-hunting" was known by many as McCarthyism. Many people were unjustly accused, including members of the Truman administration.

Truman refused to run in the election of 1952. He returned to Independence, Missouri, in 1953. After his retirement, Truman published two volumes of memoirs and several volumes of his speeches. The Harry S Truman Library and Museum (dedicated in 1957) near Independence is a popular tourist attraction and historical research center.

ALSO READ: COMMUNISM; KOREA; ROOSEVELT, FRANKLIN D.; UNITED NATIONS.

▲ *When North Korea invaded South Korea on June 25, 1950, President Truman quickly sent American soldiers into action to aid South Korea. Americans soon discovered that they had to cope with severe winter weather as well as with the enemy.*

TRUTH, SOJOURNER (1797–1883) Sojourner Truth spent much of her life working for the freedom of other black people in the United States. She was born a slave in Ulster County, New York. Her original name was Isabella Van Wagener. In 1827, New York State freed all slaves. Isabella then went to New York City, where she took a job as a household servant.

In 1843, she had a vision in which she believed she heard voices from God. She changed her name to Sojourner Truth and joined the abolitionist movement, organized by people who wanted to put an end to slavery. By then most of the northeastern states had passed laws against slavery. But in the southern states, slavery remained legal. Sojourner Truth traveled through several states preaching against slavery. She also spoke out for the emancipation (freedom) of women.

Although Sojourner Truth never learned to read or write, she was a convincing speaker She spent the last years of her life in Washington, D.C., working to bring a better standard of living to black people in the city.

ALSO READ: ABOLITION, SLAVERY.

▲*Harriet Tubman, a black heroine, helped to free many slaves.*

TUBMAN, HARRIET (about 1821–1913) Harriet Tubman was an active worker in the abolitionist movement that was organized to put an end to slavery in the United States. Harriet Tubman was born a slave on a plantation near Cambridge, Maryland. As a young girl, she was forced to work in the fields. About 1849, Harriet escaped from the plantation. She traveled to the northern states, where most of the slaves had already been freed. She became a "conductor" on the Underground Railroad. The railroad was a secret route by which slaves escaping from southern plantations could travel to the North. Harriet traveled up and down the route helping the runaway slaves and encouraging them to complete the journey. She was nearly captured herself several times. She was immensely strong and courageous, and was often called "General" Tubman.

After the Civil War broke out, Harriet worked as a nurse and cook for the Union Army. She also traveled behind enemy lines as a spy. After the war, she built a house in Auburn, New York, which was open to any black person who needed help. Harriet could not read or write, but she told her life story to her friend Sarah Bradford, who published it in the book *Scenes from the Life of Harriet Tubman.*

ALSO READ: ABOLITION, SLAVERY, UNDERGROUND RAILROAD.

TUNDRA The tundra is a flat, treeless area that extends across the Arctic lowlands in North America, Europe, and Asia, and the Antarctic region of South America.

The tundra is a snow-covered, marshy prairie for about ten months of the year. Most of the soil under the snow, except for a thin top layer, stays frozen all year long. This frozen soil is called permafrost. When the snow and ice melt in June, the water cannot seep into the permafrost, so it forms lakes and ponds of all sizes.

Summer on the tundra lasts from about mid-June to mid-August. During those two months, the tundra brightens with

◀*A nomadic Laplander follows his herd of reindeer in a search for new grazing land in the tundra region of northeastern Lapland.*

color. Red poppies, blue lupines, and other flowers mingle with mosses, lichens, and other vegetation. Sub-Arctic animals drift up to join their Arctic neighbors during the short summer. The hardy musk ox shares grazing space with the caribou, a relative of the reindeer. Hungry wolves roam the tundra, seeking food. The king of the tundra, the mighty polar bear, hunts the seal and the walrus. Tundra animals also include white Arctic hares, lemmings, and Arctic foxes. Birds are numerous and include ptarmigans, ducks, owls, and snow buntings.

The sun never sets in the Arctic Circle in summer. With the coming of autumn, the flowers fade, leaves turn brown and gold, and most birds and other animals migrate southward. Twilight ushers in winter, and winter brings snow, freezing cold, and darkness.

ALSO READ: ANIMAL, ANIMAL DISTRIBUTION, ARCTIC LIFE, BIRD, FOX, PLANT, PLANT DISTRIBUTION, SEALS AND SEA LIONS, WOLF.

TUNISIA The Republic of Tunisia, North Africa's smallest country, lies between Algeria and Libya on the Mediterranean coast. It is slightly smaller than the combined New England states. (See the map with the article on AFRICA.) The Atlas Mountains separate the fertile northern part of Tunisia from the dry southern area.

TUNISIA

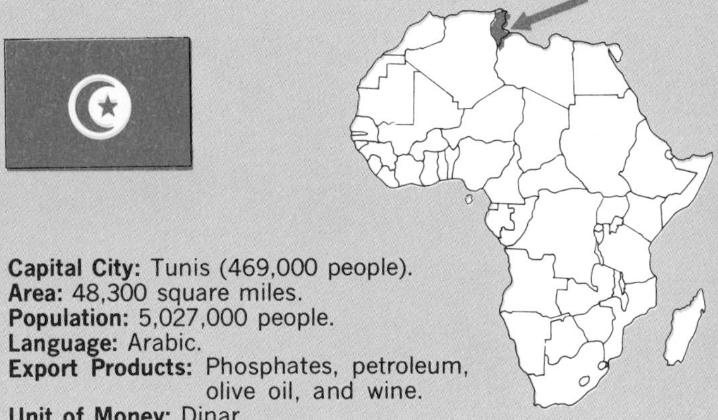

Capital City: Tunis (469,000 people).
Area: 48,300 square miles.
Population: 5,027,000 people.
Language: Arabic.
Export Products: Phosphates, petroleum, olive oil, and wine.
Unit of Money: Dinar.

▲*The Plaza of the Republic in Tunis was named to commemorate Tunisia's becoming independent in 1956.*

Tunis, the capital city, is a great port and a university center. The modern city exists with the old part, where tourists shop at *souks* (small shops) on narrow streets.

The Bedouin people of the southern desert region raise sheep, goats, and camels. Cattle graze on land near the coast. Fishing and mining of phosphates and iron ore are major industries. Oil is refined at Bizerte. Olive trees, date palms, grape vines, fruit trees, and wheat fields bring some agricultural wealth to Tunisia. The people of Tunis are mainly Arab and Berber, with some Europeans. More than one-third of all Tunisians live in urban communities.

The ancient city-state of Carthage was founded by the Phoenicians as a trading center near the site of present-day Tunis. Carthage was a powerful city until it was crushed by Rome during the Punic Wars. It became a possession of the Roman Empire in 136 B.C. Visitors to Tunis can see the ruins of Carthage and, in the Bardo Museum, a beautiful collection of Roman mosaics. Near El Djem stands a Roman colosseum built about 100 B.C. Tunisia was controlled by a succession of powers. The last was France, which took over in 1881.

Several battles in North Africa between the Allied forces and the Germans in World War II were fought in Tunisia. France recognized Tunisian independence on July 20, 1956, and the next year the old monarchy was abolished. The republic's first president was Habib Bourguiba.

ALSO READ: AFRICA, CARTHAGE, WORLD WAR II.

TUNNEL A tunnel is a tube-shaped underground passageway. Tunnels are usually designed to go through or under some obstacle, such as a river, mountain, or busy city. Tunnels under rivers and through mountains are built to make shorter and easier traveling routes. Tunnels under cities are built to divert some of the traffic from the streets.

Tunnels may be built in many sizes for a variety of purposes. Small tunnels are built to carry the lines for electricity, petroleum, water, gas, telephone, electricity, and sewers. These tunnels are rather small in diameter, but they may extend for many miles. *Vehicular* tunnels are designed as roads for vehi-

LONG TUNNELS OF THE WORLD

MOTOR TRAFFIC TUNNELS			RAIL TRAFFIC TUNNELS		
TUNNEL	LOCATION	LENGTH (MILES)	TUNNEL	LOCATION	LENGTH (MILES)
Mont Blanc	Alps (France-Italy)	7.3	Simplon	Alps (Switzerland-Italy)	12.3
Viella	Spain	3.1	Apennine	Italy	11.5
Broadway	Oakland, California	2.8	St. Gotthard	Alps (Switzerland)	9.3
Mersey	Liverpool, England	2.2	Lötschberg	Alps (Switzerland)	9.0
Kanmon	Japan	2.1	Mont Cenis	Alps (France-Italy)	8.5

◀ *Tunnels are often built to provide short cuts through mountains. This tunnel was blasted through the solid rock of Mount Blanc in the French Alps.*

cles such as cars, trucks, and railroads. Railroad tunnels are special vehicular tunnels that permit only rail traffic. Subways are commuter railroad tunnels located under cities that have heavy traffic. Other vehicular tunnels permit only cars and trucks. Some underwater tunnels are combined with bridges. A vehicle travels part of the route *over* water on a bridge and part of the route *under* water in a tunnel. Many mines consist of networks of tunnels that allow miners and their equipment to get to the ore deposits being mined.

Methods of construction depend on the material through which the tunnel is dug. To build a tunnel through solid rock, several large holes are drilled. Then explosives are placed in the holes, and the rock is blasted to pieces. Steel supports, called shoring, must be placed along the walls and top, especially in building through soft earth. These supports protect the workmen while they build the tunnel. In constructing *subaqueous tunnels* (tunnels in the soil under a river or bay), air pressure must be kept equal with the pressure of water outside so water will not enter the tunnel. A shield at the tunnel face is also used during construction to keep the water out. Tunnels are lined with iron or steel so the walls and roof will not cave in. Tunnels are ventilated by large fans that force in fresh air and suck out exhaust fumes. The next time you travel through a tunnel, look for air vents along the sides near the floor and on the roof.

ALSO READ: CAISSON, RAILROAD, STREETS AND ROADS, SUBWAY, TRANSPORTATION.

▲ *These men are performing caulking operations. They are filling in cracks in the walls of a tunnel in order to keep it watertight.*

TURBINE see ELECTRIC POWER, JET PROPULSION, PUMP.

TURKEY A visitor to the Middle Eastern city of Istanbul, Turkey, could travel from Asia to Europe on a ferry and still be in the same city! Located on a peninsula known as Asia Minor, Turkey lies mostly in Asia but partly in Europe.

The Turkish Straits separate the continents and connect the Black Sea with the Aegean and Mediterranean seas. The Straits (narrow passages of water) are made up of the Dardanelles, the Sea of Marmara, and the Bosporus Strait.

TURKEY

Capital City: Ankara (979,000 people).
Area: 296,185 square miles.
Population: 34,375,000 people.
Language: Turkish.
Export Products: Cotton, tobacco, fruit, and nuts.
Unit of Money: Turkish pound.

▲*The University of Istanbul, which dates back to the 1400s, is Turkey's most respected center of learning.*

Turkey's Asian neighbors are the Soviet Union, Syria, Iraq, and Iran. The European part of Turkey is bordered by Bulgaria and Greece. Turkey is a little larger than Texas. (See the map with the article on the MIDDLE EAST.)

Central Turkey is mainly a high plain, called the *Anatolian Plateau.* It is a land of salt lakes and hot springs. Earthquakes often take place. High mountains, some of them active volcanoes, almost completely surround the plateau.

The warm and sunny garden area by the Aegean Sea around Izmir (Smyrna) yields figs and other fruits. Turkish farmers also grow wheat, cotton, and tobacco. Turkey is the world's largest producer of *mohair*—fleece from the Angora goat. Chromite, coal, and iron are mined. State-owned factories produce steel, textiles, paper, and farm machinery. The people, who are mostly Muslims, speak Turkish. In eastern mountain villages, people called the *Kurds* have kept their own language and customs.

Istanbul, divided by the Bosporus Strait, has been an important city under several different names. The Roman Emperor Constantine established the capital of the Eastern Roman Empire at Byzantium in 324 A.D., and called it New Rome. But it was soon known as Constantinople. The Turks captured Constantinople in 1453, made it the capital of the Ottoman Empire, and later changed its name to Istanbul. It is the cultural and economic center of Turkey, although the capital is Ankara.

The Ottoman Empire at its height extended into Hungary, included the northern coast of Africa, and reached to the Persian Gulf. Turkey was one of the countries defeated in World War I and, as a result, it lost much of its land to Britain and France. Turkey became a republic on October 29, 1923, with Mustafa Kemal, or Kemal Ataturk, as the first president. He took the name *Ataturk*, meaning "Father of the Turks."

ALSO READ: OTTOMAN EMPIRE.

Noah's Ark came to rest on "the mountains of Ararat" when the great flood ended, according to the Book of Genesis in the Bible. The highest mountain in Turkey is called Ararat. Some people think it is the Biblical peak.

TURPENTINE see PLANT PRODUCTS.

TURTLE Turtles are reptiles with shells. The top shell and the bottom shell join at the sides. The head, legs, and tail can be pulled at least partly inside to protect the turtle from its enemies. Some turtles, such as the box turtle, have a hinged bottom shell that can be pulled up for even more complete protection.

The turtle, like all reptiles, is cold-blooded. This does not mean that its blood is always cold, but that its body temperature varies with the temperature of its surroundings. So turtles cannot live in very cold places.

About 200 different species (kinds) of turtles live in the warmer parts of the world. Turtles live in the ocean, in fresh water, and on land. Turtles that live on land are commonly called tortoises, and those that live in the ocean are called sea turtles. All turtles, even those that spend most of their lives in water, lay their eggs on land.

Turtles are of many different sizes. The tiny bog turtle averages 3½ inches. Giant Galapagos turtles can grow to weigh more than 500 pounds. The huge leatherback sea turtle is the heaviest of all reptiles. An adult may be 8 feet long and can weigh over 1,200 pounds. Turtles, large and small, are usually long-lived. Some have been known to live a hundred years, although few live much longer than that. Some turtles add "growth rings" to their shells as they grow. A young turtle's growth rings can be counted, but it is not a very accurate way to tell the turtle's age. Not all turtles grow a new ring every year.

Turtles do not have teeth. The edges of their jaws are sharp, hard ridges, similar to a bird's beak. Some turtles eat fish and animals that live near water, such as frogs and ducklings. Others eat insects and plants.

Land turtles, or tortoises, are slow-moving animals, so they usually have especially strong, tight shells to protect them from enemies. The box turtle is a common tortoise. Gopher turtles are tortoises that dig burrows in the ground. In rocky areas of Africa, some tortoises have flexible shells. When threatened they wedge themselves into a crevice and fill their lungs with air.

Freshwater turtles, like other turtles, can be beautiful or ugly. Their names often tell you which they are. The painted turtle and the mud turtle both live in ponds, but you know which is handsomer. The ugliness of a turtle can be to its advantage. The matamata, a South American turtle, looks like a floating log, and this helps it to hide from its enemies. All turtles have to put their heads out of water to breathe, but strangely, some pond turtles cannot swallow unless their heads are under the water. Many of the baby turtles sold as pets must eat and swallow under water.

"Terrapin" is an American Indian name sometimes given to turtles, especially those turtles people eat. The diamondback terrapin is often made into terrapin soup.

▲*Some sea turtles have flippers and others have webbed toes to enable them to swim more easily.*

▼*Box turtles, which inhabit the eastern United States, are found mainly on land.*

Large sea turtles spend almost all their lives in the sea. The female comes out on land only to lay her eggs. Turtles lay from 2 to 200 eggs at one time, depending on the variety of turtle.

ALSO READ: GALAPAGOS ISLANDS, REPTILE.

TUSCANY see ETRUSCAN, ITALY.

TUTANKHAMEN see EGYPT, ANCIENT.

▲*Mark Twain, American author.*

TWAIN, MARK (1835-1910) Mark Twain's real name was Samuel Langhorne Clemens, and he was one of America's most popular writers. He was born in Florida, Missouri, but grew up in Hannibal, Missouri, on the Mississippi River. Twain worked at many jobs. He was a printer, a steamboat pilot on the Mississippi River, a silver miner, and a reporter. The words "mark twain" mean "two fathoms deep." The phrase was used on Mississippi River steamboats in calling out the water's depth. When Clemens began writing, he adopted this phrase as his pen name.

Twain went to California in 1864. The following year a story about frontier life, "The Celebrated Jumping Frog of Calaveras County," made him famous. In the next few years, Twain traveled all around the world and began giving humorous lectures. Twain married in 1870 and moved to Hartford, Connecticut. In 1884, he became a partner in a publishing firm. But the firm failed, and Twain began lecturing again to pay his debts.

Twain wrote about his travels in *Innocents Abroad* and *Following the Equator. Life on the Mississippi* is an account of his experiences working on Mississippi River steamboats. Twain's most popular books are *The Adventures of Tom Sawyer* and its sequel, *The Adventures of Huckleberry Finn. Tom Sawyer* is about a boy growing up in a small town on the Mississippi with his good friends Becky Thatcher and the independent, mischievous Huck Finn. *Huckleberry Finn*, which carries Huck's story further, is considered Twain's best book. Twain modeled Tom, Becky, Huck, Aunt Polly, and even the villain, Injun Joe, on real people he had known in his own life. The book tells of the adventures of Huck and the runaway slave, Jim, as they travel down the Mississippi River on a raft.

ALSO READ: LITERATURE, NOVEL.

When John Tyler married his second wife in 1844, he became the first President to wed while in office. He also had the most children—15—of any President.

TYLER, JOHN (1790-1862) "His Accidency," as John Tyler was called by some of his enemies, was the first Vice President to succeed a President who had died in office. When President William Henry Harrison died on April 4, 1841, Vice President Tyler decided to become President rather than serve as Acting President until new elections could be held. Two days later, Tyler took the Presidential oath of office, but some leaders in government did not believe he had the right to that title. Tyler insisted that he had both the responsibility and the privilege that went with the highest office in the land.

TENTH PRESIDENT APRIL 6, 1841—MARCH 4, 1845

JOHN TYLER

Born: March 29, 1790, Charles City County, Virginia
Parents: John and Mary Armistead Tyler
Education: College of William and Mary, Williamsburg, Virginia
Religion: Episcopalian
Occupation: Lawyer
Political Party: Democratic, then Whig
State Represented: Virginia
Married: 1813 to Letitia Christian Tyler (1790–1842)
1844 to Julia Gardiner Tyler (1820–1889)
Children: 3 sons and 5 daughters (one died in infancy) by first wife; 5 sons and 2 daughters by second wife
Died: January 18, 1862, Richmond, Virginia
Buried: Hollywood Cemetery, Richmond, Virginia

John Tyler, born on a large plantation in Charles City County, Virginia, was the son of a distinguished judge and former governor of Virginia of the same name. The younger Tyler graduated from The College of William and Mary at 17 and then studied law. At 21 he was elected to the state legislature. He served in the House of Representatives from 1817 to 1821 and as governor of Virginia from 1825 to 1827. Tyler was elected to the Senate in 1827, where he served until 1836. Although Tyler was elected to the Senate as a Democrat, he disagreed with some of President Andrew Jackson's policies. Tyler believed strongly in a very strict interpretation of the Constitution. He believed in states' rights opposed to the power of the central (federal) government. Nationalism (pride in one's country and its destiny) was growing at this time and, as a result, the Federal Government was growing. So Tyler's views were not very popular. In 1840, the rival political party, the Whigs, hoped to gain the votes of dissatisfied Democrats. They nominated Tyler, a Democrat, for Vice President. Harrison, the Whig Presidential nominee, was known as "Old Tippecanoe." Their campaign slogan–which has since become famous–was "Tippecanoe and Tyler, too."

During his administration, the nation made a trade agreement with China for the first time. President Tyler urged that Texas be admitted as a state, and Congress finally passed a resolution to that effect. Tyler signed the bill just three days before he went out of office in 1845.

In 1842, while Tyler was still in the White House, his first wife (Letitia Christian) died. He married his second wife, Julia Gardiner, two years later. Sixteen years after retiring to Sherwood Forest, his Virginia plantation, the former President returned to Washington to preside over a peace convention. The representatives who attended from both North and South

▼A key event in Tyler's Presidency was the invention of a reaping machine by Cyrus H. McCormick. This reaper, a great improvement over an earlier model, created a revolution in farming methods. The drawing shows the machine which McCormick patented in 1845.

hoped to settle the differences between the two sections of the country and avoid a civil war. When the convention failed, Tyler favored secession. He was elected to the Confederate House of Representatives but died before he could take his seat.

ALSO READ: CHINA; CIVIL WAR; HARRISON, WILLIAM HENRY; PRESIDENCY; TEXAS.

TYPESETTING Have you ever looked at a book or magazine and wondered how the words and letters are put on the page? Look at the right-hand margins of the columns in this book. How are they made so straight and even? Compare the type used in this book with the type used in several other books, magazines, and newspapers. Notice the differences. On the top surface of a piece of metal type is a raised character called the *type face.* The face is the part that is inked for printing. In photographic typesetting, the characters are photographed on film. The characters on the negative are then transferred by a chemical process to a metal plate which is inked for printing. Type cast from metal is called *hot metal type.* Photographic typesetting is called *cold type.*

Type is made in several thousand sizes and styles. Each style gives a different feeling to a page. The choice of type styles depends on the purpose and kind of material being printed. The type used for advertisements is often unusual-looking and is chosen to draw attention to the ad. Newspaper headlines are printed in large, heavy, dark type to get you to read the article. Books are usually printed in clear, plain type that is easy on the eye and not difficult to read. Invitations and formal documents are often set in very fancy type to emphasize the importance or formality of the material.

▼Each time a Linotype operator presses a key, a brass mold is released from the flat, sloping part at the top of the machine. When a line of molds is in position, molten metal is forced against the molds to form a line of raised type.

Type styles are divided into four classes according to certain characteristics. *Roman type* is the class most used in modern-day printing. The type you are reading is a Roman type called "Times Roman." The Roman types all have *serifs* (little finishing strokes) on the characters. You can see the tiny little serifs at the ends of the lines that form each letter.

Sans serif type has no serifs on the letters. The letters are straight, clean, and squared off at the ends. The tables and charts in this encyclopedia are printed in a sans serif type called "News Gothic."

Script type is easy to recognize. It looks like fancy handwriting, and all the letters are connected. *Black letter type* has an old fashioned look. It is similar to the handwriting used in many European countries during Gutenberg's time.

All the characters included in the same style and size of type is called a *font* of type. One font may include several different *faces.* For example, the font of Times Roman type you are reading includes an *italic face that looks like this.* Times Roman also includes a **bold face that looks like this.** Fonts also include characters for CAPITAL LETTERS, SMALL CAPITALS, and lowercase letters. Some fonts even have ***bold face italic*** and other variations. Also included in some type fonts are symbols used in mathematics, astronomy, science, music, and other fields.

Setting type is the process of assembling type pieces in words and lines. Up until the late 1800s, most typesetting was done by hand. Each piece had to be selected from a case and inserted into a frame. Blank spacer pieces of various sizes were inserted to make blank spaces between words and to *justify the lines* (make them come out even on the right-hand side). Hand-setting is still done today for advertisements, expensive books, and material that cannot be set by machine.

Machine typesetting is of two kinds—hot metal and cold type. The two main hot-metal processes are Linotype and Monotype. The primary cold-type process used today is phototype.

A Linotype machine has metal molds, or matrices, for all the characters in a particular font. When the operator depresses a key, a matrice (mold) moves into place in the line. When the line is complete, a casting mechanism forces molten metal into the matrices. When hardened, the resulting metal slug has raised letters, forming the line of type.

Ottmar Mergenthaler invented the Linotype machine in 1884. It was first used by *The Tribune* newspaper in New York City in 1886. Another slug-casting machine, called *Intertype,* works on the same principle as the Linotype.

Linotype machines cast a whole line of type, whereas Monotype machines cast one character at a time.

Monotype was invented by Tolbert Lanston in 1887. It is not often used nowadays. The more flexible methods of film typesetting have largely taken over the jobs that used to be done by Monotype machines.

Phototypesetting is the most modern method of setting type. Characters are rapidly photographed by a high-speed camera. The camera is usually operated by a computer. The computer is programmed for the size and style of type, the line length, and so on. The computer can justify the lines automatically, and the operator need only feed it the correct program. The photographed lines of type are prepared for printing through a chemical process that transfers the image of the photographed characters onto a metal plate. This encyclopedia was set with phototype.

Phototype is an extremely fast method of typesetting. New processes are being discovered all the time to increase its speed and accuracy.

ALSO READ: BOOK; GUTENBERG, JOHANNES; MAGAZINE; NEWSPAPER; PRINTING; PUBLISHING.

TYPEWRITER see OFFICE EQUIPMENT.

▲*As a phototype operator types the copy to be set, the paper tape at the left* (above) *is perforated as it moves through the machine. The perforated tape is run through a machine* (below) *that controls a camera which reproduces the type photographically.*▼

U u

UGANDA Uganda is a country in the highlands of East Africa. It has no seacoast and is surrounded by other countries. (See the map with the article on AFRICA.)

Uganda lies on the equator. But because it is on a plateau about 4,000 feet high, the climate is mild. Temperatures range from 60 to 90 degrees. The Ruwenzori Mountains, sometimes called the Mountains of the Moon, rise from the plateau along Uganda's border with Zaire in the west. Lake Victoria, the source of the Nile River, borders Uganda on the southeast. Uganda shares the lake with its neighbors, Tanzania and Kenya.

The Victoria Nile, which branches off from Lake Victoria, is the home of many hippopotamuses and crocodiles. Wildlife is also abundant in the plains. Uganda has two of the finest parks in all Africa. The Queen Elizabeth National Park is an animal sanctuary for waterbucks, lions, leopards, wart hogs, and huge herds of buffaloes. Road markers read, "Elephants have the

▼*A member of the Karamojong tribe, a people who live in northeastern Uganda.*

UGANDA

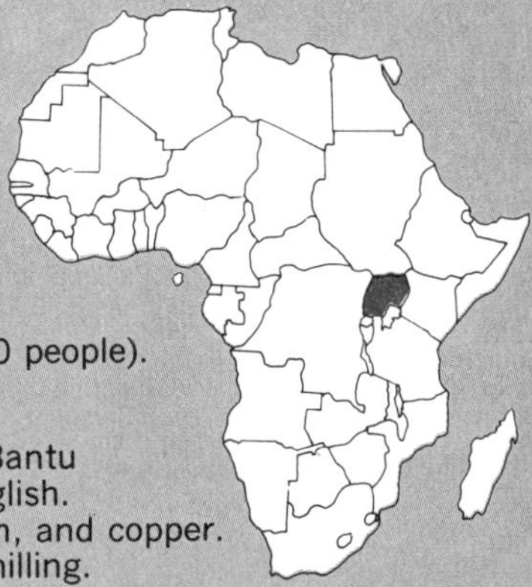

Capital City: Kampala (123,000 people).
Area: 80,301 square miles.
Population: 9,500,000 people.
Languages: Ganda and other Bantu languages and English.
Export Products: Coffee, cotton, and copper.
Unit of Money: East African shilling.

right-of-way." Murchison Falls National Park has giraffes and rhinoceroses, as well as parrots, storks, ostriches, and cranes.

Farming is Uganda's largest industry. Plantain, a type of banana, is the main crop. Coffee and cotton are grown for export. A huge water-power dam built at Owens Falls on the Victoria Nile is helping Uganda's industry grow.

The Baganda are the most important of the more than 30 tribes living in Uganda. For centuries, the Baganda had their own king, called the *kabaka.* The last kabaka became the first president of Uganda. The Baamba and the Bakonja, who live near the Ruwenzori Mountains, are small people related to the pygmies of the Congo.

John Speke, a British explorer searching for the source of the Nile River, became the first European to reach Uganda. The year was 1862. In 1896, the British made Uganda a protectorate. Uganda finally won its independence in 1962.

Kampala, on Lake Victoria, is Uganda's capital and chief commercial center. Makerere University is located there. Oinja, near the site of the Owens Falls Dam, is the second largest city.

ALSO READ: AFRICA; EQUATOR; NILE RIVER; PYGMY; STANLEY, HENRY MORTON.

UNCLE REMUS see HARRIS, JOEL CHANDLER.

UNCLE SAM Uncle Sam is a nickname for the United States government. It was first used during the War of 1812, and eventually "Uncle Sam" grew to represent the United States.

The name Uncle Sam may have come from the initials U.S. stamped on uniforms and government property during the War of 1812. According to one story, the name originated with Samuel Wilson, an upstate New York patriot and merchant during the War of 1812. He owned a meat-packing business that supplied provisions to U.S. troops. When the governor of the state visited the plant, he asked what the initials U.S. on bar-

Several other countries include the names of men in their national symbols. John Bull, a stout, jolly figure, sometimes represents Britain and its people.

rels in the factory stood for. He was told that they stood for Uncle Sam Wilson. The hard-working, honest Wilson seemed to symbolize the ideal American. Before the end of the war, the name Uncle Sam was commonly used to mean the United States itself. In 1961, the U.S. Congress adopted a resolution saluting Uncle Sam as the country's national symbol.

Uncle Sam has often been pictured in cartoons and on patriotic posters. He usually wears a white beard and top hat with striped pants and a long-tailed jacket.

▲*This poster by artist James Montgomery Flagg, showing that Uncle Sam needed volunteers, was widely displayed during World War II.*

UNDERGROUND RAILROAD The Underground Railroad was a secret system by which people helped runaway slaves escape from their masters to freedom in Canada in the days before the Civil War. As many as 75,000 slaves may have used the Underground Railroad to escape between about 1830 and 1860.

The name Underground Railroad did not mean that an actual railroad was used. But railroad terms were used for many parts of the escape system. For example, the places where slaves were hidden along the way—usually the homes of abolitionists, Quakers, and other people who hated slavery—were called *stations.* The people who guided the slaves from station to station were called *conductors,* and the slaves themselves were sometimes referred to as *freight.* Because many people were against helping runaway slaves, and rewards were offered for the capture of slaves, the system was kept "underground," or secret.

Underground Railroad lines extended from Kentucky, Maryland, and Virginia up into Ohio, Pennsylvania, New York, and New England. Moving from station to station, usually at night, most slaves tried to escape over the Canadian border.

Both black and white people helped the slaves to use the Underground Railroad. One of the best-known conductors was a black woman named Harriet Tubman. She made many daring trips into the South to bring slaves north. She became known as Moses to her fellow blacks, because like the character from the Bible, she helped her people find the "Promised Land." Thomas Garrett, a Pennsylvania Quaker, was another well-known conductor. He is said to have helped more than 2,500 blacks escape.

ALSO READ: ABOLITION; SLAVERY; TUBMAN, HARRIET.

UNICORN see ANIMALS OF MYTH AND LEGEND.

UNIDENTIFIED FLYING OBJECT Many objects fly across the sky—airplanes, helicopters, stars, planets, satellites, and clouds. Most of these objects can be easily identified, but occasionally someone sees an unidentified flying object, or UFO.

The first written report of a UFO was made in Egypt in 1500 B.C. A few hundred more UFOs were seen over the next few thousand years. A rash of UFOs was reported in 1896 and 1897.

These were often described as cigar-shaped silver airships. Some passengers were even observed. The most dramatic UFO of 1897 was that which landed in a Kansas farmer's field, carried off his heifer, and dropped it a few miles away. Several neighbors vouched for the farmer's honesty and sanity.

UFOs are sometimes called "flying saucers." This name was first used in 1947 when an American pilot reported sighting ten saucers flying in formation near Mount Rainier in Washington. Shortly afterwards more sightings were reported, and the Air-Force began a study of UFOs. Over the next 15 years the Air Force received more than 11,000 reports of UFOs.

Most of the reported UFOs were eventually identified as known objects—airplanes flying in the vicinity, weather balloons, peculiar cloud formations, satellites, or meteors. Those few that could not be explained had not usually been very carefully described by the observers. A study group formed by the Air Force reported no evidence that any of the UFOs were likely to have come from outer space.

ALSO READ: AIRPLANE, SPACE TRAVEL.

▲*Four unidentified flying objects zoomed across the sky near Salem, Massachusetts, in July, 1952. The mysterious objects were spotted by members of the U.S. Coast Guard who took this photograph.*

UNIFORM see CLOTHING.

UNION OF SOVIET SOCIALIST REPUBLICS see SOVIET UNION.

UNITED KINGDOM The United Kingdom of Great Britain and Northern Ireland is a nation made up of four regions—England, Scotland, Wales, and Northern Ireland. The name of the kingdom is usually shortened to "Great Britain" or "United Kingdom." Often the name "England" refers to the whole United Kingdom, which covers all of the British Isles except for the southern part of Ireland, which is the Republic of Ireland. (See the map with the article on BRITISH ISLES.)

Wales was united with England by an Act of Union in 1536. In 1603, the king of Scotland, James VI, also became king of

UNITED KINGDOM

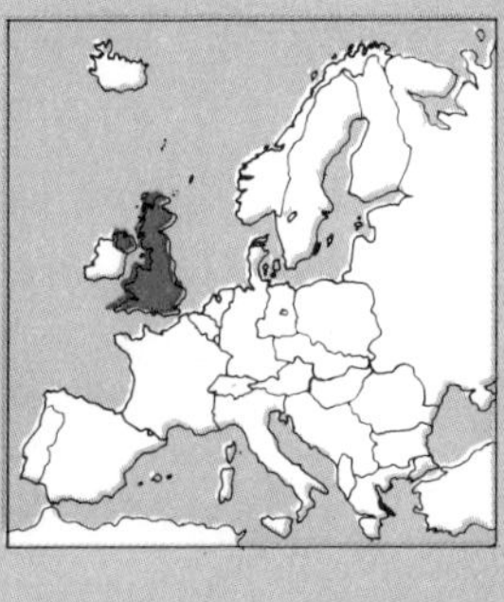

Capital City: London (7,764,000 people).
Area: 94,214 square miles.
Population: 55,534,000 people.
Languages: English and Welsh.
Export Products: Machinery, transportation equipment, automobiles, and textiles.
Unit of Money: British pound.

▲*The houses of Parliament in Westminster, London, are the seat of the legislature for the United Kingdom. Parliament consists of the House of Commons* (right) *and the House of Lords* (left). *Big Ben, a world-famous clock, can be seen on the far right.*

England and Wales, as James I. His successors ruled both kingdoms during the 1600s. In 1707, an Act of Union joined Scotland with England and Wales as the Kingdom of Great Britain. Ireland became part of Great Britain by an Act of Union in 1800, and the whole nation became known as the United Kingdom of Great Britain and Ireland. In 1922, The Irish Free State was formed. Later it broke all ties with Britain and became an independent republic. Six counties in the north of Ireland voted to remain a part of the United Kingdom.

The capital of the United Kingdom is London, England, and the official language is English. But Scotland, Wales, and Northern Ireland have their own capitals. The three areas have kept their own traditions, religious faiths, and local languages, although English is spoken throughout the United Kingdom. Each region sends representatives to the British Parliament.

ALSO READ: BRITISH ISLES, ENGLAND, ENGLISH HISTORY, IRELAND, NORTHERN IRELAND, SCOTLAND, WALES.

UNITED NATIONS On October 24, 1945, 51 nations created the international peace organization called the United Nations. By 1972, the UN had grown to a membership of 132 nations. The UN was first proposed by Franklin D. Roosevelt and Winston Churchill in the Atlantic Charter, issued in 1941. The first plans for the UN were made at a conference at Dumbarton Oaks in Washington, D.C., in 1944. When Roosevelt died in 1945, Harry Truman carried out the plans. At a conference in San Francisco in the same year, the UN charter was drawn up and signed. Plans for the United Nations were based on the League of Nations, a peace organization formed after World War I. But the United States had refused to join the League, and it had never been successful in forcing nations to keep the peace.

▼*The seating of the delegation of the People's Republic of China in the United Nations General Assembly was a historic event. As of November 15, 1971, over 700 million Chinese were represented in the world organization.*

The UN has five major goals: to promote peace and security; to bring about friendly relations among all nations; to encourage respect for the rights and freedoms of others; to improve living conditions, education, and health; and to develop an effective system of international law. Nations must agree to these principles in order to become members of the United Nations. The UN works toward its goals through six major bodies.

The *Security Council* has 15 members. Ten are elected for two-year terms, and five are permanent. The ten temporary members are chosen from all areas of the world in an effort to assure fair geographical representation on the council. The five permanent members are the People's Republic of China, France, the U.S.S.R., the United Kingdom, and the U.S. If just one permanent member votes against a Security Council resolution, the measure is automatically defeated. This is called the *power of the veto.* The members of the council take turns acting as chairman. Each one serves for one month.

◀*The headquarters of the United Nations are in New York City on the banks of the East River. The glass-faced skyscraper is the Secretariat. The low building in front of it is the Conference Building where the different councils meet.*

The Security Council's duty is to maintain peace. It studies aggression and disagreements that might lead to war and recommends ways to solve them. The Security Council usually tries to negotiate a settlement. It may set up a fact-finding commission to determine which nation is at fault in committing aggression and persuade that nation to stop. It may convince quarreling nations to submit their dispute to the International Court of Justice (World Court). If these measures fail, the Security Council may ask the UN to impose some kind of sanction (economic punishment) to try to force the offending nation to cooperate. The UN has sometimes used force to bring peace.

The largest body of the UN, the *General Assembly,* is made up of the delegates from every member nation. Each nation has one vote. The General Assembly discusses and makes recommendations on any problem relating to the welfare of member nations. But the General Assembly cannot discuss matters that are under discussion in the Security Council, unless the Security Council is unable to agree upon a course of action. Then the General Assembly may recommend ways to maintain order or restore peace. A new president is elected each year.

Nations may fight over politics, but everybody wants to improve the quality of life for mankind. In the UN, this is the duty of the 27-member *Economic and Social Council,* supervised by the General Assembly. The Council studies living conditions in many lands and sends experts to teach people the skills they need to survive. Fifteen specialized agencies are attached to the UN by treaties or agreements. They work through the Economic and Social Council to help people everywhere. The International Atomic Energy Agency works for the peaceful use

▼*A flag-raising ceremony is held to welcome new members to the United Nations.*

of atomic energy. The Food and Agriculture Organization helps to improve nutrition and farming methods in member nations. The United Nations Educational, Scientific, and Cultural Organization (UNESCO) works to improve education around the world and to extend communications among various cultures. There are other agencies for health, international trade, labor standards, communications, and transportation.

One special branch of the UN is devoted to children—the United Nations Children's Fund (UNICEF). UNICEF helps to combat disease by vaccinating children and improving nutrition-scarce diets in underdeveloped nations.

The day-to-day work of the UN is done by the fourth major body, the *Secretariat,* the administrative branch of the UN. The Secretariat, which employes over 4,000 people, is headed by the Secretary-General, a delegate appointed for a 5-year term by the General Assembly. The Secretary-General can alert the Security Council to any matter he thinks threatens international peace. He often tries to ease conflicts by personally visiting troubled areas of the world. The Secretary-General is also responsible for carrying out tasks assigned to him by the General Assembly and the various councils.

▼*Representatives of the United Nations, such as this man in Guinea, travel around the world to investigate problems.*

The *International Court of Justice* is the main judicial body of the UN. Its 15 judges, who serve for nine years, are elected by the General Assembly and the Security Council. The Court is located at The Hague, Netherlands. Any nation involved in a dispute may refer its case to the Court, but decisions are not binding unless all parties agree beforehand to accept the decision. The Court also strives to establish a system of international law so that disputes can be settled by reasonable discussion, not war. The UN may ask the Court for advice in interpreting the UN Charter.

The *Trusteeship Council,* also supervised by the General Assembly, is the least active of the UN bodies today. Its task is to guide colonies toward independence. Nine of the eleven original trust territories have now gained independence.

UN headquarters are located in New York City. The UN has its own post office that issues stamps and has its own police, fire department, and school. UN headquarters are a popular international tourist attraction. If possible, visitors are given a tour by guides who speak their native languages.

There are five official languages at the UN—English, French, Russian, Spanish, and Chinese. Each seat is provided with earphones and a dial. Whenever a delegate speaks, his words are immediately translated into the five languages. A listener can listen in any of the languages.

ALSO READ: BUNCHE, RALPH; HAMMARSKJOLD, DAG; INTERNATIONAL LAW; INTERNATIONAL RELATIONS; INTERNATIONAL TRADE; LEAGUE OF NATIONS; WAR.

◀ *The Capitol is the seat of Congress, the legislative branch (the Senate and the House of Representatives) of the U.S. government.*

UNITED STATES GOVERNMENT The national government of the United States is that of a constitutional federal republic. It is *constitutional* because the powers and operations of the government are designated by long-established written law (the Constitution) and not by any person or group, as is often the case with monarchies, oligarchies, and dictatorships. The U.S. government is *federal* because it represents the union, or federation, of all the states. It shares authority with state governments and cannot take over the powers of the states in matters under their rule. The U.S. government is *republican* in form because the citizens elect the people who represent them.

Four basic features make the United States government different from the governments of other nations–the relationship of the states to the Federal Government; the U.S. Constitution; the separation of powers among three branches of government; and the broad powers of the U.S. President.

The Federal Government and the States

When the colonies won their war for independence against England in 1783, they knew they would have to join together in order to survive as a nation. But the colonies wanted to retain their newly won independence and were against too much control from a central government. In 1781, the original 13 states adopted a constitution, called the Articles of Confederation. Under this constitution, each state had almost as much power as an independent nation.

The states soon realized that the Articles of Confederation were not building a strong nation. Because each state was acting as if it were a separate nation, the union of states was in danger of collapse. State leaders had to come up with a better system if the United States were to survive as a single, whole nation.

In 1787, representatives from every state met in Philadelphia to revise the Articles of Confederation. Instead, they wrote the present U.S. Constitution, in which the states agreed to give up some of their powers in order to form a more perfect union.

▼ *Federal Hall in New York City was the first Capitol of the U.S. government. This is how it looked in 1797.*

Representatives from the 13 states wished to construct a stronger, more workable central government. But they wanted limits on the powers of the central government so that it could not become too strong and all-powerful, like the rule of a king.

The representatives wrote a constitution that specifically defines the powers of the Federal Government. All other powers not specifically given to federal authority belong to the states. The Federal Government handles services that cross state boundaries and that affect the nation as a whole. Transportation, road building, electric and gas power, and natural resources lie within the federal authority. Can you explain why?

►*The Department of Commerce is part of the executive branch of the United States Government.*

In modern times, there has been a shift of power and control away from the states and toward the Federal Government in order to solve the increasingly complicated problems confronting people living in a large modern nation. Increased transportation and communication, as well as greater U.S. involvement in foreign affairs, have produced more situations in which the Federal Government must act for the nation.

The U.S. Constitution

The U.S. Constitution differs from the constitutions of many other nations in its brevity, simplicity, and flexibility. The Constitution has survived with only 26 changes for almost 200 years. Some nations change their constitutions quite often. The same brief U.S. Constitution has seen the United States through the early frontier years, Indian wars, the Industrial Revolution, a Civil War, two World Wars, the terrible Depression of the 1930s, and the troubled Cold War period culminating in the Vietnam Conflict. Throughout these great upheavals and changes, the Constitution has remained a basic source of law with which the actions and decisions of the United States can be guided. Very few new words have been added to its original language.

Much credit for the Constitution must go to men like Alexander Hamilton, Thomas Jefferson, and James Madison, who had to devise general principles of government for specific situations they could not possibly foresee. At the Constitutional Convention in 1787, they composed a document that they knew must serve the nation for many years to come.

Separation of Powers

The men who designed the Constitution did not want a system of government that in any way resembled a monarchy. The colonists had fought long and hard to free themselves from the rule of a hostile king and parliament. They were determined that the power of the Federal Government would never be allowed to come under the control of an all-powerful king or group of rulers. They outlined a system whereby power is divided among three branches of government—the Presidency, called the *executive branch;* the Congress, called the *legislative branch;* and the courts, called the *judicial branch.*

In their operations, these three branches of government check and balance each other so no one man or group can gain complete control of the government at any time. The Congress, for example, can pass a law, and the President can sign it, but if the law runs contrary to the Constitution, the Supreme Court can void it. The President commands the army, but only Congress can declare war and supply funds for the military services. A President who has acted corruptly may be impeached and convicted by Congress and removed from office.

The Federal Government, according to the Constitution, can coin money, tax, borrow money, set up federal courts, and in other ways run the nation. The Congress, as the lawmaking body, enacts new laws, levies taxes, and spends the tax money. The Supreme Court, as the highest court in the nation, interprets the laws of the nation. Decisions of the Supreme Court become law, and its decisions can change laws that are deemed unconstitutional. By declaring a law unconstitutional, the Supreme Court has power over both the Congress and the executive branch and therefore a great role in shaping the nation. Where Constitutional language is vague, the Court can interpret it according to the just needs of the nation.

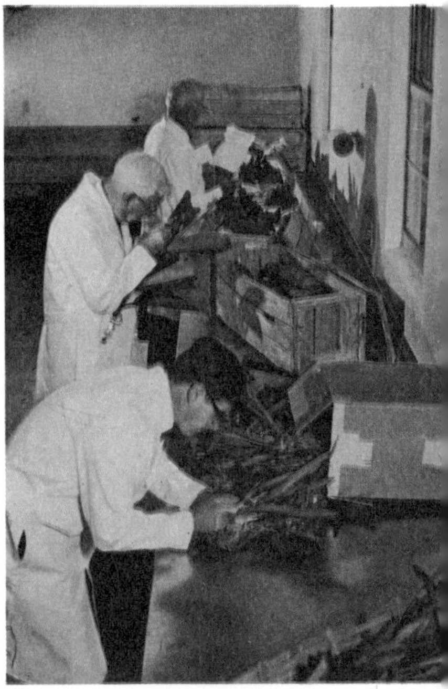

▲*Officers of the Bureau of Customs regulate all goods that enter the United States. Merchandise suspected of bearing contagious disease germs may be quarantined, or detained for a period of time, until it is judged to be harmless.*

The Party System

The system of political parties in the United States has a great effect on the President and Congress. The two major parties, Democrat and Republican, as well as independent parties, perform special duties in the political system. U.S. political parties select candidates for elective office, provide the means for a candidate to make his views known to the public, and allow for individuals to participate in the selection process through nominating conventions and primary elections.

The Democratic, Republican, and other parties serve as checks on each other. Within each party are members with widely differing political views. The candidate of a party must usually be able to bring the various views of party members together on most issues. He must try to represent the political views of the people who nominate him. If a candidate does not represent the views of the majority of his party, there is danger of members voting for the candidate of the opposing party.

For further information on:

Agencies Within U.S. Government, *see* FEDERAL BUREAU OF INVESTIGATION, FOREIGN SERVICE, LIBRARY OF CONGRESS, PEACE CORPS, POSTAL SERVICE, SOCIAL SECURITY, UNITED STATES GOVERNMENT AGENCIES.

Branches of U.S. Government, *see* CABINET, UNITED STATES; CONGRESS, UNITED STATES; COURT SYSTEM; PRESIDENCY; SUPREME COURT; VICE PRESIDENT.

Formation of U.S. Government, *see* AMERICAN COLONIES; AMERICAN HISTORY; AMERICAN REVOLUTION; ARTICLES OF CONFEDERATION; BILL OF RIGHTS; CONSTITUTION, UNITED STATES; CONTINENTAL CONGRESS; DECLARATION OF INDEPENDENCE; ELECTION; MAYFLOWER COMPACT; POLITICAL PARTY.

Powers of U.S. Government, *see* CITIZENSHIP, CIVIL RIGHTS, IMPEACHMENT, INTERNATIONAL RELATIONS, INTERNATIONAL TRADE, LAW, MONEY, PASSPORTS AND VISAS, PATENTS AND COPYRIGHTS, TAX, TREATY, WAR.

UNITED STATES GOVERNMENT AGENCIES Besides the three branches of the United States government–the Presidency, the Congress, and the federal court system–the United States has many administrative agencies to handle special problems in governing a large nation. These agencies vary in size and importance. Many were created during President Roosevelt's New Deal administration to cope with bank failures, widespread unemployment, and other problems during the Depression of the 1930s. Other agencies, such as the Lend-Lease Administration and National War Labor Board, were formed as temporary measures during and after World War II.

▼*Buyers crowd around as* America Illustrated, *a publication of the United States Information Agency, goes on sale at a Moscow newsstand. In exchange,* Soviet Life *is for sale in the United States.*

The President appoints and the Senate confirms the heads of government agencies and commissions. A commissioner's term usually runs seven years. Directors of agencies, such as the U.S. Information Agency, are appointed every four years at the beginning of each new presidential term. Commissions grew out of a definite need for small independent bodies, apart from the regular government structure, to investigate unfair practices and to settle disputes in areas affecting the public, such as transportation, business, international trade, and foreign loans.

Once the work of a commission is completed, it is usually disbanded. After World War II, for example, the U.S. Foreign Claims Settlement Commission was set up. This agency was

SOME IMPORTANT INDEPENDENT FEDERAL AGENCIES

ACTION—controls programs for aid to needy areas at home and abroad. It includes the former Vista and Peace Corps organizations.
Atomic Energy Commission—controls the use and development of atomic energy in the United States.
Central Intelligence Agency—is responsible for the intelligence operations of the United States government.
Civil Aeronautics Board—determines air routes used by U.S. airlines and the prices charged by them.
Civil Service Commission—has responsibility for the selection of applicants for government jobs.
Environmental Protection Agency—leads the government's fight against pollution.
Equal Employment Opportunity Commission—is responsible for the prevention of discrimination in employment.
Export-Import Bank of the U.S.—provides aid in financing exports and imports of commodities.
Federal Communications Commission—licenses broadcast stations and regulates some aspects of the programming of broadcast stations as a whole.
Federal Deposit Insurance Corporation—insures the deposits of most banks in the United States.
Federal Maritime Commission—administers federal laws relating to U.S. shipping operations.
Federal Power Commission—regulates the prices charged by electric and gas companies that engage in interstate commerce.
Federal Reserve System—influences the flow of credit and money in the United States.
Federal Trade Commission—attempts to keep business fair and competitive.
General Accounting Office—examines the accounts of most federal agencies and provides Congress with reports.
General Services Administration—manages federal property.
Government Printing Office—is responsible for government publications.
Interstate Commerce Commission—enforces federal laws concerning transportation of people or property across state lines.
Library of Congress—provides research and other materials to Congress and members of the public.
National Academy of Sciences—advises the United States government on scientific matters.
National Foundation of the Arts and Humanities—provides financial and other assistance to the arts and humanities.
National Labor Relations Board—prevents unfair labor practices by either unions or employers.
Office of Economic Opportunity—controls government programs in education and job training.
Securities and Exchange Commission—enforces federal laws concerning the purchase and sale of securities.
Selective Service System—is responsible for providing enough men for the Armed Forces.
Small Business Administration—tries to help small businesses by use of loans and government contracts.
Tennessee Valley Authority—is responsible for the development of resources in the Tennessee Valley.
United States Information Agency—provides information to foreign countries about the United States.
Veterans Administration—administers laws concerning benefits for men who served in the Armed Forces.

empowered to check into damage claims against the United States made by citizens of countries where U.S. troops fought. The Commission then recommended payment if the U.S. was at fault. By the early 1960s, no more war claims were being made against the United States, and the Commission was dissolved.

Commissions are created by Acts of Congress. The nine-member Federal Trade Commission (the FTC), which checks into unfair trade and business practices, and the Federal Communications Commission (the FCC), which regulates communications by wire and airwaves, are examples of commissions set up by Congressional Acts. One of the oldest commissions is the Interstate Commerce Commission. It was established in 1887 during a public furor over railroad abuses in the 1880s. The ICC continues to investigate the rates, safety, and management of interstate commerce.

A government corporation, the Reconstruction Finance Corporation, was started by an Act of Congress in 1932. Its purpose

▲*The Atomic Energy Commission is the independent federal agency in charge of atomic energy and its uses in the U.S. Its laboratory in Oak Ridge, Tennessee, developed a machine (shown here) to achieve thermonuclear fusion.*

was to make emergency loans to banks and trust companies during the depression. Another government corporation, the Export-Import Bank, makes loans to American companies that export products abroad. It also supervises various types of trade relations between the United States and foreign nations. The Bank is run by a full-time, five-member board.

Government agencies that are not corporations or commissions are established by Acts of Congress and are each run by a director. The directors are appointed by the President with the approval of the Senate. The U.S. Information Agency was set up in 1949 to distribute information to foreign countries about the United States and its policies. The U.S. Arms Control and Disarmament Agency was established in 1960. It is empowered to negotiate disarmament treaties for the United States and to research and develop arms control measures for negotiation with foreign governments. The Central Intelligence Agency is the office of government engaged in espionage work overseas. There are many more agencies and commissions within the U.S. government. The independent agencies (those not connected with any larger governmental department) are listed in the table accompanying this article.

ALSO READ: CONGRESS, UNITED STATES; PEACE CORPS; PRESIDENCY; UNITED STATES GOVERNMENT.

UNITED STATES OF AMERICA The United States of America is a large country centered on the North American continent. It was founded in 1776, when 13 colonies along the Atlantic coast broke away from England to form an independent nation.

Today, the U.S. consists of 50 states and several outlying dependencies, including partially independent Puerto Rico, the Virgin Islands in the West Indies, and Guam in the Mariana Islands. The U.S. is the fourth largest country in the world both in area and population. Only China, India, and the Soviet Union have more people, and only the Soviet Union, Canada, and China are bigger in size.

The Land and Climate

The United States covers many different geographical regions. The Appalachian Mountains run southwestward along the Atlantic Coast from New England to Alabama. But from New York south, a coastal plain widens to include most of Georgia and all of Florida. Vast plains cover the huge central area of the U.S. West of the central plains rise the Rocky Mountains. Between them and the Pacific is an uneven, high tableland, ending with coast ranges along the Pacific Ocean. The coast ranges include the Sierra Nevada, a mountain chain which extends for about 400 miles through eastern California. The highest peak in

◀ *Summer in the United States is a lovely time for strolling through high mountain meadows carpeted with wildflowers.*

the original 48 states, Mount Whitney (14,945 feet), rises in the Sierra Nevada. The Cascade Mountains run north from the Sierra Nevada through Oregon and Washington.

In the state of Alaska are the highest mountains in North America. Mount McKinley (20,320 feet), the country's tallest mountain, is located there. The mountains in Alaska gradually taper off to an Arctic coastal plain.

The islands of Hawaii are located about 2,000 miles off the Pacific Coast of the continental United States. They were formed by volcanoes that built up from the ocean floor. The islands have many volcanoes that are still active.

Most of the United States is drained by six great rivers—the Mississippi and its branches (which include the Missouri) in the center, the Columbia in the northwest, the Colorado and the Rio Grande in the southwest, the St. Lawrence-Great Lakes system in the northeast, and the Yukon in central Alaska.

Because the U.S. is so large, it has many different types of climate. The southern part of the West Coast has what is called a Mediterranean climate. It is warm and sunny most of the year, with some rain in winter. North of California the coast has a marine climate. The winds come mostly from the sea and carry much moisture—rain is common and forests are dense.

The sea winds are forced upward by the coastal mountains and lose their moisture. This creates a long band of dry country just east of the coast. In the south, this arid belt produces deserts as dry as Death Valley in California. Farther north, the land is often dry and barren, but usually has some sparse growth and stunted trees.

The land near the Rockies has a highland climate. It is cooler, because of its high altitude, and has more rain and snow. The central plains have what is called a continental climate. Summers are hot and winters are very cold.

When the winds come from the sea, as they do on the West Coast of North America, they keep winters mild. Even a coastal

UNITED STATES OF AMERICA

Capital City: Washington, D.C. (756,510 people).
Area: 3,615,211 square miles.
Population: 210,000,000 people.
Language: English.
Export Products: Machinery, aircraft, automobiles, and chemicals.
Unit of Money: U.S. dollar.

▲*The rich green fields of an Iowa farm are typical of agricultural land in the United States.*

▲*A family relives history at the National Battlefield Park in Yorktown, Virginia. The British surrender here ended the Revolutionary War.*

▲*The United States looks out into space from the Naval Observatory in Washington, D.C. Scientists here send out exact time signals every day.*

▲*A church in a small Vermont town symbolizes the American devotion to religion. The church is typical of the kind of architecture to be found in New England during the early years of the Republic* (above). *Whatever goes up must come down! Skiers ride to the top of a New Hampshire mountain on chair lifts and then ski down the snow-covered slopes* (right).▶

◀*Waikiki Beach in Hawaii, the newest state, is a vacation paradise. Diamond Head rises in the background* (left). *Portland, Oregon, stretches from the meeting point of the Columbia and Willamette rivers to the distant hills* (right).▶

CANADA
BRITISH COLUMBIA
ALBERTA
SASKATCHEWAN
MANITOBA
ONTARIO
QUEBEC
NEW BRUNSWICK
NOVA SCOTIA
PRINCE EDWARD I.
Vancouver I.
WASHINGTON
OREGON
CALIFORNIA
IDAHO
NEVADA
MONTANA
WYOMING
UTAH
ARIZONA
COLORADO
NEW MEXICO
NORTH DAKOTA
SOUTH DAKOTA
NEBRASKA
KANSAS
OKLAHOMA
TEXAS
MINNESOTA
IOWA
MISSOURI
ARKANSAS
LOUISIANA
WISCONSIN
ILLINOIS
MICHIGAN
INDIANA
OHIO
KENTUCKY
TENNESSEE
MISSISSIPPI
ALABAMA
GEORGIA
FLORIDA
SOUTH CAROLINA
NORTH CAROLINA
VIRGINIA
WEST VIRGINIA
PENNSYLVANIA
NEW YORK
MARYLAND
DELAWARE
NEW JERSEY
CONNECTICUT
RHODE ISLAND
MASSACHUSETTS
VERMONT
NEW HAMPSHIRE
MAINE
Seattle
Olympia
Salem
Boise
Helena
Sacramento
San Francisco
Carson City
Los Angeles
Salt Lake City
Phoenix
Cheyenne
Denver
Santa Fe
Bismarck
Pierre
Lincoln
Topeka
Oklahoma City
Dallas
Austin
Houston
St. Paul
Des Moines
Jefferson City
Little Rock
Baton Rouge
New Orleans
Jackson
Madison
Chicago
Springfield
St. Louis
Lansing
Detroit
Indianapolis
Nashville
Montgomery
Atlanta
Tallahassee
Miami
Columbus
Cleveland
Frankfort
Charleston
Columbia
Raleigh
Richmond
Washington D.C.
Annapolis
Dover
Baltimore
Philadelphia
Harrisburg
Trenton
New York
Hartford
Providence
Boston
Albany
Montpelier
Concord
Augusta
CASCADE RANGE
SIERRA NEVADA
GREAT BASIN
Mt. Whitney (14,495 ft.)
ROCKY MOUNTAINS
GREAT PLAINS
APPALACHIAN MOUNTAINS
Great Salt Lake
Columbia R.
Snake R.
Missouri R.
Yellowstone R.
Colorado R.
Arkansas R.
Platte R.
Canadian R.
Red R.
Pecos R.
Rio Grande
Red River of the North
Mississippi R.
Ohio R.
Tennessee R.
St. Lawrence R.
Lake Superior
Lake Michigan
Lake Huron
Lake Erie
Lake Ontario
PACIFIC OCEAN
ATLANTIC OCEAN
GULF OF MEXICO
MEXICO
BAHAMA ISLANDS
CUBA
45°
30°
120°
90°
N
S
E
W
ALASKA
YUKON TERRITORY
Yukon R.
Mt. McKinley 20,320 ft.
Bering Sea
Bristol Bay
Kodiak
Unimak Island
Gulf of Alaska
Juneau
HAWAII
Kauai
Oahu
Honolulu
Maui
Hawaii
PACIFIC OCEAN
PLAINS
HIGHLANDS
MOUNTAINS
0
200
400
Scale of Miles

▲*Scott Lake in Oregon* (left), *and Cape Hatteras off the coast of North Carolina* (right) *are two examples of the great natural beauty to be found in the United States.*

city as far north as Juneau, Alaska, is warmer in January than inland Milwaukee or Buffalo, New York. On the East Coast, however, the wind brings weather mostly from the west, so the climate is generally but not always continental. South Florida and Hawaii are warm and humid all year round. Most of Alaska, by contrast, has the nation's coldest temperatures. Alaska's long, southeastern arm, called the panhandle, has a cool marine climate, but its central portion has a cold, continental one.

People

U.S. citizens, usually called Americans, are descended from people from almost every country in the world. Only about 800,000 U.S. citizens are of American Indian descent. Most non-slave immigrants to the United States came from Europe. Of those from Europe, the greatest numbers came from Germany, Italy, Great Britain, Ireland, Austria, and Hungary. Many came from the Scandinavian countries and settled in middle and northwestern areas of the United States. Some of America's earliest immigrants were from Africa. Negro slaves were brought by force to the colonies in the early 1600s. More than 20 million of their descendents live in the U.S. today. Roughly one out of every ten Americans is black.

America is also a land of many religions. Most Americans who belong to a religious group are Christians. Of these, about two-thirds are Protestants, while one-third are Roman Catholic. About 5 of every 100 Americans are Jewish.

There are more women than men in the U.S. by the ratio of 51 to 49. The largest number of men are "blue-collar workers." They work at jobs requiring physical effort or skill, such as most factory jobs. Most women and the next largest group of men work at "white-collar" jobs, which include working in offices, teaching, and selling.

One-third of all Americans still live in the country or in small villages. However, this is changing. More rural Americans are moving to the cities or suburbs each year.

Almost all Americans can read. The U.S. has more newspapers than any other nation, and is second only to the Soviet Union in the numbers of new books it publishes each year. Americans do not read as much as people in other developed nations, but they have considerably greater choice in television programs.

In only one other country in the world, the tiny, oil-rich nation of Kuwait, is the average income of the population higher than in the U.S. In the total amount of money earned, the United States is well ahead of any other nation. Other countries, however, have incomes that are growing more rapidly than those of the people of the United States. Incomes in Japan, for example, are increasing three times as fast.

▲ *Petroleum is one of the great natural resources of the United States. Each one of these derricks outside Oklahoma City represents a producing oil well.*

Land and Resources

The United States leads the world in developed natural resources. It produces more oil, zinc, copper, and aluminum than any other country. Many other minerals of commercial use are found in the U.S. The country still has vast forests, particularly in the West. But careless use of its resources in the past have made modern Americans more aware of the need to preserve their natural resources.

About one-half of the United States land area is used for farming or ranching. There are about four million separate farms in America, but the number is declining steadily. Small farms cannot compete with the bigger farms, where food for people and livestock can be produced in greater amounts more economically.

Crops of cotton, corn, oats, and tobacco in the U.S. are the largest in the world. Only the Soviet Union grows more wheat. Very few other countries can compete with the U.S. in production of cattle, sheep, pigs, poultry, fruits, vegetables, and many other farm crops.

To a large extent, the climate determines the type of farming found in the different areas of the United States. On the Arctic slopes of Alaska, only a few days each year are without frost,

▼ *The American Indian is proud of his culture and customs. These Hopi Indians are performing in a ceremonial parade in Gallup, New Mexico* (left). *The United States is known as the "melting pot" of the world because of the varied mixture of peoples who came here. These children are Japanese-Americans parading in San Francisco's Cherry Blossom Festival* (right).

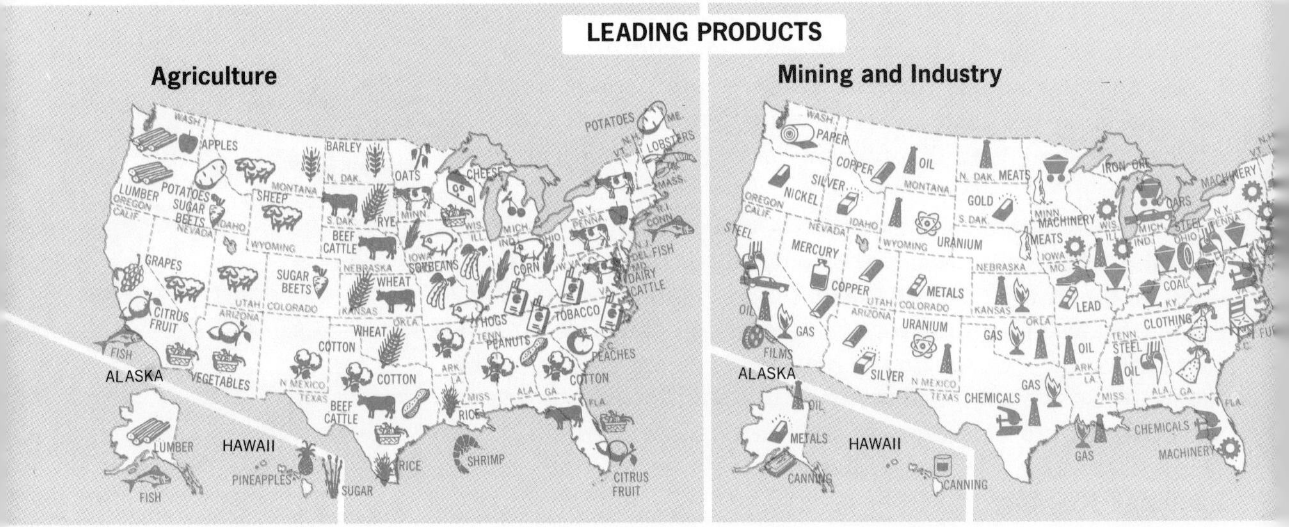

and only mosses and lichens can survive. But central Alaska has two or three months without frost, and fast-growing crops such as vegetables thrive during the long summer hours of sunlight.

The midwestern states have four to six months without freezing. This growing season is long enough to grow the huge grain crops of the prairies—wheat, oats, rye, barley, and corn. Around the cities, fruit and vegetable farming flourish.

The seven frost-free months of the southern states permit the growing of such crops as cotton, peanuts, and tobacco. The subtropical climates of Florida and Hawaii, where it rarely freezes, are good for growing delicate citrus fruits such as oranges and grapefruit. Citrus fruits, as well as grapes, figs, olives, and almonds, are grown in the Mediterranean climate of southern California.

▼*The United States is the world's leading industrial country. A skilled glassblower is shown heating a blob of glass in a factory at Corning, New York.*

Industry

The United States is one of the world's industrial leaders. The manufactured goods produced by U.S. factories account for about one-third of the world's total industrial output. The production of transportation equipment, steel, chemicals, and machinery are some of the most important industries. Food processing and the production of textiles, paper, and clothing are also major industries. Most of the country's manufacturing states, such as New York, Ohio, Pennsylvania, and Michigan, are located east of the Mississippi River. California, a leading industrial state, is one very important exception.

ALSO READ: AMERICA; AMERICAN HISTORY; APPALACHIAN MOUNTAINS; DISTRICT OF COLUMBIA; GREAT LAKES; GREAT PLAINS; GULF OF MEXICO; INDIANS, AMERICAN; MISSISSIPPI RIVER; NEGRO HISTORY; NORTH AMERICA; PILGRIM SETTLERS; PUERTO RICO; ROCKY MOUNTAINS; SIERRA NEVADA MOUNTAINS; WEST INDIES; *each individual state.*

UNITED STATES SERVICE ACADEMIES The armed forces of the United States have five separate branches—the Army, the Navy, the Air Force, the Marine Corps, and the Coast Guard. Each branch is composed of enlisted men and officers who lead them. Many young men become officers in the armed forces without graduating from a military service academy, but the United States does provide schools for training potential officers for each of these branches. The U.S. Military Academy, founded in 1802, trains future army officers at West Point, New York. Future naval officers are trained at the U.S. Naval Academy at Annapolis, Maryland. It was established in 1845. The Air Force Academy, founded in 1954, is at Colorado Springs, Colorado; and the Coast Guard Academy, founded in 1915, is at New London, Connecticut. Marine Corps officers are trained at West Point or Annapolis.

Qualifications and requirements for appointment vary somewhat among the service academies. But generally, candidates must be physically, mentally, and morally qualified male citizens 17 to 22 years old and unmarried. Nominations for appointment to all but the Coast Guard Academy are made by the President, Vice President, members of Congress, or other high government officials. Other appointments are reserved for members of the regular or reserve armed forces, qualified sons of deceased veterans and Medal of Honor winners, and members of other special groups. Coast Guard cadets are selected by means of a competitive examination.

Each academy provides a four-year program of study, equal to a regular college course of study, plus an athletic and physical education program. This is in addition to military and professional training. Every student receives free room and board. He also receives a salary each month from the Federal Government to pay for his uniforms, books, and some personal expenses. When the student graduates, he receives a bachelor of

◀ *The color guard of the United States Military Academy passes in review on the parade grounds at West Point, New York.*

▶ *Midshipmen, students at the United States Naval Academy in Annapolis, Maryland, leave a class in the science building.*

▲*The modernistic chapel at the Air Force Academy in Colorado Springs, Colorado.*

science (B.S.) degree and a commission (a government certificate stating his military rank and authority).

A newly graduated officer in the U.S. Army, U.S. Air Force, or U.S. Marine Corps is commissioned as a second lieutenant in his branch of service. A newly graduated officer in the U.S. Navy or the U.S. Coast Guard is commissioned as an ensign in his branch of service. In exchange for their education, these new officers agree to stay in military service for a certain number of years.

The U.S. Merchant Marine also operates a service academy at Kings Point, New York. Cadets there study navigation, seamanship, oceanography, and other technical subjects. These cadets are appointed by members of Congress. Graduates of the Merchant Marine Academy receive commissions as ensigns in the U.S. Naval Reserve.

ALSO READ: AIR FORCE, ARMY, COAST GUARD, MARINE CORPS, MERCHANT MARINE, MILITARY CAREER, NAVY.

UNIVERSAL LANGUAGE Wouldn't it be wonderful if there were one universal language that people from all over the world could learn to use! No interpreters would be needed at international conferences. Nobody would feel like a stranger when traveling, because everyone could communicate.

The universal language so far invented that has met with most success is *Esperanto.* The inventor was Lazarus Ludwig Zamenhof, a Russian physician, who presented his new language in 1887. It is based on words from several European languages, making it easy for people who speak one or two of these languages to understand Esperanto. It is pronounced phonetically, as it is written, and uses a 20-letter alphabet.

The following paragraph is in Esperanto. Can you read it?

"Elefanto estas tre granda besto, kiu vivas en Afriko kaj Azio. La homo rigardas la elefanton kiel amiko, kaj ili ofte kunlaboras. Oni diras, ke elefantoj nemian forgesas."

Here are some hints for translating Esperanto. (1) All nouns end in "o," and plurals are made by adding a "j." (2) *Estas* means "is," *kaj* means "and," *kiu* means "who," *kiel* means "as," *oni diras* means "they say."

Another universal language that has become very useful in recent years is *Interlingua.* It was developed by the scientist Giuseppe Peano and presented in 1903. Since then, it has been modified. The words are based on scientific and technological terms that are the same in almost all languages.

Other universal languages and their dates of presentation are *Volapük* (1880), *Idiom Neutral* (1898), *Ro* (1906), *Ido* (a simplified Esperanto, 1907), *Novial* (1928), *Basic English* (during the 1920s). Basic English is interesting because it uses only 850 English words. This small vocabulary is very powerful because the words can be combined to do the work of thousands of other words. For example, the word "go" in Basic English can combine with prepositions to make hundreds of other verbs. Here are a few of them:

enter–go into	exit–go out of
break–go against	leave–go away
fetch–go for	fall–go down
return–go back	rise–go up
precede–go in front of	pass–go by
turn–go right (left)	approach–go up to
encircle–go around	avoid–go past

ALSO READ: LANGUAGES.

UNIVERSE The universe includes the stars, planets, comets, galaxies, meteors, dust, and everything else in space, including space itself. In short, the universe is everything–not only those things that we know, but also those things that exist but are unknown to us. The universe is not just what men know, the universe is that which *is.*

Until the 1500s, men thought that the Earth was the center of the universe. This idea was so pleasing that they held to it even when astronomical observations showed that it was unlikely.

In 1514 Nicolaus Copernicus poked a hole in the Earth-centered view of the universe by suggesting that the Earth probably moved around the sun. In the 1600s, the telescope was invented, and this instrument drastically changed men's notions of the size of the universe. It was much larger than they had imagined. The nearest stars were so far away that their distances had to be measured in light-years–the distance light, moving at 186,000 miles a second, travels in a year. One light year is 5.88 million million miles.

Today it is thought that the universe is about 20 billion light-years across. The Earth is merely one planet moving around one star–the sun. The sun is one of about 100 billion stars in one *galaxy* (groups of stars)–the Milky Way. The Milky Way is about 80,000 light-years across and 13,000 light-years thick. It is one of 10 to 100 million galaxies. The nearest large galaxy to the Milky Way is the Andromeda nebula, over two million light-years away.

You might well wonder how astronomers can measure the universe. They can observe it with optical telescopes and radio telescopes. But how can they tell whether a star or a galaxy is one or a million light-years away? The answer, in part, is that they cannot always tell. In some cases they just assume that a galaxy that looks bright is closer than a galaxy that looks dim.

It might seem even more difficult to tell where a star is going and how fast it is moving than to tell where it is. But it is often much easier. When a light source, such as a star or galaxy, is

▼ *The constellation Cygnus, or Northern Cross, is one of the star formations studied by astronomers seeking answers about the formation of the universe.*

moving away from an observer, its light appears red. If the light source is moving closer, its light appears blue. These "red shifts" and "blue shifts" help astronomers to calculate the speed and direction in which stars and galaxies are moving. It was discovered that almost all galaxies showed red shifts. None showed blue shifts. This meant that almost all of the visible galaxies were moving away from the Earth. It was also discovered that the farther away a galaxy was, the faster it was moving. Two American astronomers, E. P. Hubble and Milton Humason, calculated that galaxies 10 billion light-years away from the Earth would be moving at the speed of light. According to the theory of relativity, it is impossible to travel at the speed of light. Even if it were possible, light from a galaxy moving at that speed would never reach the Earth. So 10 billion light-years came to be considered the radius (distance from the center of the edge) of the observable universe.

The discovery that all galaxies are moving apart led to the *big bang theory* of the origin of the universe. According to the big bang theory, the universe started with a huge explosion—the big bang. At the instant of this explosion, all matter was collected at one point. The explosion sprayed matter in all directions. The matter was formed into elements, and the elements eventually lumped together to form stars, planets, and galaxies. The big bang took place 10 billion years ago, and the galaxies, and all other matter in space, have been rushing apart since then.

The main flaw of the big bang theory is that the Milky Way has been estimated to be 20 to 30 billion years old. This would make it older than the universe, and this is clearly impossible.

Another modern theory of the universe is called the *steady state theory.* According to this theory the universe has no age. It has always existed and never changes. While the galaxies are moving apart, matter is being created to fill in the empty space they leave behind. And although galaxies are very large and are moving very fast, this would not take very much matter. The creation of one hydrogen atom every fifty cubic feet once every million years should be enough to keep the universe in a steady state. Unfortunately, the supporters of the theory have not been able to explain how this matter is to be created. Recent discoveries have supported the big bang theory, and it is still the most widely accepted explanation of the origin of the universe.

ALSO READ: ASTRONOMY; COMET; COPERNICUS, NICOLAUS; GALILEO GALILEI; MILKY WAY; OBSERVATORY; ORBIT; RELATIVITY; SOLAR SYSTEM; SPACE; STAR; SUN; TELESCOPE.

▼*Agricultural scientists in Upper Volta check the growth of an experimental plant.*

UPPER VOLTA The landlocked Republic of Upper Volta lies in the heart of West Africa. It is about the size of Colorado. (See the map with the article on AFRICA.) Upper Volta gets its name from its location at the headwaters of the Volta River.

UPPER VOLTA

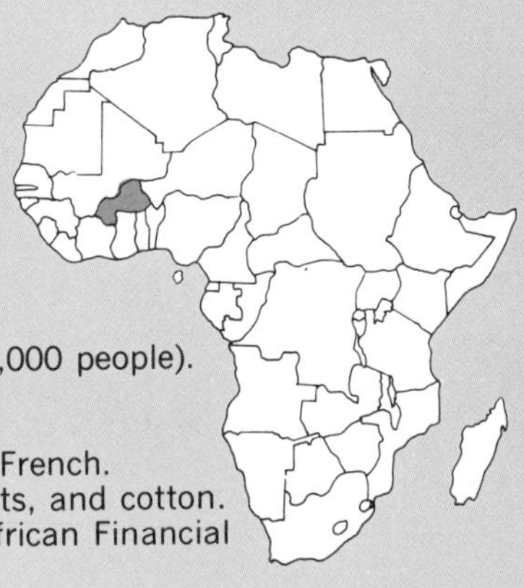

Capital City: Ouagadougou (77,000 people).
Area: 105,841 square miles.
Population: 5,278,000 people.
Languages: Mossi, Samo, and French.
Export Products: Cattle, peanuts, and cotton.
Unit of Money: Franc of the African Financial Community.

The country is on a plateau, with an altitude of between 650 and 1,000 feet above sea level.

The soil is not fertile. The country lacks water, good forests, and mineral resources, making Upper Volta's economy one of the most limited in West Africa. The country's wealth lies in livestock. It is one of the great cattle areas of Africa.

Two distinct groups of people live in Upper Volta. The primitive tribes in the west, which include the Cobo and the Lobi, are farmers and hunters. They live in large villages. The other group are the descendants of the founders of Upper Volta's medieval empire. The main tribe is the Mossi. They live in family groups called *yiris* and work as farmers and herdsmen. Most of the people of Upper Volta have kept their traditional religions, although a minority are Muslims and Christians. Tribal religions may center around a supreme god, secondary gods, and cults of ancestors.

The Mossi people, who probably came from Ghana, established feudal kingdoms in Upper Volta in the 1000s. The emperor of the Mossi established his throne at Ouagadougou, which is the capital city today. Royal courts with ministers, vassals, and pages were held until this century. Although the Mossi were peaceful farmers, they fought against the people of the north who tried to conquer and convert them to Islam. The French took control of the country in 1896. Upper Volta became independent on August 5, 1960.

ALSO READ: AFRICA, ISLAM.

URAL MOUNTAINS The Ural Mountains are a chain of low mountains in the Soviet Union. They extend 1,300 miles from the Arctic Ocean southward to the Caspian Sea, and form the traditional boundary between Europe and Asia. They also form a nature boundary–plants and animals on each side are often different.

The Ural chain has three main divisions. The Northern Urals are craggy and narrow. Their crests average between 1,000 and 1,500 feet high, but several peaks are more than 5,000 feet high. The highest peak, Narodnaya (6,184 feet), is one of these. The Northern Urals are generally treeless.

The Middle Urals consist of numerous high hills surrounded by deep valleys. They average between 1,000 and 2,000 feet in height. Dense forests cover the entire Middle Ural region.

The Southern Urals are made up of three parallel mountain chains. Their summits reach between 2,000 and 3,000 feet high. All of them are covered with plant life and provide rich pasture.

The Urals are rich in mineral wealth. They contain deposits of copper, zinc, iron, platinum, silver, and gold. One of the Soviet Union's most important industrial areas is located in the Middle and Southern Urals.

ALSO READ: ASIA, EUROPE, MOUNTAIN, SOVIET UNION.

URANIUM see ELEMENT, NUCLEAR ENERGY.

▲*Montevideo, the capital and largest city of Uruguay, has modern apartment houses rising behind fine, wide beaches.*

URUGUAY Uruguay is sometimes called "The Purple Land" because of its vast pasture lands of blue-purple grass. It is the smallest South American country, only slightly larger than North Dakota. Argentina and Brazil border Uruguay. (See the map with the article on SOUTH AMERICA.)

It is the only South American country that has no large uninhabited area. People are found in almost every part, although about half live in the south, in or near the capital city of Montevideo. The city has recently become overcrowded because of the many people who have moved there from the interior.

Much of the country is covered with grassy plains and low hills. The climate is temperate, producing good pasture on the rich land. Freezing temperatures occur only rarely. Livestock raising is the major agricultural activity, and wool, meat, and hides are the main exports.

URUGUAY

Capital City: Montevideo (1,154,000 people).
Area: 72,172 square miles.
Population: 2,852,000 people.
Language: Spanish.
Export Products: Wool, meat, and hides.
Unit of Money: Uruguayan peso.

Most of the population is of European background, mainly Spanish and Italian. There are almost no *mestizos* (people of mixed Spanish and Indian descent) because the native Indians were killed off in the very early colonial days.

International conferences, such as meetings of the Organization of American States, have been held at Punta del Este, a popular beach and resort area on Uruguay's coast.

Spanish adventurers were the first to explore Uruguay, but the Portuguese founded the first town there. Spain and Portugal vied for control of Uruguay, and later Brazil and Argentina fought to possess it. Jose Gervasio Artigas, who led the fight against the Spanish government in the early 1800s, was defeated and driven into exile. Then Portuguese Brazil annexed Uruguay in 1821. Under the leadership of Juan Antonio Lavalleja, a group known as the Immortal Thirty-Three declared independence in 1825 and had the country temporarily joined to Argentina. Independence was finally won in 1828, but the country had a stormy history until Jose Batlle y Ordoñez became its president in 1903.

ALSO READ: ARGENTINA, BRAZIL, SPANISH HISTORY.

UTAH The Great Salt Lake of Utah is a small leftover part of an ancient inland sea, Lake Bonneville. The billions of tons of salt in the lake provide such buoyancy that it is almost impossible to sink while floating in it. The Jordan River flows from Utah Lake to the Great Salt Lake. West of the lake is the Great Salt Lake Desert.

Utah's state flower is a dainty wildflower that grows from a bulb. When Mormon pioneers were short of food, Indians told them that the sego lily bulbs were good to eat. Families dug thousands of them.

The Land and Climate

Utah lies on the western side of the Rocky Mountains. Idaho and Wyoming are north of it. Nevada is on its western side. Utah's southeastern corner is the only point where four states meet.

Utah is divided into two almost equal parts. Its western part is in the Great Basin. Its eastern part belongs to the big Colorado Plateau. The dividing line follows the highest ridge of a north-south highland. The Wasatch Mountains, a branch of the Rockies, are at its northern end.

The highland is the state's most important part. It has most of the farmland and many of the mines. The factory centers are here, too. Most of Utah's people live in the highland. At its southern end, the highland curves westward. Here is beautiful canyon country. The canyons are straight-sided valleys where colored rocks have been carved by wind and water. In two national parks, Zion and Bryce, you can follow winding trails through the canyons.

The Great Basin Region, west of the dividing line, is gray and barren. It is sagebrush land. White salt flats show where lakes have dried up and left salt behind.

▼*It's great fun to climb the weird rock formations in the well-named Goblin Valley in Utah.*

In the Colorado Plateau, the Uinta Mountains rise in the north near the Wyoming border. They have high, wooded peaks and deep canyons. Southward lies dry, yellow country.

Most of Utah has little rain. Only the mountains in the north receive much precipitation. A large part of this comes in the form of snow. As the snow melts in spring and summer, it feeds mountain streams.

The little rainfall that Utah receives falls mainly on the western side of the mountains. People therefore started farms in a strip along the western slopes of the Wasatch Range. They widened the strip of crop land by irrigating with water from the mountain streams.

UTAH

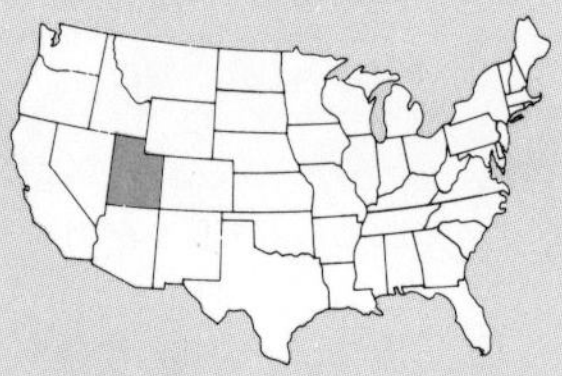

State flower
Sego lily

State bird
Sea gull

State tree
Blue spruce

Capital and largest city
Salt Lake City
(175,885 people)

Area
84,916 square miles
(ranks 11th)

Population
1,059,273 people
(ranks 36th)

Statehood
January 4, 1896
(45th state admitted)

Principal rivers
Sevier River
Green River
Colorado River

Highest point
Kings Peak, in the
Uinta Mountains
(13,498 feet)

History

Dry, barren country has one advantage for the people who live there. Outsiders aren't likely to try to take their land from them.

For three hundred years, white men left Utah to the Paiute, Shoshone, and Ute Indians. But a change came in 1847. It came

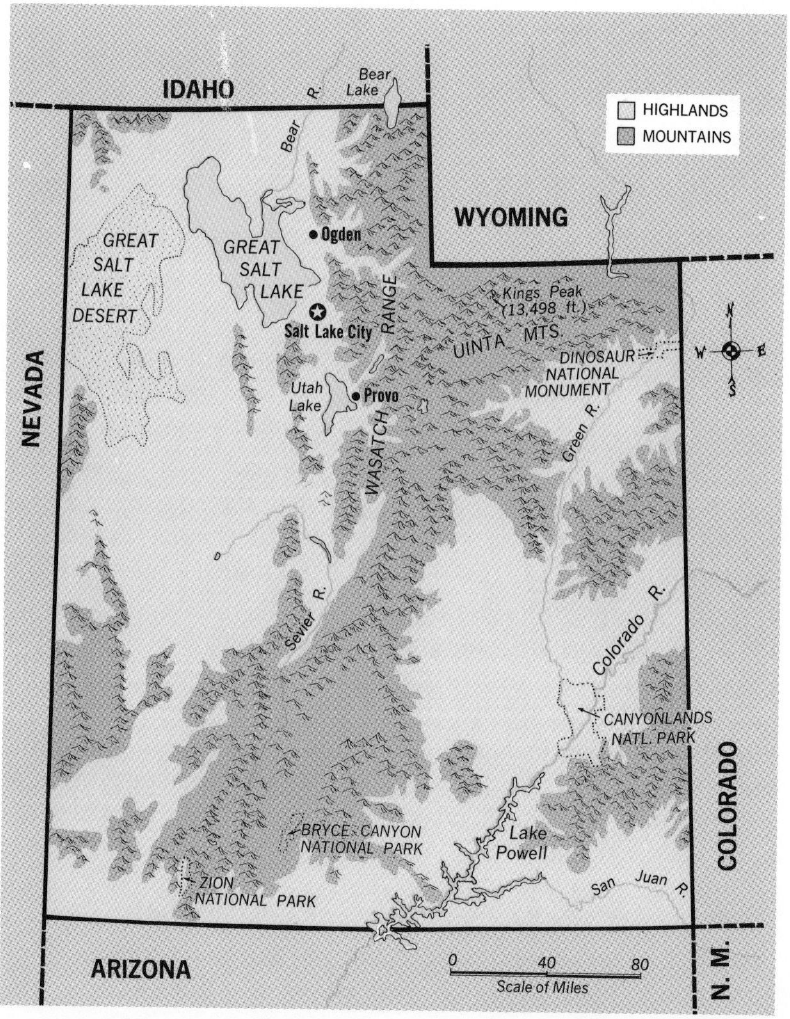

because a group of people wanted land where they could live as they pleased and be left alone by other people. They were a religious group, the Church of Jesus Christ of Latter-day Saints. Most people called its members *Mormons.*

Mormon customs were different from those of the other settlers. The differences made their neighbors unfriendly. Mobs often attacked the Mormons. When they did, the Mormons fought back. In search of peace, the Mormons moved from the East to the West. They reached the Great Salt Lake in 1847.

"This is the place," said their leader, Brigham Young. They had left their former neighbors almost a thousand miles behind them—east of the Rockies. Other people of different beliefs were 600 miles away on the Pacific Coast. And the mountains and deserts of the Great Basin were in between.

The first settlement in Utah was named *Great Salt Lake City.* Nearly all the people were farmers in the beginning. As their population grew, the Mormons started other settlements. Their land was made a United States territory. Congress named it *Utah.* The word is a form of the Indian name *Ute.* Brigham Young was the territory's first governor.

People other than the Mormons settled in Utah. There was trouble between them and the Mormon majority. In time, though, the different groups of people learned to live peaceably together. The territory became a state in 1896.

The People at Work

Brigham Young liked farming. He liked manufacturing and trade. But he did not like mining. He felt it would give people get-rich-quick ideas. They might stop their useful labors and wander about hunting gold and silver. And if these were found, Young believed, Utah might be overrun by hordes of rough fellows who would be hard to handle. But mining did start in Utah. It is now the state's second-largest industry. Manufacturing earns even more money than mining today. The leading manufacture is food products. Cattle, sheep, and poultry bring in more money than crops do.

Tourism is growing rapidly. Historic Salt Lake City is a great attraction. Many tourists visit the Mormon Tabernacle. This hall seats five thousand people. It was put up over a hundred years ago *without nails.* Wooden pins and rawhide thongs held it together. Nails have since been used in repairing it, however.

Utah has ski resorts and some unusually interesting recreation areas. Dinosaur National Monument (partly in Colorado) is known all over the world for the remains of huge dinosaurs found there.

ALSO READ: DINOSAUR; GREAT SALT LAKE; IRRIGATION; ROCKY MOUNTAINS; SHOSHONE INDIANS; SMITH, JOSEPH; WESTWARD MOVEMENT; YOUNG, BRIGHAM.

▲This is the Place Monument *was erected in 1947 to commemorate the 100th anniversary of the settling of the Great Salt Lake Valley by Mormon pioneers.*

Although Utah is not located by the sea, a monument honoring sea gulls stands in Salt Lake City. In 1848, great flocks of sea gulls came to Utah, probably from the Pacific Ocean. The birds saved the crops of the pioneer Mormons by eating the plague of locusts attacking the crops.

▼*Two young boys are awed by a model of a dinosaur standing in a field in Utah.*

V

VACUUM A perfect vacuum would be a space that had absolutely nothing in it—not even air, not even a single atom or molecule. A perfect vacuum is almost certainly impossible to find. Even in outer space there are molecules or particles of very fine dust. Even inside a glass or steel container, molecules would break away from the surface faster than they could be removed. So, the word "vacuum" usually refers to a partial vacuum—a space from which *almost* everything has been removed.

Vacuum pumps have been invented that can suck the air out of containers. Vacuum pumps work much like ordinary pumps except they pump the air from inside a container until only a partial vacuum is left. A vacuum cleaner, for example, has a pump inside it that sucks air through a long hose. If a container were attached to the front end of the hose, the vacuum cleaner would create a partial vacuum within the container. Without a container, the vacuum cleaner continuously sucks dirt into the hose. This is how a vacuum cleaner cleans rugs and floors.

[illegible] vacuum-packed." This means that [illegible] ated in the container. With almost [illegible] he food does not spoil so easily. [illegible] ontainer, the container is closed [illegible] it is still hot. Both the air and the [illegible] ot, so the container will hold less [illegible]. When the container is shut tight, [illegible] container. When you open a "vac- [illegible] can hear a hissing sound as the [illegible]

[illegible] he radio tube, was one of the most important inventions in electronics. Early light bulbs also con- [illegible] y "vacuum tubes" and most light bulbs [illegible] acuums. But vacuums are still im- portant to scientists and engineers. Certain scientific experi- ments and industrial processes are performed in vacuums.

ALSO READ: [illegible] PUMP, SPACE.

VALENTINE'S DAY Valentine's Day is a romantic holiday celebrated on February 14. Gentlemen send flowers or candy to their favorite ladies, and many people send Valentine cards. "Valentines" are greeting cards which are often decorated with red hearts, lace, ribbons, and pictures of cupids. Many carry messages of love, and some are humorous.

Valentine's Day can be traced back to the ancient Roman festival called Lupercalia. This festival, held every February 15, was in honor of young lovers. Later, the Christian church established Saint Valentine's Day on February 14, in honor of two saints named Valentine who lived in the 200s A.D. The old Roman custom is now celebrated on the saints' feast day.

ALSO READ: HOLIDAY.

VALLEY see MOUNTAIN.

VAN ALLEN, JAMES A. see RADIATION BELT.

▲*An old Valentine's Day card portrays Cupid, a figure from Roman mythology who carries a bow and arrows. A wound from one of Cupid's arrows would make his victim fall in love.*

VAN BUREN, MARTIN (1782–1862) Martin Van Buren, the eighth President, was the first President born in the United States. The previous seven Presidents had been born in the British colonies before the colonies declared their independence and became the United States.

Martin Van Buren lived in Kinderhook, New York. He graduated from the village school at the age of 14. He studied law in Kinderhook and in a law office in New York City and became a lawyer at the age of 21. Van Buren then returned to his native town to practice law. In 1807, Van Buren married a cousin, Hannah Hoes. The couple had four sons. Hannah Van Buren died just 12 years after her marriage.

Van Buren served in the United States Senate from 1821 to 1828, when he was elected governor of New York. In the same

Martin Van Buren's nickname was "Old Kinderhook." In the election of 1840, a group of his friends formed the O.K. Club to work for his re-election. Van Buren was not re-elected, but one theory is that the club succeeded in making the expression "O.K." popular.

EIGHTH PRESIDENT MARCH 4, 1837—MARCH 4, 1841

MARTIN VAN BUREN

Born: December 5, 1782, Kinderhook, New York
Parents: Abraham and Maria Hoes Van Buren
Education: Village schools, studied in law office
Religion: Dutch Reformed
Occupation: Lawyer, government official
Political party: Democratic
State represented: New York
Married: 1807 to Hannah Hoes Van Buren (1783–1819)
Children: Four sons
Died: July 24, 1862, Kinderhook, New York
Buried: Kinderhook Cemetery, Kinderhook, New York

year, when Andrew Jackson was the nominee for President, some members of the Democratic-Republican Party began calling themselves Democrats. Van Buren, one of the leaders of the new party, worked hard for Jackson's election and was appointed secretary of state when Jackson took office in 1829. Only a few months after taking office, Van Buren resigned the governorship of New York to accept this new appointment. As secretary of state, Van Buren won the confidence of President Jackson, who chose him as his Vice Presidential running mate in the election of 1832. In 1836, Jackson urged the members of his party to nominate Van Buren for President.

Van Buren won the election, but soon after his inauguration, economic hard times hit the country. The Panic of 1837 developed when government funds that had been deposited in certain state banks were mismanaged. Some of the loans made by the banks with government funds had not been wise and were not repaid. As President, Van Buren urged that government funds be kept in a national treasury independent of state and private banks. After three years, Congress passed the Independent Treasury Bill (1840), but it was too late to help Van Buren win a second term. He was blamed for the hard times. Van Buren made himself even more unpopular with the American people by refusing to become involved in Canadian rebellions against Great Britain in 1837. (Many Americans sided with the Canadians.) In 1840, Van Buren lost the Presidential election to William Henry Harrison.

After his defeat in 1840, Van Buren returned to his home town to practice law. He remained active in politics for many years, and even ran again for President in 1848. His last years were spent in Kinderhook.

ALSO READ: HARRISON, WILLIAM HENRY; JACKSON, ANDREW; PRESIDENCY.

VAN GOGH, VINCENT (1853–1890) A painter whose brief, bright flash of life ended in what he thought was failure was the Dutchman Vincent van Gogh. He was born in Groot-Zundert, the eldest of six children of a Dutch Protestant minister.

The first of his many failures took place after he went to work at the age of 16 for an uncle who owned an art gallery. He fell in love with a girl who did not care for him, and he suffered a nervous breakdown. He tried another gallery, then took a job teaching in England. But he did not do well at either job. He studied to be a minister but failed the language exams. He tried being a minister to the coal miners of Belgium. He really wanted to work for the poor. He lived in a shack and slept on a pallet made of old coats. He even dressed like the miners, in clothes covered with coal dust. But van Gogh was not a good speaker, and he failed as a preacher.

At this time he began to draw and paint. Van Gogh's early works are dark and somber and show the misery of coal miners and peasant farmers. His first important painting, *The Potato Eaters,* is a dark picture of a group of work-worn peasants eating humble food after a hard day's work.

In 1886, he went to Paris and lived with his favorite brother, Theo, an art dealer. Van Gogh became friendly with many talented artists, including several of the Impressionists, who liked to paint outside in natural light. Van Gogh began to use more color in his work, and he changed his brush technique. He used many separate brush strokes, as did the Impressionists. But under van Gogh's hand, the stroke became very loose and expressive of his feelings.

Look at his painting, *The Painter on the Road to Tarascon.* The painter walking down the road could be van Gogh. The golden scene seems sun-drenched. Can't you just feel the warmth of a summer day? You do not see the sun, but you are aware of its presence everywhere. This was van Gogh in the brief happy months of his life, when he painted an amazing number of pictures.

Contrast this painting with *Road with Cypresses* (shown here) which was painted some months later. The golden colors are gone. The sun has become a yellowish-green in a wild-moody blue sky swirling with brush strokes. For no apparent reason, there is also an orange moon in the sky. The black-green cypresses reach darkly up to the sky along a hard, green, river-like road. The figures in the foreground are dark and look helpless in front of the swirling high cypresses. The wheat fields (so golden and straight in earlier paintings) are now dark and wild and choppy. Van Gogh expressed his feelings about life in his pictures so much that he is considered the first of the *expressionists,* a school of painters who showed their personal feelings in their art.

▲The Painter on the Road to Tarascon (above) *and* Road with Cypresses (below), *by Vincent van Gogh.*▼

Van Gogh's mental illness had become worse. His friend Paul Gauguin, whom he had eagerly awaited, came to vist. But they had a violent quarrel, and van Gogh ran after Gauguin with a razor. Gauguin stood his ground, and van Gogh went to his room. He then cut off a piece of his ear and sent it to a woman he knew.

After this, van Gogh was in the care of doctors until his death. In between fits of madness, he did several paintings. His colors became wilder and wilder. The next year he shot himself in the chest. He failed at this suicide attempt, but died two days later of complications.

ALSO READ: EXPRESSIONISM; GAUGUIN, PAUL; IMPRESSIONISM.

▲*The Swiss Guards in traditional uniform are the ceremonial guard at Vatican City. The artist Michelangelo designed this uniform.*

VATICAN CITY Vatican City is an independent nation located on Vatican Hill in the city of Rome, Italy. It is ruled by the pope and is the headquarters of the Roman Catholic Church. In size, Vatican City is the world's tiniest country—108.7 acres.

The main building in Vatican City is St. Peter's Basilica, with a large *piazza* (square) in front of it. Important church functions are held in St. Peter's. In the days of ancient Rome, Vatican Hill had been a burial ground. The first basilica of St. Peter was erected over what is believed to be the grave of St. Peter.

Near the basilica is the Vatican Palace, which contains the pope's living quarters and offices of the church government. The Vatican Museums, housing some of the greatest works of ancient art, are located in the Palace, as is the Vatican Library, the oldest public library in Europe. Also within the Vatican Palace are various chapels. The most famous is probably the Sistine Chapel, its walls and ceiling covered with the magnificent frescoes of the artist Michelangelo.

Vatican City has about 1,000 citizens who live in apartments surrounding the church buildings. The business of this little nation is handled by a lay governor (a man who is not a member

VATICAN CITY

Area: 108.7 acres.
Population: 1,000 people.
Languages: Italian and Latin.
Export Products: Vatican City does not engage in trade. It depends mostly on charity for income.
Unit of Money: Italian lira.

of the clergy) whose offices are located in Government Palace. The governor administers property belonging to the Vatican, the Vatican City police, and the Vatican post office (which issues its own stamps). Vatican City also has its own militia, called the Swiss Guards, whose job it is to protect the pope. The Vatican has its own telephone system, auto licenses, flag, currency, radio and television stations, and its own newspapers, the most important of which is *L'Osservatore Romano.* As an independent state, the Vatican conducts international business and political affairs and negotiates treaties.

Beginning in the 1400s, the Vatican took over and ruled large areas of land in Italy called the Papal States. Italy became a united country in 1870, and the Italian government took control of the Papal States in 1871. Throughout the next 50 years, the popes refused to accept money from the Italian government in exchange for the lands taken away. The Vatican was no longer an independent state, and the popes considered themselves to be prisoners of the Italian government. In 1929, the Lateran Treaty established the present Vatican City as an independent nation.

ALSO READ: ITALIAN HISTORY, MICHELANGELO BUONARROTTI, POPE, ROMAN CATHOLIC CHURCH, ROME.

VAUDEVILLE Vaudeville is an entertainment consisting of a variety of individual acts. These acts usually include singing and dancing, magic, animal acts, juggling, acrobatics, short humorous or dramatic skits, and comedy routines. The word "vaudeville" comes from the French words *vau-de-vire,* a name applied to comic drinking songs written in Vau-de-Vire, France, in the 1400s. The songs were often sung between acts of plays and later began to be called *vaudevilles.*

Vaudeville, as a program of variety acts, began in the United States in the 1800s. Up to that time, most public entertainment was considered vulgar, and only men went to see it. Vaudeville introduced family entertainment. In 1883, Benjamin F. Keith opened the first vaudeville theater in Boston.

Vaudeville's popularity grew rapidly. In the 1920s, vaudeville performances attracted audiences of over two million people each day in over 1,000 theaters. Tony Pastor's and the Palace in New York City were two of the most famous vaudeville houses. It was the ambition of every vaudeville actor to play in them. Some of the stars of vaudeville were Frank Fay, Pat Rooney, Bill "Bojangles" Robinson, Ted Healy and the Three Stooges, the Marx Brothers, Sophie Tucker, and Eddie Foy and the Seven Little Foys. In Great Britain, music halls presented vaudeville shows. Stars such as Charlie Chaplin performed there. Many top television and movie comedians began their careers in vaudeville—Jack Benny, George Burns and

▼ *Weber and Fields, a great comedy team of vaudeville.*

Gracie Allen, and Bob Hope, among others. Milton Berle and Sammy Davis, Jr., were child stars in vaudeville.

Vaudeville reached its height in the late 1920s. But then it began to run into trouble. There were actors' strikes and problems with theater owners. Talking motion pictures were created, and much of vaudeville's audience turned to movies and radio. Performers had to find other places to show off their talent, and the old kind of vaudeville died out.

ALSO READ: MUSICAL COMEDY.

▲*The inner clusters of the broccoli plant are the parts of this vegetable that are eaten.*

VEGETABLES All plants are vegetables, but in everyday use, the word means plants with a high water content that are grown for food. Any part of a plant can be used as a vegetable. In some cases, such as spinach and lettuce, people eat the leaves. Celery is the leaf stalk of a plant. Beets, carrots, and turnips are the roots of plants. Green peas are the plant's seeds. Tomatoes and green and red peppers are fruits, and broccoli is a flower. (The fruits of many plants, such as oranges and apples, are not generally called vegetables.) Some vegetables are grown for their oils. Corn and soy beans yield oil used for cooking and seasoning. People can buy these oils either in liquid form or as solid white shortening.

A plant (or plant part) one society considers a common vegetable might be unheard of in other parts of the world. South Sea islanders eat roots we would not recognize as vegetables. Chinese cooks use vegetables unusual to us, such as bean pods, bamboo shoots, and water chestnuts. French people eat more kinds of salad greens, such as kale, chicory, and even dandelion greens, than Americans do. Some vegetables are common in some parts of the United States, but are rarely eaten in other parts. Okra is a southern favorite, but northern and western shoppers are not accustomed to its heavy pod and somewhat sticky flesh. About 30 kinds of vegetables are commonly eaten in the United States.

▼*The large curly leaves of a lettuce plant show that the ripe head is ready to be cut from the stalk.*

Vegetables usually taste better when they are ripened on the vine or stalk, but many vegetables are picked while they are immature and ripen on their way to market. Some vegetables, such as potatoes, can be stored fresh for a long time, but others, such as asparagus and peas, must be preserved in some way. Some are dried, some are canned, and some are frozen.

Many familiar vegetables have been known for centuries, but not always as food. Tomatoes were once thought to be poisonous and eggplants inedible. Asparagus was used as a medicine 2,000 years ago, long before the Romans raised it for food. Cabbage leaves were used as a dressing for bruises and to prevent baldness. When vinegar was added, they were supposed to cure dog bites. Onions were a household cure for colds during the Middle Ages. Carrots came from Asia to England, where ladies used the leaves as hat trimmings. Persian cooks served lettuce in the 500s B.C. Melons have been grown in Africa and Asia for thousands of years. Yams were eaten by primitive African tribes. Squash, corn, and several kinds of beans are native to the Americas.

Vegetables are very important in good nutrition. But they do not all offer the same food value. Avocados are largely fat. Starchy vegetables, such as beans, potatoes, and corn, contain mostly carbohydrates. Beans and peas also contain small amounts of protein. Most vegetables provide vitamins, especially A, the B vitamins (thiamine, riboflavin, and niacin), and C. Usually, the deeper the color of the vegetable the richer in vitamins it is. Carrots, tomatoes, and spinach are nutritious vegetables with deep coloring. Cabbage, however, has abundant vitamin C, despite its pale green color. Vegetables are also rich in minerals, such as calcium, iron, phosphorus, and potassium. Spinach and asparagus provide iron, a very important nutrient. Beans are high in calcium.

Besides vitamins and minerals, vegetables offer substances that help digestion of other foods. All vegetables contain a great deal of water. *Cellulose,* the fibrous material in vegetables, adds bulk to the diet, which aids the digestive system.

ALSO READ: MEAL PLANNING, NUTRITION, PLANT, SEEDS AND FRUIT, TRUCK FARMING.

VEIN see CIRCULATORY SYSTEM.

▲*A county agricultural agent shows a Georgia farm woman how deep to plant her vegetable seeds.*

VELAZQUEZ, DIEGO (1599–1660) Diego Rodriguez de Silva y Velazquez was the master of Spanish painters and one of the greatest artists of all time. He was born in the city of Seville, then a wealthy city because of its trade with America.

At the age of 12 Velazquez became an apprentice to Francisco Pacheco, a well-known Seville painter. Many artists from other countries visited at the Pacheco home, and Velazquez was able to learn of new developments in painting. He became a master painter at the age of 17.

Velazquez soon made a reputation for himself as an excellent painter. He painted with dark brown and yellowish tones. His early paintings, both his still lifes and his religious pictures, show that he had mastery of objects and figures when he was barely 20 years old. After five years in Seville he journeyed to Madrid, hoping to have a chance to paint a portrait of the king, Philip III. He could not arrange to do so, but a year later he went to Madrid again. By this time the old king had died, and his son Philip IV had succeeded him. Velazquez became a member of the court.

King Philip IV was very fond of Velazquez, who painted many portraits of the king. In 1628, the great painter Peter Paul Rubens came to Madrid on a diplomatic visit. Velazquez was

▲*The Prince on Horseback, by Diego Velazquez.*

chosen to be his companion. It is thought that Rubens urged Velazquez to go to Italy to see the work of the great artists there. When he returned to Spain, his paintings had become more colorful. His brushstrokes were freer.

The Prince on Horseback (shown here) is a handsome portrait of Prince Baltazar Carlos, son of King Philip IV. The little boy looks very much a prince astride a beautiful, lively looking pony. The prince's sash flies out behind him as he rides. The young face looks at the painter with a fresh, alert expression. The prince is in command of the situation. Do you suppose this was his own pony he is riding? Velazquez's background here was unusual for portraits of the day. Beautiful clouds sail through the sky, a strip of oak forest lies in the near background, while snowcapped mountains rise in the distance.

Velazquez made another journey to Italy in 1649. At that time he did a portrait of Pope Innocent X that has been called one of the finest portraits ever done. Velazquez lived out his whole life at court and left a wealth of beautiful paintings. Many of his paintings are in the Prado Museum in Madrid, although fine examples of his work can be seen in most of the world's leading museums.

ALSO READ: ART; ART HISTORY; BAROQUE PERIOD; RUBENS, PETER PAUL; SPANISH HISTORY.

VENEZUELA Venezuela is one of the richest South American countries because of its oil deposits. It lies on the northern coast of South America, bordered on the north by the Caribbean Sea. Its neighbors are Brazil to the south, Colombia on the west, and Guyana on the east. Several islands off the Caribbean coast are part of Venezuela. (See the map with the article on SOUTH AMERICA.)

Venezuela is larger than Texas and Oklahoma combined. It has four main regions. In the Andes Mountains and surrounding hills, many peaks soar up over 15,000 feet. The capital city of Caracas lies at 3,000 feet and has spring weather the year round. Most of the Venezuelan people live and work in the cool mountain areas.

The hot and humid coastal plain includes Lake Maracaibo and the Orinoco River delta. This region is the source of Venezuela's oil wealth. Plains, or *llanos,* lie between the Andes and the Orinoco. This hot region, where cattle graze on large ranches, at times receives heavy rain and at other times is very dry. The Guiana Highlands, a vast area of high plateaus and plains, extends from the Orinoco River to the Brazilian border. Primitive Indian tribes live in this ruggedly beautiful country. The world's highest waterfall, Angel Falls (3,212 ft.) was discovered there in 1935 by an American airplane pilot, Jimmy Angel, after he had crash-landed near the site.

One of the buildings from Spanish colonial times that is preserved in Caracas, Venezuela, is the *Casa Natal.* It is the birthplace of Simón Bolívar, who led the fight to free Venezuela and other South American countries from Spanish rule.

VENEZUELA

Capital City: Caracas (2,064,000 people).
Area: 352,143 square miles.
Population: 10,035,000 people.
Language: Spanish.
Export Products: Oil, iron ore, and coffee.
Unit of Money: Bolivar.

Most Venezuelans are *mestizos* (people of mixed Spanish, Indian, and Negro descent). The overall standard of living is high compared to that of other Latin American countries, but many of the people are still very poor.

In 1917, oil was discovered along the shores of Lake Maracaibo, an area now one of the largest producing oil fields in the world. Oil revenues are now being used for public housing and other projects to benefit the people. Caracas, with its plazas and its University City, is a rich and modern city.

Venezuela was first discovered by Christopher Columbus on his third voyage in 1498. It was one of the first colonies to revolt against Spain but did not win independence until 1821, under the leadership of Venezuela's famous hero, Simon Bolivar. General Juan Vicente Gomez ruled as dictator from 1908 to 1935. The country was not free from dictatorial rule until 1958. It is now a republic, administered by a president. In recent years, revolutionary groups have tried to disrupt elections.

▲*Caracas, the capital and largest city of Venezuela, lies 3,000 feet above the Caribbean Sea.*

ALSO READ: BOLIVAR, SIMON; COLUMBUS, CHRISTOPHER; SOUTH AMERICA.

VENICE Venice is a beautiful Italian city built on the sea. Some Venetians do have cars, but many travel along canals instead of streets, using boats instead of cars.

When the Roman Empire collapsed in the 400s, savage invaders swept across Italy. People who lived on the northern Italian mainland fled by boat to low mud islands off the coast. On these islands and in the shallow parts of the sea nearby they began to build a city, Venice. Venice developed into a great seafaring and trading center. Its merchants controlled the growing ocean traffic to the eastern Mediterranean. From there they brought spices, silks, sugar, gems, and perfumes to Europe.

Even today, visitors to Venice come by boat, train, or plane. The city's 120 islands are connected by 400 graceful bridges.

▶*The Grand Canal winds through the city of Venice past some of the most graceful buildings in the world. The Church of Santa Maria della Salute is in the center background. Posts for mooring gondolas and other boats can be seen in front of the houses on the left.*

Boats carry people along the 177 canals. Motorized launches are common, but some people prefer to travel on elegant Venetian boats called *gondolas.* These decorative, flat-bottomed boats have high prows and sterns and are propelled by oarsmen called *gondoliers.*

Venice is a city of striking palaces, churches, and public buildings. The Grand Canal leads to the heart of town, the Square, or *Piazza,* of St. Mark. The Cathedral of St. Mark, the Palace of the Doges (Dukes of Venice), and the Campanile (bell tower) are located there. Four gilded horses made by the ancient Greeks adorn the upper tier of the cathedral. These horses were brought to Venice in the 1200s. Tourists like to feed the pigeons which flock to the square. The ancient Rialto bridge and the Bridge of Sighs are also favorite sights. Galleries contain masterpieces painted by such Venetian masters as Titian, Tintoretto, and Giorgione. Many visitors like to relax on the beaches at Lido, across the lagoon from the city.

ALSO READ: ITALIAN HISTORY, ITALY, ROMAN EMPIRE.

VENTRILOQUISM see PUPPET.

VERB see PARTS OF SPEECH.

▼*Giuseppe Verdi, Italian opera composer.*

VERDI, GIUSEPPE (1813–1901) Verdi was one of the world's greatest composers of grand opera. He created works filled with more exciting drama and richer melodies and harmonies than did previous opera composers.

Verdi's father was a poor innkeeper in the small town of Roncole, Italy. A local parish priest gave Verdi his first music lessons. He later moved to Busseto, Italy, where he studied with the local orchestra conductor, Francesco Provesi. A merchant of Busseto helped support Verdi, even paying for his musical studies in Milan, Italy. In 1833, Verdi returned to Busseto, where he became director of the orchestra after Provesi's death.

Oberto, Verdi's first opera, was produced in Milan in 1839 with some success. But his next opera was a failure. The death of his young wife and children resulted in his giving up composing for more than a year. The manager of the La Scala Opera in Milan succeeded in interesting Verdi in a new opera text, and he went back to composing.

Verdi's musical gifts developed gradually, his greatest works being written in his later years. *Rigoletto,* composed in 1851, was the first of Verdi's operas that is still regularly performed today. It was followed by *Il Trovatore, La Traviata, Don Carlos,* and *La Forza del Destino.* His greatest successes, which formed the high point of Italian opera, were *Aïda, Othello,* and *Falstaff.* He also composed a *Requiem Mass* in memory of the Italian poet Manzoni.

ALSO READ: MUSIC, MUSICIAN, OPERA.

Verdi composed the opera *Aïda* in 1871 for the khedive (Turkish ruler) of Egypt. It was written to celebrate the opening of the Suez Canal.

VERMONT Vermont is a beautiful New England state. The Vermont countryside–with its rolling hills dotted with sugar maples, peaceful villages with steepled white churches, and clear mountain lakes–gives visitors a chance to imagine what life was like in early America. Beneath this lovely countryside lies very hard rock. The city of Barre in central Vermont is sometimes called the Granite Center of the World. Vermont's early settlers chiseled millstones from granite. Today, granite blocks are used for building.

Vermont's list of famous citizens is headed by two American Presidents. Chester A. Arthur and Calvin Coolidge were both Vermont Republicans.

The Land and Climate

A long, rocky range of mountains divides Vermont into western and eastern sections. This range belongs to the Appalachian Mountains. It stretches from the Canadian province of Quebec in the north to Massachusetts in the south. The part of the range in Vermont is named the Green Mountains. A hiking path follows the range all the way through the state. Frenchmen came to this region during the 1600s and early 1700s. They may have used the name *Les Verts Monts* (The Green Mountains), which led to the name *Vermont.*

◀*Lake Champlain is part of Vermont's border with New York. Some of Vermont's best farmland borders this scenic lake.*

West of the Green Mountains, the land slopes toward Lake Champlain and the border of New York State. Burlington, the state's largest city and site of the University of Vermont, overlooks the lake. The Champlain Valley has much beautiful scenery. Part of the lake itself, as well as several islands and a peninsula, are in Vermont.

Addison County, near Lake Champlain, might be described in Biblical terms as a land of "milk and honey." Vermont's biggest honey producers are in Addison County. Dairying is also an important industry, just as it is in more than half of the entire state.

East of the Green Mountains, the land slopes mostly toward the Connecticut River. However, a branch of the White Moun-

VERMONT

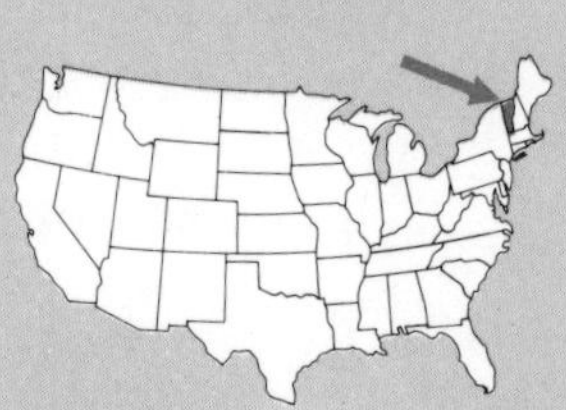

State flower
Red clover

State bird
Hermit thrush

State tree
Sugar maple

Capital
Montpelier
(8,609 people)

Area
9,609 square miles
(ranks 43rd)

Population
444,732 people
(ranks 48th)

Statehood
March 4, 1791
(14th state admitted)

Principal river
Connecticut River

Highest point
Mount Mansfield
(4,393 feet)

Largest city
Burlington
(38,633 people)

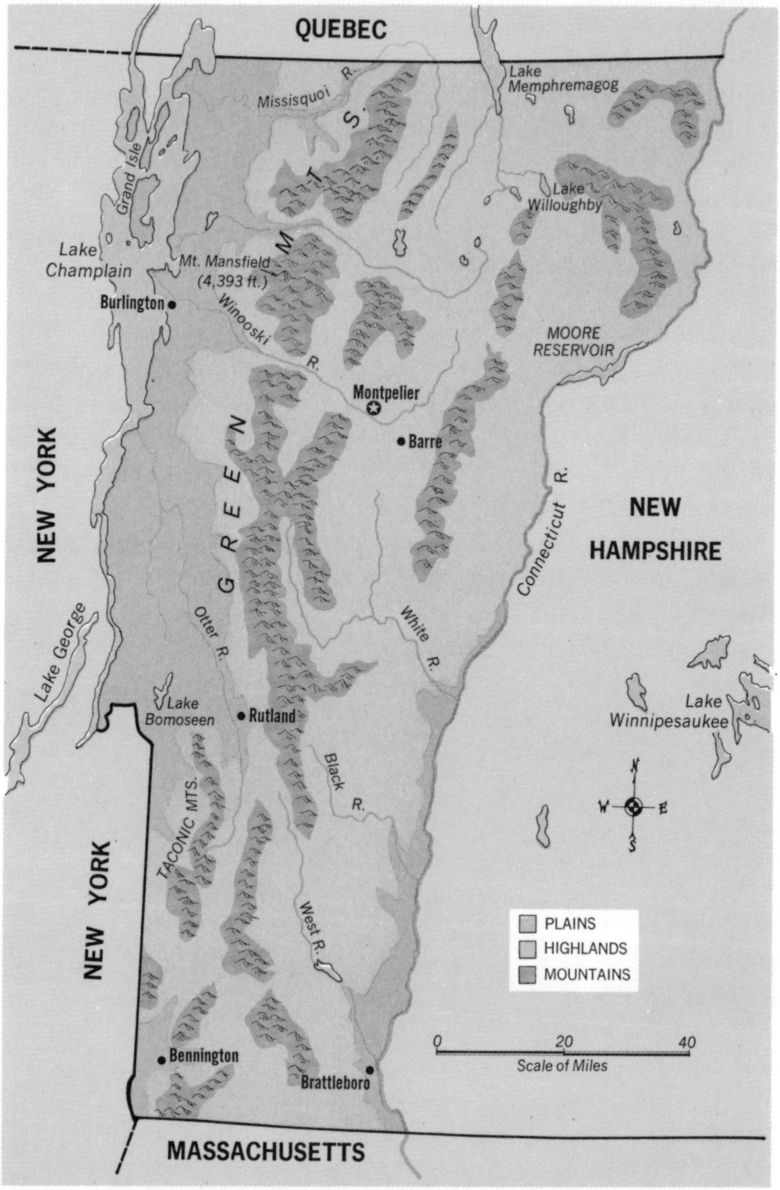

tains rises in the northeast. Most of this range is in the state of New Hampshire, just across the Connecticut River. Eastern Vermont is horse-raising country. Miles of riding trails wind through woods, along streams, and past waterfalls and lakes.

Vermont's summers are cool, and rain is usually plentiful. Vacationers from many states come to the cool, green hills to escape summer heat. From December until the end of March, the state is generally under a blanket of snow.

▲*Vermont in the fall is a place of incredible beauty. Many people come to the state during the "foliage season" to see the varied colors of the turning leaves.*

History

In the days of the Indians, Vermont was a borderland. It lay between the territory of the New York Iroquois and that of the Algonkin tribes to the east. Other Algonkin tribes lived north of Vermont. The Algonkins of Canada and their neighbors, the Hurons, were enemies of the Iroquois.

By 1609, the French explorer, Samuel de Champlain, had made friends among the Algonkins and Hurons. They persuaded him and other Frenchmen to fight the Iroquois with them. Their war party paddled south on Lake Champlain. For the first time, Europeans saw Vermont's Green Mountains. The fight with the Iroquois took place on the New York side of the lake. French guns won the battle for the Canadian Indians. Later, the French built log forts in the Champlain Valley. The first one was built on Isle La Motte in the lake itself.

The English entered Vermont from the southeast. In 1724, they built Fort Dummer where Brattleboro stands today. The fort was the first permanent English settlement. With the help of the vengeful Iroquois, the British began to fight the French. By 1758, the French had lost all their forts in Vermont.

Many people began to come from Massachusetts and Connecticut to settle in Vermont. But nobody was sure whether the area was part of New York or New Hampshire. In 1764, the English king declared that it belonged to New York. When New York tried to claim it, Vermont settlers chose Ethan Allen to take charge of their defense. He armed a force that he called the "Green Mountain Boys." But before the matter could be settled, the American Revolution broke out. The Green Mountain Boys marched on Fort Ticonderoga, west of Lake Champlain. On May 10, 1775, they took it from the British soldiers.

Vermont declared itself an independent republic. For a time, it had its own postal system and coined its own money. But in 1791, Vermont joined the Union, the first state to do so after the original 13 colonies. Vermont was the first state to ban slavery and give the vote to all adult males.

As long as farming was the main business in America, Vermont was at a disadvantage. It had little good land for growing crops, although sheep raising brought prosperity for awhile. Many farmers gave up their struggle with stony soil and moved

▼*Early spring is maple sugar time in Vermont. The sap is drawn from the trees and then boiled down to the consistency of maple syrup or sugar inside the shed.*

west. But French Canadian settlers who were unable to get fertile land in Quebec began to come to Vermont in the late 1800s. They bought the farms that Vermonters had given up. Dairy farming became the main type of agriculture.

Vermonters at Work

Today, manufacturing is Vermont's most important business. Machinery is the leading manufactured product.

Agriculture and tourism are also important. Dairying is still the principal kind of agriculture. But one of Vermont's best-known agricultural products—maple syrup—is not a dairy product. The maple sap is gathered from the state's official tree, the sugar maple. The state's natural beauty draws visitors at all times of the year, but especially in autumn when the leaves change colors. Winter brings skiers to the snowy slopes of the Green Mountains.

ALSO READ: ALGONKIAN; APPALACHIAN MOUNTAINS; CHAMPLAIN, SAMUEL DE; FRENCH AND INDIAN WAR.

VERNE, JULES (1828-1905) Jules Verne was a writer of science fiction who forecast many modern scientific inventions. Verne was born in Nantes, France. He studied law, but was more interested in writing.

▲*Jules Verne, French author of science fiction.*

Verne was deeply interested in geography and in *aeronautics,* the science of flight. He wrote a scientific essay suggesting an expedition to Africa in a balloon. His publisher persuaded him to turn the essay into a novel, called *Five Weeks in a Balloon.* This book was immensely successful, and Verne wrote several other novels of adventure and science fiction, including *A Journey to the Center of the Earth, From the Earth to the Moon,* and *The Mysterious Island.*

Long before such inventions were seriously believed to be possible, Verne wrote about helicopters, airplanes, submarines, rocket-propelled missiles, television, man-made satellites, and space travel. His book *Twenty Thousand Leagues Under the Sea* is about a sea captain named Nemo, who travels about in a submarine far beneath the surface of the seas. Many of Verne's books have been made into motion pictures, including *Around the World in Eighty Days.* This novel tells the story of Phileas Fogg's exciting trip around the world, using all sorts of transportation. To make the trip in such a short time was an unheard-of feat in those days.

ALSO READ: SCIENCE FICTION.

VERRAZANO, GIOVANNI DA (about 1485-about 1527) Giovanni da Verrazano was an Italian explorer and pirate, one of the first Europeans to explore the coast of North America.

Little is known about Verrazano's life. He is first mentioned historically in the 1520s, as a pirate paid by the French to capture Spanish ships. In 1523 the king of France, Francis I, commissioned Verrazano to find a "northwest passage" to the Orient around the northern continent of America. The Spaniards were preventing French merchant ships from using the southern route around South America. Records of Verrazano's expedition are scanty and inaccurate. He seems to have landed on the coast of present-day North Carolina. He then sailed northward and discovered what is now New York harbor. He probably also explored the coast of New England. On a later expedition to America, Verrazano explored the West Indies. He was killed there either by natives or by the Spaniards.

The entrance to New York harbor between Brooklyn and Staten Island is known as the Narrows. The Verrazano-Narrows Bridge, opened in 1964, is the longest suspension bridge in the world, with a span of 4,260 feet.

ALSO READ: EXPLORATION, NORTHWEST PASSAGE.

VERSAILLES Versailles is a city in France, southwest of Paris. The magnificent Palace of Versailles, home of the French kings for about 100 years, stands at the center of the city.

About 350 years ago, Versailles was a tiny village in the middle of a forest. King Louis XIII of France built a hunting lodge at Versailles in the 1620s. After Louis XIII died, his son Louis XIV decided to build a huge palace at the same place.

The Palace of Versailles took 21 years to build. When it was finished in 1682, Louis XIV moved there with his court. The palace is surrounded by vast gardens with hundreds of fountains and statues. The rooms of the palace are decorated with priceless works of art. Two smaller palaces, the Grand Trianon and the Petit Trianon, were built in the gardens of Versailles.

When the French Revolution began in 1789, King Louis XVI and his family were forced to leave Versailles. The palace was never again used as a residence.

Today, the Palace of Versailles is a national museum. The Treaty of Versailles, which ended World War I, was signed between Germany and the Allied Powers in the great Hall of Mirrors at Versailles.

ALSO READ: FRENCH HISTORY; FRENCH REVOLUTION; LOUIS, KINGS OF FRANCE.

◀*The Palace of Versailles is a historic building that is now a museum. Beautiful formal gardens and elegant sculptures lie at the back of the palace.*

VERTEBRATE Vertebrates include all the animals that have backbones, from giant whales to tiny field mice. All mammals, such as deer, cats, and humans are vertebrates. Reptiles, amphibians, birds, and fish are also vertebrates. Besides having backbones, all vertebrates are alike in other important ways. They have a body plan that makes them different from *invertebrates,* or animals without backbones, such as mollusks, insects, and worms. A vertebrate has a skeleton inside its body. A skeleton is a framework that supports muscle and tissue. It is made of bone and cartilage. Invertebrates often have hard outside coverings, like shells. Or they may have no supporting framework at all.

An important part of a vertebrate's skeleton is its skull. It holds and protects the animal's brain. Eyes, ears, and a nose are all found in the skull of vertebrate animals. Almost all vertebrates have jaws. One exception is the lamprey eel, which has a sucking device instead of jaws. Most vertebrates have limbs, such as arms or legs. Fish have fins which take the place of legs. The limbs and fins are always found in pairs. Vertebrates never have more than two pairs. Humans and apes, for example, have two arms and two legs. Most other mammals have two pairs of legs. Birds have two legs and two wings. Snakes once had limbs like other vertebrates, but lost them in the process of evolution. The number of legs varies among invertebrates. Insects, for example, have six legs. Some invertebrates have no limbs.

ALSO READ: AMPHIBIAN, ANIMAL KINGDOM, BIRD, EVOLUTION, FISH, MAMMAL, REPTILE, SKELETON.

▲*Amerigo Vespucci, Italian navigator.*

VESPUCCI, AMERIGO (1451-1512) Amerigo Vespucci was an Italian businessman and ship's pilot, or navigator. He is mainly remembered as the man after whom America was named. Vespucci was born in Florence. He traveled to South America as a ship's pilot on a Spanish expedition in 1499, and on a Portuguese expedition in 1501. During these voyages, Vespucci explored the coast of South America and discovered the mouth of the Amazon River. In a letter written in 1504, Vespucci stated that he had also made an earlier voyage to the New World in 1497. He claimed that he was the first European to set foot on the continent. Before 1498, Christopher Columbus had landed only on the islands of the West Indies.

Scholars today doubt that Vespucci actually made the voyage in 1497. But Vespucci certainly was one of the first Europeans to realize that the new lands being discovered were not part of Asia but a whole new continent. In 1507, a German map maker Martin Waldseemuller, who perhaps had not heard of Columbus, decided to name the new continent after the Latin form of Amerigo's name, "Americus."

ALSO READ: AMERICA, EXPLORATION.

VESUVIUS see POMPEII, VOLCANO.

VETERANS DAY Veterans Day is a national holiday in the United States. Since 1971, it has been celebrated on the fourth Monday in October, in honor of all the men and women who have served in the U.S. armed forces during wartime. On this day veterans parade, patriotic speeches are made, and a special ceremony takes place at Arlington National Cemetery in Virginia, at the Tomb of the Unknowns.

Veterans Day was originally called Armistice Day. It commemorated the end of fighting in World War I, which took place on November 11, 1918. President Woodrow Wilson first proclaimed November 11 as Armistice Day in 1919. In 1954, the U.S. Congress changed the name of the holiday to Veterans Day, to honor the veterans of all wars.

ALSO READ: HOLIDAY, PARADE, TOMB OF THE UNKNOWNS.

VETERINARY MEDICINE Animals become sick, just as human beings do. And animals can be injured. A doctor who treats sick or injured animals is a veterinarian, or a veterinary.

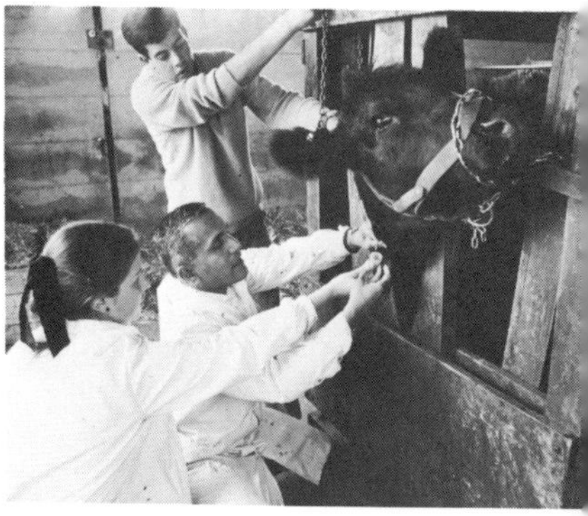

▲*A veterinarian, helped by his assistant, takes a blood sample from a cow in order to find if the animal is healthy or diseased.*

Veterinarians working in cities usually have private practices and treat mostly pets. These doctors often have animal hospitals where owners can leave their sick pets. People who are going to be away from home can also leave their healthy pets with veterinarians. The veterinarian who treats pets should know how to get along with people. The owners of sick animals often become so worried that they are hard to deal with.

Veterinarians in rural areas usually specialize in treating cattle and other livestock, including poultry, sheep, and horses. These animals are often treated on the farm, rather than being taken to clinics or hospitals.

The office of a veterinarian has modern medical equipment, including examining and operation tables and X-ray machines. The veterinarian takes X-rays and runs tests to find out what is wrong with a sick animal. If necessary, he performs surgery or gives drugs to make the animal well again.

In government service, veterinarians protect American livestock from foreign diseases by inspecting animals brought into this country from other countries. Within the borders of this country, veterinarians safeguard public health by inspecting meat, poultry, eggs, and butter. They also inspect the farms, dairies, and packing plants where these foods are produced.

The agricultural services of the states have many veterinarians working to advise farmers on the health of their poultry and other livestock. Some veterinarians teach in schools of veterinary medicine. Many others teach in agriculture colleges. One of the most interesting jobs in veterinary medicine is being a veterinarian in a zoo. These veterinarians must treat the diseases of hundreds of kinds of animals from every part of the world.

ALSO READ: ANIMAL, MEDICINE, PUBLIC HEALTH, SURGERY.

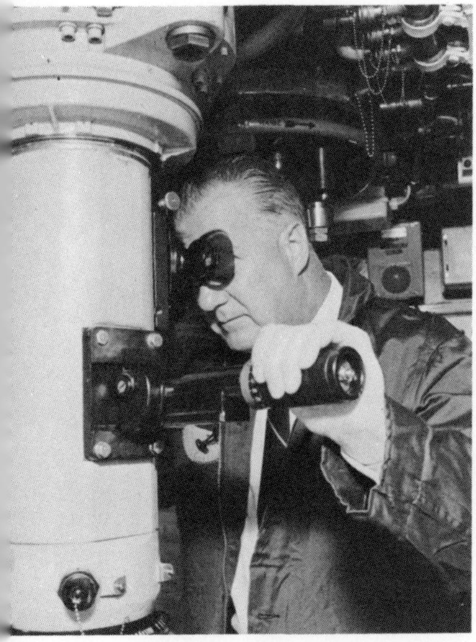

▲*Vice President Spiro T. Agnew tours the nuclear-powered submarine, U.S.S.* Hammerhead.

VICE PRESIDENT The Vice President is second in rank to the President of the United States and is elected along with the President. According to the Constitution, the Vice President must have the same qualifications as the President—he must be a native-born citizen at least 35 years old, and he must have lived in the United States for 14 years.

If a President dies in office, the Vice President automatically succeeds (follows) him and becomes the President of the United States. The Constitution is vague about whether the Vice President actually becomes President or merely performs the duties. The custom for the Vice President to assume the Presidency was established by John Tyler in 1841, when he succeeded William Henry Harrison, the first President to die while in office.

The President is the head of the executive branch, so the duties of a Vice President are largely defined by the Chief Executive. The only specific duty given to a Vice President by the Constitution is to serve as President of the Senate. The Vice President presides over Senate sessions, but he has no voting power unless there is a tie. When a vote is tied, the Vice President casts the deciding vote to break the tie. The Vice President also attends Cabinet meetings, and he is a member of the National Security Council, which advises the President on defense and foreign policy.

Historically, many men have disliked their job as Vice President and have felt powerless to guide government affairs. John Adams, in a letter to his wife, made his feelings known about his role in the job: "My country has in its wisdom contrived for me the most insignificant office that ever the invention of man contrived or his imagination conceived. . . ." Theodore Roosevelt, as Vice President, thought he was being "laid on the shelf," but the assassination of President McKinley in 1901 thrust him into the nation's highest office.

Since World War II, two Vice Presidents have come to the White House because a President died in office. Harry Truman succeeded Franklin Roosevelt in 1945, and Lyndon Johnson took over as President when John Kennedy was killed in 1963. Both won election on their own right.

In 1965, Congress passed the Twenty-fifth Amendment. This change authorizes a Vice President who has succeeded to the Presidency to appoint, with the approval of Congress, his own Vice President. This amendment also defines the procedures by which a Vice President can assume Presidential duties when a President is too ill to do his work. The Amendment was ratified by the states in 1967.

ALSO READ: ADAMS, JOHN; CONSTITUTION, UNITED STATES; JOHNSON, LYNDON BAINES; PRESIDENCY; ROOSEVELT, FRANKLIN D.; ROOSEVELT, THEODORE; TRUMAN, HARRY S; TYLER, JOHN; UNITED STATES GOVERNMENT.

VICTORIA (1819–1901) Victoria was Queen of the United Kingdom of Great Britain and Ireland and Empress of India. Her reign, which lasted for 63 years, was the longest in British history. While she was queen, Britain became the richest and most powerful nation in the world.

Victoria was born in London. Her father Edward, Duke of Kent, died when she was very young, and Victoria was brought up by her strict German mother. Victoria became queen at the age of 18, after the death of her uncle King William IV. By this time, Britain was a *constitutional monarchy.* The monarch was expected to follow the advice of the prime minister and not attempt to influence government policies. But Victoria took a keen interest in government affairs, and soon began to state strongly her approval or disapproval of her ministers' policies.

In 1840, Victoria married her cousin, a German prince, Albert of Saxe-Coburg-Gotha. Their marriage was extremely happy and became an inspiration to other families throughout Britain. Victoria and Albert had nine children, most of whom married into other royal families in Europe.

In 1861, Prince Albert died suddenly of typhoid fever. Victoria was grief-stricken and went into deep mourning for several years. She later returned to public life at the encouragement of Prime Minister Benjamin Disraeli. Victoria now ruled over a mighty empire, and in 1876 she took the title Empress of India. The Industrial Revolution had brought immense prosperity to Britain. In 1887, the British people celebrated the fiftieth year of Victoria's reign with a great festival, the Golden Jubilee. A Diamond Jubilee was held ten years later, on her sixtieth anniversary.

Victoria was a small, plump woman with an air of immense dignity. To the British people she became a symbol of strength and virtue. Her reign is often called the "Victorian Age."

ALSO READ: ENGLISH HISTORY.

◀*The coronation of Queen Victoria took place in Westminster Abbey in 1838. It was an occasion full of pomp and ceremony as the young woman was crowned queen.*

▲*A South Vietnamese soldier stands near a war memorial in a square in Saigon, South Vietnam's capital.*

VIETNAM Vietnam is the name shared by two countries that form the eastern coast of the Southeast Asian peninsula. North Vietnam touches China in the north, and South Vietnam stretches to the Gulf of Thailand in the south. (See the map with the article on ASIA.)

The Vietnamese people have had few years of peace since before World War II. The Japanese occupied their country during the war. Then fighting broke out with the French, who had controlled Vietnam before the war.

A Communist leader named Ho Chi Minh led a guerrilla force called the Vietminh to victory, and the French were driven out. The battle of Dien Bien Phu, when the French forces were overrun by the Vietminh on May 7, 1954, ended French power there. A civil war between the northern Communist government (Democratic Republic of Vietnam) and the government of South Vietnam (Republic of Vietnam) began in 1957. A truce was declared in January, 1973.

At its narrowest point, Vietnam is less than 40 miles wide. It is there that a dividing line, called the seventeenth parallel, separates North Vietnam from South Vietnam. This division was suggested as a temporary measure in 1954 at the Geneva Conference. The conference set the peace terms between France and Vietnam, called for general elections (which were never held), and allowed for resettlement of people.

SOUTH VIETNAM

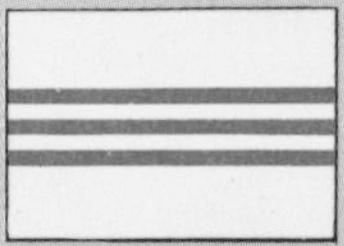

Capital City: Saigon (1,682,000 people).
Area: 65,726 square miles.
Population: 17,867,000 people.
Language: Vietnamese.
Export Products: Rubber.
Unit of Money: Piaster.

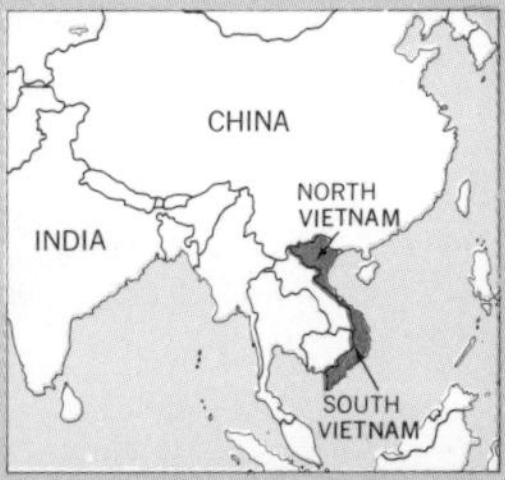

NORTH VIETNAM

Capital City: Hanoi (644,000 people).
Area: 63,370 square miles.
Population: 21,430,000 people.
Language: Vietnamese.
Export Products: Coal, handicrafts, cement, and lumber.
Unit of Money: Dong.

Today North Vietnam is Communist, ruled from the capital at Hanoi. The leaders would like to win control of all Vietnam. They gave aid to the Vietcong (Communist guerrilla fighters in the south). South Vietnam has been ruled in recent years by generals, and has struggled to stay free of Communist control. The United States helped South Vietnam in the war against the Vietcong and armies of North Vietnam.

North Vietnam is slightly larger than Georgia. About half the land is mountainous and covered by forest. Most people live in the Red River delta, where rice is cultivated. Haiphong is the chief port. Coal and iron are mined. The main industries are food processing, textiles, and steel making.

South Vietnam is an area curving along the South China Sea. It is a little larger than the state of Florida. In the lower part, where the Mekong River system spreads, the land is low and flat. The soil here is very rich, especially for rice-growing. Rubber trees grow on plantations here.

The Vietnamese people have been some of the most energetic people of Asia. Their culture is influenced by China, and partly by India. There have been European influences also, as a result of nearly 100 years of French rule. Most of the people are Buddhists, but many are Catholic, especially in South Vietnam. People called *Montagnards* (mountain men) live in the central highlands of Vietnam. Other minority groups in the country are the Chinese and the Cambodians.

▲*These people are citizens of Hanoi, North Vietnam's capital city.*

Vietnamese history is said to be 2,000 years old. The first people are believed to have come from China and parts of southeast Asia. China controlled Vietnam for nearly 1,000 years, until 939 A.D. Vietnam remained free until the 1800s, when France conquered Laos, Vietnam, and Cambodia and governed these regions as *French Indochina.* The areas of Tonkin (North Vietnam), Annam (Central Vietnam), and Cochin China (South Vietnam) made up Vietnam.

ALSO READ: ASIA, CHINA, INDOCHINA.

VIKINGS Also called *Norsemen, Northmen,* or *Normans,* the Vikings were a warlike, seafaring people—the ancient inhabitants of Norway, Sweden, and Denmark. In the 700s A.D., the Vikings became known to the people of Europe when Viking pirates began to raid settlements along European coastlines.

The Vikings were organized by tribes, and lived in small villages along the lengthy Scandinavian coastlines. They took great pride in their military skills and in their ability to sail the seas. They were extremely loyal to their tribal chiefs, especially during battle. Viking men considered it the greatest honor of all to die while fighting.

▼*Most Viking ships had a beautifully-painted dragon's head for a prow.*

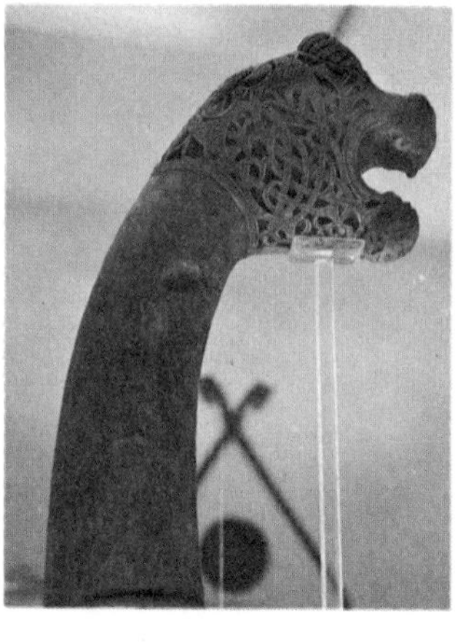

The Vikings had a written language spelled with the runic alphabet of 16 letters. Norsemen considered runic letters to be magic, and they often tried to predict the future by "casting the runes." As craftsmen, the Vikings were highly skilled carpenters and ironworkers. They fashioned excellent tools, weapons, and armor from iron and leather. Viking ships were probably the best fitted and most seaworthy vessels of ancient times. Both their warships and merchant vessels were swift and easy to maneuver—powered both by oars and sails.

▶*Leif Ericson, a Viking explorer, and his men approaching the coast of North America hundreds of years before Columbus.*

In the 700s, the Viking population in Scandinavia became too large and their poor land could not support the people. Areas of land away from the coasts were covered with dense forests that were almost impossible to get through, let alone start new settlements in. These circumstances forced the Vikings to move southward to find new places to live.

The first recorded Viking attack upon England came in 787, after which the Norsemen raided towns along the shores of present-day Belgium and France. In 878 the Saxon king Alfred the Great drove many of the invaders from England. But between 1017 and 1035, the Danish king Canute ruled a Norse empire that included Norway, Denmark, and England.

According to the Smithsonian Institution, the Vikings may have discovered America in 2000 B.C. An expedition to Labrador was undertaken in 1972 to try to prove this theory.

Charles III of France was unable to defeat the Vikings. Instead, Charles gave lands in northern France (modern-day Normandy) to the Viking chief Rollo, on condition that Rollo become his vassal. Rollo agreed, and in the year 911 he married King Charles's daughter and converted to Christianity. Rollo's descendant, William II of Normandy, invaded England in 1066 and became the English king William I.

In other lands, Vikings were equally successful. Along the Irish coast, they established the kingdoms of Dublin, Limerick, Waterford, and others in the 800s A.D. During that same century, Iceland was discovered and colonized. From Iceland, the Norsemen sailed still farther west, settling along the coasts of Greenland and eventually reaching the area of Vinland (present-day Newfoundland) in North America. Two of the best-known Viking seamen and explorers are Eric the Red and his son, Leif Ericson. Eric the Red discovered and named the great island of Greenland. Leif Ericson discovered Vinland and explored the coast of North America. In 1963, a team of Norwegian archeologists announced the discovery of a Viking settlement in Newfoundland. The digs have uncovered the foundations of nine buildings constructed in Norse style. Scientific tests show that the buildings were built about the year 1000.

By the 1100s, Christianity had become the religion of most of

Europe. Vikings converted and adapted themselves to this new religion. Their way of life had changed from that of a fierce, warring people to that of peaceful landowners and farmers. The Vikings had mixed with other Europeans and were no longer considered a separate people.

ALSO READ: CANUTE, DENMARK, ENGLISH HISTORY, NEWFOUNDLAND-LABRADOR, NORSE MYTH, NORWAY, RUSSIAN HISTORY, SCANDINAVIA, SCANDINAVIAN LANGUAGES, SHIPS AND SHIPPING, SWEDEN.

VIOLIN see STRINGED INSTRUMENTS.

VIRGINIA You can't go backward in time to the Virginia of George Washington and Thomas Jefferson. But perhaps you can do the next best thing. You can visit Williamsburg. Williamsburg was made the capital of Virginia in 1699, after Jamestown burned. It remained the capital until 1779.

Part of the town has been rebuilt to look as it did when Virginia was an English colony. The British flag flies from the brick Governor's Palace. Restored Williamsburg is a town of pretty houses. Its inns serve delicious meals in colonial style. In its shops, craftsmen make furniture, cloth, and iron articles by hand.

Virginia was started earlier than any of the other 13 English colonies. Settlement began on the Atlantic Coastal Plain. Later it spread inland to the Piedmont. By the time of the Revolution, settlers were in the Appalachian Mountains.

VIRGINIA

State flower
American dogwood

State bird
Cardinal

Capital
Richmond
(249,621 people)

Area
40,817 square miles
(ranks 36th)

Population
4,648,494 people
(ranks 14th)

Statehood
June 25, 1788
(10th of the original 13 states to ratify the Constitution)

Principal rivers
Rappahannock River
York River
James River

Highest point
Mount Rogers (in the southern Blue Ridge, 5,729 feet)

Largest city
Norfolk
(307,951 people)

The Land and Climate

Virginia's part of the Atlantic Coastal Plain is the lowest section of the state. It is called the Tidewater area. Much of the plain is almost level. In places, the low, flat land drains poorly. Such land is marsh. A good example is the Dismal Swamp, which extends into North Carolina.

Chesapeake Bay lies between the easternmost part of Virginia and the mainland. This eastern part of the state is the southern end of the Delmarva Peninsula. (The peninsula's name comes from the names of three states. What are they?) In 1964, the Chesapeake Bay Bridge-Tunnel was completed. It links the eastern shore to the mainland at a point near Norfolk. The bridge-tunnel is more than 17 miles long.

The principal rivers of the main part of Virginia flow southeastward across the coastal plain to Chesapeake Bay. Near the bay, they divide the bay's western shore into peninsulas.

Because the rivers flow to the southeast, you know that the land rises to the northwest. Virginia's middle section, the Piedmont, is higher than the coastal plain. The Piedmont is rolling, well-drained land that rises to mountains called the Blue Ridge. The fertile Shenandoah Valley is part of the Appalachian Valley that lies beyond the Blue Ridge.

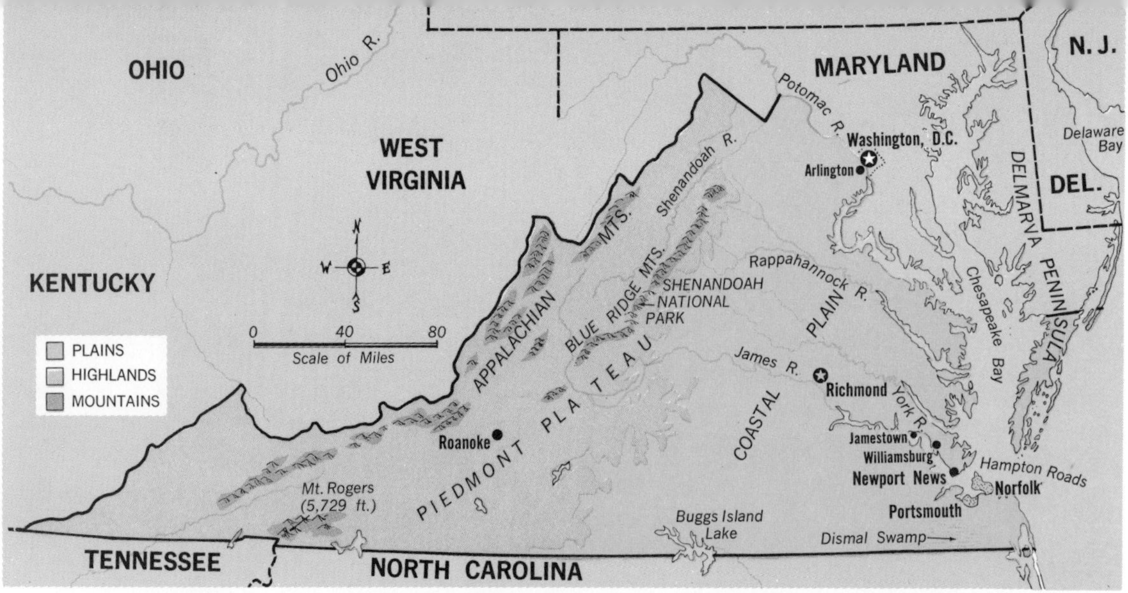

To the west, Virginia's mountains are part of the Appalachians. Their forested ranges slant from southwest to northeast. Green valleys lie between the ridges. The West Virginia border is in the mountains.

Summers are very warm in the coastal plain and the Piedmont. Winters are mild, with occasional snow.

▼*The Natural Bridge of Virginia, located just south of Lexington, is one of the natural wonders of the world. This great arch, 215 feet high and 90 feet long, was carved by a mountain stream over hundreds of thousands of years.*

History

This pleasant land had a large Indian population. When the Europeans arrived, there were about 200 Algonkin villages in Virginia's coastal plain. The 30 or more tribes here were ruled by a chief whom the English called Powhatan. Other tribes lived in the Piedmont.

The first English ships sailed up the James River in the spring of 1607. Full-sized models of them are tied up in the James today. They are moored not far from the place where the settlers landed. The settlers built a log fort and some huts. They named the settlement *James Towne* in honor of their king.

Hunger, disease, and Indian attacks almost wiped out the colony during its first years. The colonists had to buy tools, weapons, and clothes from England. They needed some way of paying for them. One of the settlers, probably a man named John Rolfe, suggested the raising of tobacco. This crop proved to be valuable. The first shipload went to England in 1614.

That same year, Rolfe aided the colony in another very different way. He married Pocahontas, the daughter of Powhatan. The marriage brought the colony years of peace.

In 1619, the first elected lawmaking body in the New World met at Jamestown. It was called the House of Burgesses. With the governor and his council, it made laws for the colony.

Also in 1619, the first Negroes reached English North America. A Dutch ship landed them at Jamestown. The men were not slaves. Like many white newcomers, they were indentured servants. Colonists paid their passage money. Each Negro then worked for the colonist until the debt was paid off.

The Negroes did so well as farm workers that English colonists decided to buy slaves from Africa. The result was decades of slavery, which brought suffering to millions.

Virginia played a big part in the Revolution. General Washington was a Virginian. So were Thomas Jefferson, Patrick Henry, George Mason, George Wythe, and other leaders. In the 1790s, Virginia and Maryland gave land to the new Federal Government to be used as the site of the capital, later named Washington, D.C. When the land given by Virginia had not been developed by 1846, it was returned to the state.

In 1861, Virginia joined the Confederate States of America. Richmond, now the state capital, was the capital of the Confederacy during most of the Civil War. Many Civil War battles were fought in Virginia. The first Battle of Bull Run was an early battle. On April 9, 1865, Confederate General Robert E. Lee surrendered to Union General Ulysses S. Grant at Appomattox. The war left the state poor—and smaller. The northwestern part of the state had refused to leave the Union. It had become a separate state, West Virginia.

Virginia finally recovered from the war. But evils that came from slavery continued to trouble it. As in other states, Negro citizens were treated as second-class citizens. The 1960s brought changes for the better. But in Virginia, as elsewhere, Negroes are still fighting their battle for full equality.

▲ *Virginia Beach is a popular resort area in Virginia. Some visitors stroll the boardwalk and admire the art exhibit, while others sun themselves on the beach or take a dip in the ocean.*

Virginians at Work

In and near Virginia cities, you see smoking factory chimneys. This state is one of the many where manufacturing is the biggest industry. The leading manufactures, in order of importance, are chemical products, cigarettes and other tobacco articles, foods, and textiles.

Agriculture is second to manufacturing in dollars earned. Eggs, milk, cattle, poultry, and hogs together earn more money than all crops. Winchester is a center of the apple-growing area.

Virginia's mountains and beaches draw vacationers. So do the spots where history was made in colonial times, in the Revolution, and in the Civil War.

The giant port area of Hampton Roads on Chesapeake Bay includes the harbors of Norfolk, Portsmouth, and Newport News. The U.S. Navy has a big base at Norfolk. Ships are built and repaired at the Portsmouth and Newport News shipyards.

ALSO READ: ALGONKIAN; APPALACHIAN MOUNTAINS; CHESAPEAKE BAY; CONFEDERATE STATES OF AMERICA; HENRY, PATRICK; JAMESTOWN; JEFFERSON, THOMAS; LEE, ROBERT E.; POCAHONTAS; SMITH, CAPTAIN JOHN; TOBACCO; WASHINGTON, GEORGE.

VIRGIN ISLANDS see WEST INDIES.

▼*Luray Caverns are a fascinating wonderland of underground caves near Luray, Virginia. Visitors are able to pass through giant rooms where sharp stalactites hang from the ceiling and cone-like stalagmites rise from the floor.*

VIRUS A virus is a tiny bit of matter that is not definitely living or non-living. A virus can infect living cells. When it is within living cells a virus acts like a living organism and it reproduces. When it is outside of a cell it seems to be non-living.

Viruses are smaller than the smallest bacteria. Viruses are too small to be seen with a light microscope, but they can be photographed with an electron microscope.

When a virus infects a living cell it can cause disease. Among the human diseases caused by viruses are poliomyelitis, yellow fever, chicken pox, smallpox, measles, mumps, and the common cold. In animals, distemper, rabies, hoof-and-mouth disease, and parrot fever are caused by viruses. Tobacco mosaic disease and the curly top disease of sugar beets are two plant diseases caused by viruses.

In 1892, Dmitri Ivanovski, a Russian scientist, showed that whatever caused tobacco mosaic disease was small enough to pass through a filter that would trap the smallest bacteria. Later, a Dutch scientist named the filter-passing substance a virus. This name means "living thing."

▼ *The influenza virus is so tiny that it cannot be seen through an ordinary microscope. This photograph of it was taken through an electron microscope.*

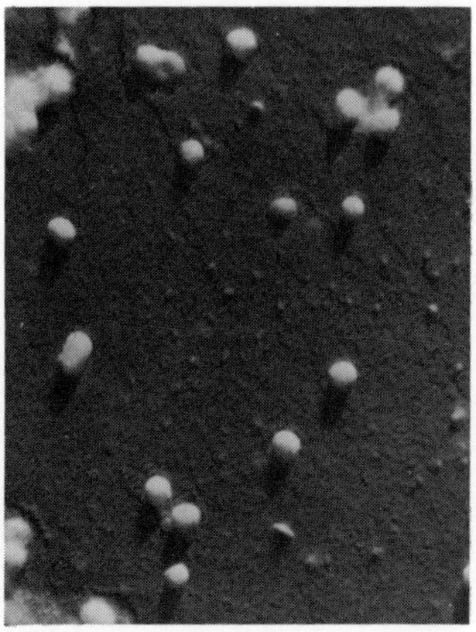

In 1935, Wendell M. Stanley, an American scientist, prepared some pure tobacco mosaic virus substance. He found that when this substance was dried, it formed non-living crystals. The crystals were harmless, but when they were dissolved in water, the virus could again cause the disease. Dr. Stanley had shown that a virus can be both a living and a non-living thing.

The electron microscope showed that some viruses look like tadpoles, with heads and tails. Other viruses are shaped like coils, and still others are solid 20-sided figures. All viruses are made up of an outer shell of protein enclosing a core of nucleic acid (a genetic material). Proteins are the basic substances of living matter. The nucleic acids, DNA (deoxyribonucleic acid) and RNA (ribonucleic acid), carry reproductive information for living cells and for viruses.

In order to infect a living cell, a virus must first attach itself to the cell. A tadpole-shaped virus attaches itself with its tail. Other viruses form a chemical bond with the cell. A virus can only attach itself to—and therefore infect—certain cells.

The nucleic acid of the virus then invades the cell. It takes over the cell's activities to produce new virus particles. The new viruses leave the cell and can infect other cells. Some viruses destroy cells. Other viruses cause cells to reproduce rapidly.

ALSO READ: BACTERIA, CELL, CRYSTAL, DISEASE, GENETICS, PARASITE, PROTEIN.

VITAMINS AND MINERALS Vitamins are food substances that you need if you are to remain in good health. The amounts you need are very small—only a few thousandths of an ounce of each vitamin each day. If the foods you eat daily include balanced amounts of meats, eggs, cheese, butter, milk, fruit, and cooked and uncooked vegetables, you are probably getting all the vitamins you need. People who do not eat the right kinds of food can still get enough vitamins by taking vitamin capsules. But it is better to get your vitamins from a variety of foods.

Vitamins were named A, B, C, and so on in the order in which they were discovered. Then, it was discovered that some vitamins are combinations of several others. The new vitamins were called B_1, B_2, and so on. They also were given names. A list of some vitamins is given in the table.

Minerals are also necessary for good health. Among the minerals needed is *calcium,* which is an important part of bones and teeth. You get calcium from milk, cream, and cheese. *Phosphorus* is an important part of certain compounds that help your body cells store and exchange energy. Your body uses *iodine* in making the thyroid hormone that regulates the pace

IMPORTANT VITAMINS

Vitamin	What Foods It Is Found In	What It does for Health
A	Butter, carrots, liver, green leafy vegetables, cod liver oil	Helps body to make *visual purple,* a substance that enables you to see in dim light; helps body resist infections; aids in the growth of cells.
B-complex		
B_1 (thiamine)	Bran, dried beans, peanuts, peas, meat, yeast, wheat germ	Increases your appetite; helps digestion; helps your nervous system work properly; reduces tiredness.
B_2 (riboflavin)	Eggs, liver, meat, milk, green vegetables, yeast	Enables cells to oxidize food for energy; controls growth; prevents certain eye, mouth, and skin diseases.
Niacin (nicotinic acid)	Eggs, fish, meat, poultry, whole wheat, yeast	Prevents the disease called *pellagra;* also prevents certain skin and nerve diseases.
C (ascorbic acid)	Citrus fruits (oranges, lemons, limes), tomatoes, raw leafy vegetables	Helps in forming teeth and bones; aids the healing of wounds; prevents the disease called *scurvy.*
D	Milk, butter, cheese, cod-liver oil (When sunlight shines on your skin, your body manufactures vitamin D.)	Regulates the absorption of the minerals calcium and phosphorus, keeping bones and teeth strong.
E	Margarine, vegetables, wheat germ	Needed by some animals for reproduction; helps your body use vitamin A.
K	Cabbage, cauliflower, spinach (K is the only vitamin your body can manufacture.)	Needed for the clotting of blood in cuts and wounds.

▲*Smoke pours from the crater of an active volcano in the Central American country of El Salvador.*

of your body's activities. *Iron* is needed for *hemoglobin,* the coloring matter in red blood cells which carries oxygen from your lungs to your tissues. *Sodium, potassium,* and *chlorine* are minerals needed to regulate the amount of water in your tissues and for proper activity of your nerves and muscles. Other minerals your body needs are *cobalt, magnesium,* and *manganese.*

ALSO READ: BLOOD, HORMONE, MINERAL, NUTRITION.

VOICE see ANIMAL VOICES, SPEECH.

VOLCANO A volcano is a mountain that has an opening through which melted rock, gases, and ashes are forced out. Underneath the Earth's rocky crust are masses of hot, melted rock. This rock material is called *magma.* Pressure pushes the magma upward through the cracks in the Earth's crust. If a crack leads to the Earth's surface, the magma pours out upon the surface. It is then called *lava.*

Magma contains large quantities of gases. When the magma rises close to the Earth's surface, the gases escape. They push outward with great force, blowing a hole in the surface. The outrushing gases carry up into the air huge amounts of dust and ashes. The tons of ashes form a cone around the hole in the Earth. Lava pours out of the hole and runs down the ash cone. In this way, a volcano is built. The outpouring of lava, gas, and ashes is called an *eruption.*

Most of the world's volcanoes were formed several million years ago. The Earth's newest volcano is located near Paricutín, Mexico. On February 20, 1943, a farmer there saw a wisp of smoke rise from a field he was plowing. A few hours later, dense clouds of smoke were pouring out of a crack in the Earth. Ashes shot out of the crack and began to form a cone as they fell to earth. Two days after the eruption began, lava started to flow out of an opening in the cone of ashes. By the time the volcano stopped erupting in 1952, the ashes and lava had built a volcano 1,350 feet high. It was named Mount Paricutín. Scientists have learned much about how volcanoes start and grow from studying this young volcano.

▼*A conduit, or passage, carries hot magma from the Earth's interior to the surface of a volcano.*

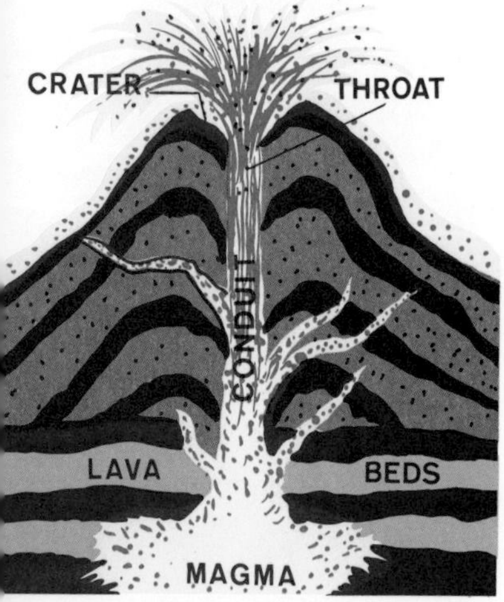

Most of the Earth's volcanoes are found in two main regions, or volcanic belts. The Pacific Ocean is surrounded by a belt of active volcanoes called the Circle of Fire. The shores of the Caribbean and Mediterranean seas also have many volcanoes.

Not all volcanoes shoot forth smoke and ashes. Some simply pour out lava. Mauna Loa in Hawaii is one of these. The Hawaiian Islands are the upper parts of volcanoes that erupted on the bottom of the Pacific Ocean.

Volcanoes that have not erupted for tens of thousands of years are called *extinct* volcanoes. Crater Lake in southwestern Oregon was formed in a depression that covers the top of an extinct volcano. Other volcanoes that have not erupted for

◀ *Lava fountains in the crater of Kilauea in Hawaii spew forth beautiful spurts of molten magma.*

thousands of years, but show signs that they may erupt again, are called *dormant* (sleeping) volcanoes. Popocatepetl is a dormant volcano near Mexico City. Volcanoes that have erupted many times in history are called *active* volcanoes. Lassen Peak, in California, is one of these. It last erupted in 1917.

The ancient Roman towns of Pompeii, Herculaneum, and Stabiae once stood at the foot of Mt. Somma, in Italy. In 79 A.D., this volcano erupted and buried the towns and their inhabitants. The eruption also destroyed Mt. Somma, but a new volcanic cone, Mt. Vesuvius, emerged. Since that time, Vesuvius has erupted many times.

One of the world's greatest volcanic explosions took place in Indonesia in 1883. Mt. Krakatoa blew apart in a number of tremendous eruptions. Nearby islands were swept by a tidal wave, and thousands of people were killed.

Although volcanoes are highly destructive and dangerous, they do help the Earth in some ways. They allow some of the tremendous pressure building up inside the Earth to be gradually released. The ashes given off by volcanoes eventually break down into rich soil, and volcanic steam is now being used in some parts of the world to generate electricity.

▲ *A stream of red-hot lava flows down the side of a volcano on a small island near Sicily.*

ALSO READ: EARTH, EARTH HISTORY, EARTHQUAKE, GEOLOGY, MOUNTAIN.

VOLGA RIVER One of the best-known Russian folk songs is the "Song of the Volga Boatmen." It is the rhythmic chant of the men who once worked along the Volga River pulling heavy boats with ropes. Although it is frozen during the long Russian winter, the Volga River has always been an important transportation route. It is 2,290 miles long—the longest river in Europe. It flows entirely within the Soviet Union. (See the map with the article on SOVIET UNION.)

The land on either side of the Volga is the most heavily populated and highly industrialized area in the Soviet Union. The cities of Moscow, Gorki, Kazan, and Volgograd are located on

►*For many years Russian serfs (peasants) were used to pull boats along the Volga River.*

the Volga and its branches. Besides providing a means of transportation, the river serves the Russian people as a source of electric power and water.

ALSO READ: SOVIET UNION.

VOLLEYBALL Volleyball is a game in which two teams hit a ball back and forth over a net. Each team tries to make the other miss a *volley* by dropping the ball or hitting it out of bounds. Volleyball can be played by people of all ages, indoors or out. The only equipment needed is a ball and a net. The ball should never touch the ground, so no special court is needed.

A volleyball court is 60 feet long and 30 feet wide. In the middle of the court is a net held up by poles. The top of the net is 8 feet above the ground. The ball is about 26 inches around and weighs about 10 ounces.

There are six players on each team. The three closest to the net are called *forwards.* The three in the back row are *backs.* The right back always serves, or *starts* the play. He may hit the ball with the palm of his hand or with a fist in an *underhand* serve or an *overhand* serve. The underhand serve is easier to control. The overhand serve sends the ball across the net harder and faster. The server has only one chance to hit the ball into the opposing team's court.

▼*The ball has just been hit over the net in a game of volleyball.*

After the ball is served, the opposing team usually uses three hits to return it across the net. The first person to hit the ball is called the *receiver.* The receiver passes it to a second player, called the *setup man,* who in turn passes it to a forward. This forward, called the *spiker,* returns the ball over the net as hard as he can, trying to hit it so that the opposing team will not be able to return the ball before it hits the ground.

The rules for volleyball are simple. The ball may not touch the ground. The ball may not be caught or held. A team may hit the ball no more than three times before returning it over the net. No player may hit the ball twice in a row, but he may give the first and third hits.

Only the team which serves the ball may score. If the opposing team cannot return the serve, the serving team scores one point. If the serving team does not return the ball, no points are lost. The other team serves and gets a chance to score. When a team loses the serve, every man moves one position clockwise.

When the serve returns to the team, a new man is in the right back position. This rule lets everyone have a chance to serve.

A special set of rules has been made for boys and girls. The United States Volleyball Association ruled that juniors may use a net seven feet high. They get two serves instead of one. There is no limit to the number of hits juniors may have before the ball goes over the net. Even the server's hit may be assisted over the net by his team.

VON BRAUN, WERNHER (born 1912) The world's foremost rocket and aerospace scientist, Dr. Wernher von Braun, is the man largely responsible for making space flight a reality.

Born in Wiritz, Germany (now Wyrzysk, Poland) on March 23, von Braun became interested in science at an early age. He studied science and engineering at the Zurich (Switzerland) Institute of Technology, the Berlin Institute of Technology, and the University of Berlin. While still a student, he worked with German rocket scientists H. Oberth and W. Dornberger.

In 1930, at age 18, von Braun began a number of successful experiments with small liquid-fuel rockets. In 1932, when von Braun was only 20, Dornberger put him in charge of the German army's rocket program. Von Braun's research team developed the V-2 rocket that was first used in 1944 during World War II. The V-2 was a large supersonic missile that was launched vertically. Its path took it out of Earth's atmosphere where it arched and descended to the ground at speeds several times faster than sound. Von Braun resigned from the rocket program when Hitler took personal control of it. Von Braun was put in jail for resigning.

▲*Wernher von Braun, German-born rocket engineer and space scientist.*

After World War II, von Braun was invited to the United States to develop rockets for the U.S. Army. For five years, he was project director for the rocket program at White Sands Proving Ground in New Mexico. He became a U.S. citizen in 1955. In 1958, when the National Aeronautics and Space Administration (NASA) was created, von Braun became director of the space flight center in Huntsville, Alabama. Von Braun led the team that developed and launched the first U.S. Earth satellite, Explorer I, on January 31, 1958.

In his work with NASA, Dr. von Braun has been involved with almost all U.S. space flight projects. He has received thousands of honors and awards from governments and organizations all over the world.

As of July 1, 1972, Dr. von Braun resigned from NASA in order to work at Fairchild-Hiller Industries, a private U.S company engaged in aerospace research.

ALSO READ: GODDARD, ROBERT H.; HITLER, ADOLF; MISSILE; ROCKET; SPACE RESEARCH; SPACE TRAVEL; WORLD WAR II.

VOTING see ELECTION.

W w

WAGNER, RICHARD (1813–1883) Richard Wagner was a German composer whose music brought about great changes in the art of opera composition. Wagner was born in Leipzig. As a boy, he became interested in the theater. But later he decided to study music. Operas at this time were written mainly to show off the voices of the singers. The story was not important. But Wagner believed that an opera should be a "music drama," vividly expressed in the music, the words of the singers, and the scenery. Wagner wrote his own *librettos* (stories) for his operas, based on exciting and romantic legends.

▼*Richard Wagner, German composer.*

On a stormy sea voyage in 1837, Wagner had an idea for an opera about a ghostly sea captain. This opera, *The Flying Dutchman,* was produced in 1843 in Dresden, Germany. His next operas, *Tannhauser* and *Lohengrin,* were very unpopular at first. Wagner's powerful music had few of the sweet tunes that people were used to hearing in operas.

In 1848 Wagner took part in a political revolution in Germany. Many of the rebels were arrested, but Wagner escaped to Switzerland. In a little cottage near Zurich, he began to write his greatest work, *The Ring of the Nibelung*. This work consists of four music dramas based on old German legends. They tell the story of a magical ring and the adventures of the hero Siegfried and the beautiful Brunnhilde. Wagner represented each person or idea in the operas with a different musical theme. Wagner was allowed to return to Germany in 1861. At Bayreuth, he designed a Festival Theater especially for his operas. *The Ring of the Nibelung* was first performed there in 1876. A festival of Wagner's music is still held at Bayreuth every summer.

ALSO READ: MUSIC, OPERA.

WALES The principality of Wales is part of the United Kingdom of Great Britain and Northern Ireland. Wales occupies a broad peninsula to the west of England on the island of Great Britain. The island of Anglesey off the northwest coast is also part of Wales. The coast of Wales is bordered on the north by the Irish Sea, on the west by Saint George's Channel and Cardigan Bay, and on the south by the Bristol Channel. (See the map with the article on the BRITISH ISLES.) Wales has been joined with England for more than 400 years.

Wales is a land of rugged sea cliffs, heather-covered mountains, and deep, green valleys. The Cambrian Mountains run north to south through most of Wales. In the northwest, the great Snowdon peak rises to 3,560 feet–the highest point in England and Wales. Many of the most beautiful Welsh valleys are in the southeast, such as those of the River Usk and the River Wye. Wales has a mild climate.

Nearly three million people live in Wales, mostly in the cities such as Swansea and Cardiff, the capital. English is the official language, but many people also speak Welsh.

The Welsh are a very musical people. Nearly every village or town has its own choir. Every year, poets, painters, musicians, and other artists from all over Wales enter competitions at a national festival called the Eisteddfod.

Coal mining is the chief occupation. Most of the mines are in the valleys of south Wales. Steel is manufactured in the cities of the south. Tourism is also an important industry. People travel from all over Britain to enjoy the Welsh mountains and beaches.

▲ *Two Welsh girls, dressed in their best, look forward to a happy time at a music festival in Wales.*

◀ *A magnificent castle built by the Normans in 1090 stands near Cardiff, Wales.*

Among the earliest settlers in Wales were a small, dark-haired people, who may have come from southwest Europe. Around 600 B.C., Wales was overrun by tall, fair-haired Celts, from central Europe. These two types of people can still be seen in Wales. Today, the language and traditions of the Welsh are still mainly Celtic. Until the 1200s, Wales was ruled by a series of princes and chieftains. Some traditions tell that the legendary British hero, King Arthur, lived in Wales. In 1282, an English king, Edward I, defeated the great Welsh prince, Llewellyn ap Gruffydd. Edward made his eldest son prince of Wales.
ALSO READ: ARTHUR, KING; BRITISH ISLES; EDWARD, KINGS OF ENGLAND; ENGLISH HISTORY; UNITED KINGDOM.

WALLACE, ALFRED RUSSEL (1823–1913) Alfred Russel Wallace was an English naturalist who worked out an idea of how plants and animals evolve slowly over millions of years into new varieties. Wallace and another English naturalist, Charles Darwin, both developed this idea of *natural selection* at the same time.

▲*Alfred R. Wallace, British naturalist and explorer.*

Wallace was born in Monmouthshire, England. He became interested in botany and started collections of plants. When he was 25 years old, he and another naturalist went on an expedition to the Amazon River in South America to collect plants and animals. He wrote a book about his travels and discoveries.

From 1854 to 1862, Wallace studied plants and animals in the islands of Malaysia. He noticed basic differences between the animals of Asia and those of Australia. He began thinking about a theory of natural selection. He wrote a paper expressing his thoughts and sent it to his friend Darwin. Darwin's own ideas of evolution, which were like those of Wallace, were ready to be published. Parts of the manuscripts (papers) of both men were published in July, 1858.

Although most people know Darwin as the discoverer of the idea of natural selection in evolution, scientists call both Darwin and Wallace co-discoverers of the theory.
ALSO READ: DARWIN, CHARLES; EVOLUTION.

WALL STREET see STOCKS AND BONDS.

WALRUS The walrus belongs to the same family of animals as the seal. The walrus and seal look much alike, but the walrus is larger than all but the largest seals. The walrus is also fatter. Both the seal and the walrus have a layer of fatty blubber under the skin, but the walrus's layer is thicker. The blubber holds in warmth. The walrus doesn't have fur, so it needs more blubber. The blubber also provides energy when food is scarce.

Walruses live together in herds on the islands, coasts, and ice floes of the Arctic Ocean. They migrate south in the winter and return to the Arctic in the summer.

◀*A herd of walruses swimming closely together. You can easily see their long tusks.*

A walrus can be most easily recognized by its tusks. The tusks are a pair of upper canine teeth that never stop growing. Some walruses have tusks three feet long. The walrus uses its tusks to dig mussels and clams from the floor of the ocean. It cracks the shells of the mussels and clams with its blunt back teeth. The walrus also uses its tusks to move itself about on land. The scientific name of the walrus (*Odobenus*) means "those who walk with their teeth."

The male walrus is called a *bull.* A full-grown bull can be 12 feet long and weigh over 2,000 pounds. The female, or *cow,* is about two-thirds the size of a bull. A baby walrus is a *pup* or *calf.* Only one pup is usually born at a time, and it stays with its mother for about two years. Walruses become mature at 5 or 6 years, and may live to be 40 years old.

The Eskimos hunt the walrus with harpoons and with bows and arrows made of bone. They eat the meat and blubber, burn the blubber in lamps, and make clothes from the walrus's skin. They use the bones to make weapons, and they make artistic carvings of the tusks. In recent years the hunting of the walrus with guns has put the animal in some danger of extinction.

ALSO READ: ANIMAL, ARCTIC, MAMMAL, SEALS AND SEA LIONS.

WAR A saying holds that "war is older than man." Certainly there are few nations in the world that have not been at war at one time or another. A war is an armed conflict between nations or groups within a nation.

People go to war usually in an effort to increase their power—over their own lives or country or perhaps over the lives or countries of other people. Revolutions and civil wars are started by discontented groups who try to overthrow the existing government and establish a new one. In such wars, the aggressors are trying to increase their power by gaining more freedom and control over their own lives. The American and French revolutions are examples of this type of war.

Governments frequently try to arouse the patriotism of their citizens in order to justify going to war. If people fear another nation or believe that that nation's form of government (democratic, socialist, communist) is evil, these people will be willing to go to war when their government tells them to go.

▲*Wars were once fought by armies that faced each other in battle. Mounted knights and foot soldiers are shown here* (left) *in close combat during a battle fought in the 1400s. Modern wars are fought at a distance. A fighter taking off from an aircraft carrier* (right) *may fly hundreds of miles to attack the enemy.*

Nations have also tried to keep the peace by making *non-aggression treaties*—agreements not to start wars. Such agreements have almost always been ineffective. In this century, two international peace organizations have been established to try to end war and promote better understanding among nations. The League of Nations was established in 1920 but failed. The United Nations was founded in 1945, and it has had only limited success as a peacemaking organization.

ALSO READ: GUERRILLA WARFARE, INTERNATIONAL RELATIONS, LEAGUE OF NATIONS, REVOLUTION, TREATY, WEAPONS.

WAR OF 1812 Since 1793, England and Napoleonic France had been in a state of war. During their conflicts, the policy of the United States had been to remain neutral (not to take sides), but both the British and the French ignored the rights of neutrals. U.S. merchant ships were stopped on the high seas and American crews impressed (forced) into military service on British naval vessels. Any U.S. ship trading with France was seized by the British, and any U.S. ship trading with England was seized by the French.

Relations between the U.S. and Britain worsened. Two U.S. Senators—Henry Clay (of Kentucky) and John C. Calhoun (of South Carolina)—charged that British army officers in Canada were equipping and encouraging Indian raids across the U.S. frontier. Clay and Calhoun wanted the U.S. to declare war on Britain in order to defeat the Indians and their British supporters. The Senators claimed that a British defeat would keep England from seizing American trading ships. The U.S. might also be able to acquire British territory in Canada.

Congress declared war on Britain on June 18, 1812. At that time the U.S. Navy had only several small warships, but it had a skilled staff of officers who had fought in wars against the Barbary pirates between 1801 and 1805. In 1812, the U.S. Army had only 10,000 regular soldiers, half of whom were recruits.

Three military invasions were begun against the British in Canada, their goal being to take the city of Montreal. All were defeated by the British.

Beginning in August of 1812, several sea battles resulted in victories for the United States. The frigate U.S.S. *Constitution* captured the British frigates *Guerriere* and *Java,* and the U.S.S. *United States* captured the British ship *Macedonia.* Both U.S. ships were armed with 44 guns, which were faster and more accurate weapons than the 38 guns on the British ships.

By the spring of 1813, an American fleet commanded by Oliver Hazard Perry had been organized on Lake Erie. William Henry Harrison had moved his Kentucky militia into Ohio. There he successfully defended Fort Meigs and Fort Stephenson against British and Indian attacks. Perry's ships completely crushed the British in a battle on Lake Erie, capturing the entire fleet. Harrison's troops were then able to invade Canada, where they again defeated British and Indian forces. The famous Indian chief Tecumseh died while fighting with the British against Harrison's forces.

In the spring of 1814, Britain defeated France and began to send reinforcements to fight the United States. The British fleet set up a blockade of U.S. ports. A British landing force came ashore, moved inland, and burned the city of Washington, D.C., including the Capitol and the White House. President Madison and other high officials had to flee to the countryside. British land and sea forces then tried to take the city of Baltimore, Maryland.

On January 8, 1815, about 8,000 British troops landed in New Orleans, Louisiana, and attacked the 5,000 troops under the command of General Andrew Jackson. In only 25 minutes of fighting, the British lost 2,036 men, while Jackson's forces lost only 71. The British immediately retreated and left the country. The Battle of New Orleans actually took place after a peace treaty had been signed between Britain and the U.S. Negotiators had met at Ghent (in Belgium) and concluded the Treaty of Ghent on December 24, 1814. The treaty gave no new territory to either side and left many other issues unsettled. However, the war forced the United States to defend herself for the first time as a unified nation.

ALSO READ: AMERICAN HISTORY; CALHOUN, JOHN C.; CLAY, HENRY; GREAT LAKES; HARRISON, WILLIAM HENRY; JACKSON, ANDREW; JEFFERSON, THOMAS; MADISON, JAMES; NAVY; PERRY FAMILY; STAR-SPANGLED BANNER; TECUMSEH; TREATY.

▼*General Andrew Jackson* (with sword raised, center) *leads the American forces to victory over the British in the Battle of New Orleans on January 8, 1815.*

WARSAW PACT The Warsaw Pact is a treaty among the Communist nations of eastern Europe to band together for mutual defense. The Soviet Union, Bulgaria, Czechoslovakia, East Germany, Hungary, Poland, and Rumania agreed to sign the 20-year alliance on May 14, 1955. The pact calls for an army made up of soldiers from each nation. The supreme commander of the army is from the Soviet Union.

After World War II, a number of European nations and the United States and Canada formed a military alliance called NATO, or the North Atlantic Treaty Organization. The purpose of NATO was to protect Western Europe from attack by an enemy nation. When West Germany joined NATO in 1955, Eastern European nations reacted by forming the Warsaw Pact to provide for their own defense.

On August 20, 1968, about 200,000 Warsaw Pact troops invaded Czechoslovakia. They claimed that the socialist government of that country was being undermined by liberal forces within the country. After the invasion, many Czech government reforms were reversed.

ALSO READ: NORTH ATLANTIC TREATY ORGANIZATION, WORLD WAR II.

▲*Margaret of Anjou, the wife of Henry VI, was a leader of the house of Lancaster in the Wars of the Roses.*

WARS OF THE ROSES The Wars of the Roses were a series of civil wars fought in England during the 1400s between two great families—the house of Lancaster and the house of York. Both claimed to be rightful rulers of England. The name of the wars comes from the badges used by the two houses—the red rose of Lancaster and the white rose of York.

Henry VI was only a child when he became king of England in 1422. A powerful nobleman, Richard, duke of York, ruled England for the young king. Henry and Richard were both descended from the same king, Edward III. The duke of York was descended from the third son of Edward III, so he claimed that he had more right to be king than Henry, who was only descended from Edward's fourth son, the duke of Lancaster. York formed a league of several great noblemen in England. Henry was by this time insane, but his young queen, Margaret of Anjou, valiantly defended the house of Lancaster. In 1455, civil war broke out, and Henry was captured by the Yorkists at a battle near Saint Albans. In 1460, Henry agreed to make Richard of York his successor. But Margaret supported the rights of Henry's son, Prince Edward, and defeated the Yorkists at the Battle of Wakefield. Richard of York was killed during the battle. But in 1461, his son was proclaimed king as Edward IV.

▼*Henry VII, the king whose victory in the Battle of Bosworth Field ended the Wars of the Roses.*

Edward IV was succeeded by his son Edward V, in 1483. The new king was only a child, and his uncle, Richard, duke of Gloucester, was chosen to rule the kingdom. Richard immediately imprisoned the young king, and proclaimed himself King Richard III. Richard made many enemies by this act. When Henry Tudor (the young leader of the house of Lancaster) marched into England with an army, many people supported him. Henry of Lancaster was descended from John of Gaunt, and was a half-brother of King Henry VI. The Yorkists were defeated at the battle of Bosworth Field in 1485. Richard III was killed during the battle, and Henry was crowned as King Henry VII. He later married Elizabeth, heiress of the house of York, and the rival families of York and Lancaster were united.

ALSO READ: EDWARD, KINGS OF ENGLAND; ENGLISH HISTORY; HENRY, KINGS OF ENGLAND; RICHARD, KINGS OF ENGLAND.

WASHINGTON The state of Washington was named in honor of the first President of the United States and is the only state named for a President. It is also called the "Evergreen State" because of its many forests of evergreen trees.

The inhabitants of Washington live close to natural beauty. Green islands lie in Washington's blue Puget Sound. Forests and meadows of wildflowers are found in the state's national parks. There are many lakes and rivers. And the great Columbia Plateau stretches for miles under a cloudless sky.

WASHINGTON

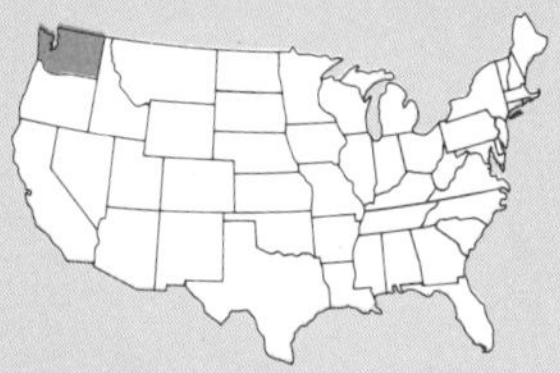

State flower
Western rhododendron

State bird
Willow goldfinch

State tree
Western hemlock

Capital
Olympia
(23,111 people)

Area
68,192 square miles
(ranks 20th)

Population
3,409,169 people
(ranks 22nd)

Statehood
November 11, 1889
(42nd state admitted)

Principal river
Columbia River

Highest point
Mount Rainier, in the Cascade Range
(14,410 feet)

Largest city
Seattle
(530,831 people)

The Land and Climate

Washington faces the Pacific Ocean. It lies in the northwest corner of the old block of 48 states. Canada is north of it. Idaho is to the east. The Columbia River forms most of Washington's southern border with Oregon. On the western shore of Washington, the Coast Ranges rise on the Olympic Peninsula. The Olympic Mountains are the highest part. Their name comes from that of the tallest mountain in the range, Mount Olympus (7,954 feet). Glaciers, lakes, and waterfalls are found in these mountains.

East of the Coast Ranges is the Puget Sound lowland. The sound is an arm of the Pacific Ocean. Large ocean-going ships sail past its islands to Seattle and Tacoma.

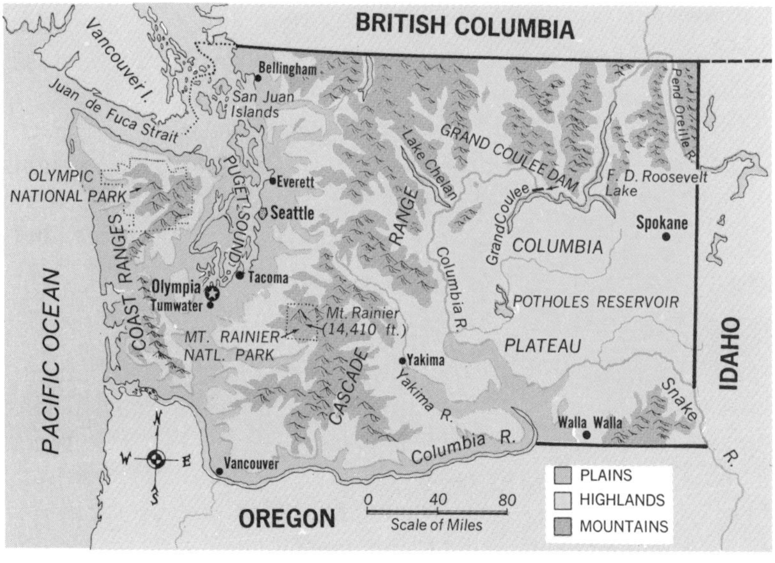

▲*Hikers on the trail stop to rest in a cool green forest on the Olympic Peninsula of Washington.*

The Cascade Range separates the green and often rainy western part of the state from the drier eastern part. Many cascades, or waterfalls, are formed by water pouring over rocks in the mountain streams. Mount Rainier, 14,410 feet high, is the highest peak in the Cascades. A beautiful national park stretches around Mount Rainier.

Eastern Washington is mainly made up of the Columbia Plateau. Nature made the plateau brown and dry. But irrigation with river water and modern farming methods have made it a rich farming region. It is called the "Inland Empire," with Spokane as its major city. Wheat is grown by *dry farming.* Such farming uses the rain of two years to grow *one* crop. Eastern Washington produces a huge amount of wheat by dry farming.

Rain makes all the difference in Washington. Precipitation is heavy in the western part of the state and light in the eastern part. The Columbia Plateau receives little rain. West winds bring moisture from the Pacific Ocean. When they reach the Coastal Ranges, the winds turn upward to cross the mountains. The air becomes chilled and then cannot hold so much moisture. Some falls in the form of rain.

The winds continue eastward. When they reach the high Cascade Range, the air is chilled even more. Much rain falls. Eastern Washington has rather warm summers and cold winters. West of the Cascades, summers are cool and winters mild.

History

Indian tribes with greatly differing ways of life once lived in what is now the state of Washington. West of the Cascade Range there were two groups of tribes. One was on the Pacific Coast. The other lived farther inland, beside rivers and bays. On the coast were the Quinault, the Quilleute, and the Makah.

East of the Cascades, on the dry Columbia Plateau, food was scarce. The Sahaptian Indians gathered berries and dug the bulbs of wild plants. But they had animal foods, too. They fished for salmon in the Columbia and Snake rivers. In the forests of nearby mountains, they hunted deer and elk. Nez Perce and Cayuse Indians lived in the southeast.

▼*Digging for clams is a popular pastime when the tide is out on the coast of Washington.*

Spaniards reached the coast of Washington in the 1770s. Englishmen were only a few years behind them. In 1792, a British naval officer, George Vancouver, explored Puget Sound. That same year, Robert Gray of Boston discovered the great river of the Northwest. He named it "Columbia," after his ship.

The first Americans to come by land reached Washington in 1805. They were led by Meriwether Lewis and William Clark. The explorers floated down the Snake River to the Columbia. Fur trading was the earliest business of the Northwest. At first, the traders came by ship. Later they came by land. They followed the route of Lewis and Clark. The first permanent settlement was Tumwater. This point was the end of the long Oregon Trail. Olympia, the capital of Washington, grew up just north of Tumwater.

As the white population increased, the Indians of the region saw their danger. Some tribes fought small, hopeless wars. The white men had the advantages of numbers and better weapons. A large council of many tribes, the Walla Walla Council, met in 1855 and ceded land to the U.S. through several treaties. Tribes were moved to reservations. One tribe, the Palouse, refused ever to live a reservation life. By 1889, when Washington became a state, Indian wars were things of the past. In the 1950s, the Nez Perce Indians asked and finally received more payment from the Federal Government for lands ceded in the 1800s.

▲*The Space Needle dominates the skyline of Seattle, the largest city in Washington. The tower, built for the 1962 World's Fair, has an observation deck at the top.*

Washingtonians at Work

The Puget Sound lowland is Washington's most thickly settled area. Most of the state's manufacturing is done here. Manufacturing airplanes is the largest industry. Foods, wood products, and paper are important manufactures, too.

Agriculture is the second-biggest business. Crops earn more money than livestock. Wheat is the leading crop. In western Washington, dairying is the main livestock industry. Beef cattle are raised in the east. The fertile valley of the Yakima River has been called the "Fruit Bowl of the Nation" because of the apples and other fruits grown there.

Tourism is another lively business. The lakes and mountains of the national parks and forests attract people for boating, fishing, and skiing. The great forests of Washington have made it one of the top lumbering states. Sawmills—mostly on the shores of Puget Sound—turn logs into lumber. The state has a big fishing industry, with salmon the most important catch.

ALSO READ: COLUMBIA RIVER; FUR TRADER; IRRIGATION; LEWIS AND CLARK EXPEDITION; OREGON TRAIL; WESTWARD MOVEMENT.

WASHINGTON, BOOKER T. (1856-1915) Booker Taliaferro Washington was born a slave. He grew up to play an important part in helping Negroes improve their economic and social lot. He was an educator, a statesman, and one of the best-known American leaders of the late 1800s and early 1900s.

▼*Booker T. Washington, American Negro educator.*

Booker T. Washington was born on a plantation near Hale's Ford, Virginia. From the age of nine, he worked in the coal mines all day and taught himself to read and write at night. At the age of 20, he graduated from Virginia's Hampton Normal and Agricultural School where he later became an instructor.

In 1881, Washington was asked to establish a new school for black students in Tuskegee, Alabama. He founded and became the first president of Tuskegee Institute. Under his direction,

Tuskegee Institute became famous as a vocational, industrial, and agricultural training school. In 1900, Washington founded the National Negro Business League to help Negroes succeed in business. He also wrote a number of books, including *Up from Slavery* and *The Future of the American Negro.*

Washington believed that Negroes would advance best through having greater opportunities in education and in the business world. He placed less emphasis on social and political equality. Although many other black people have disagreed with him, Washington is still remembered for his achievements at the Tuskegee Institute and his efforts to provide better opportunities for black people to live with dignity in a largely white society. His birthplace is now a national memorial.

ALSO READ: NEGRO HISTORY.

WASHINGTON, D.C. see DISTRICT OF COLUMBIA.

WASHINGTON, GEORGE (1732–1799) Few leaders have ever served their country more unselfishly or in more different ways than did George Washington. After the Revolutionary War, he was so popular that he might easily have made himself king or dictator. But he wanted no reward, he said, except the "affection of a free people."

Washington was born on a farm in Virginia. His father died when he was eleven years old and Lawrence, his older half brother, became like a second father to him. Lawrence was the owner of a plantation named Mount Vernon, and George was a frequent visitor there. George received little formal schooling, but he studied surveying and practiced measuring the fields around Mount Vernon. He drew such accurate maps that Lord Fairfax, the owner of a nearby plantation, was impressed.

Fairfax, who had recently come from England, had inherited thousands of acres of land west of the Blue Ridge Mountains. He decided to send out some surveyors to map the land. George Washington was asked to be a member of the surveying team. He was only 16 years old. After his return, he was appointed a public surveyor.

When he was 21 years old, Washington was asked by Robert Dinwiddie, governor of Virginia, to deliver a message to the French commander of a fort in the Ohio Valley. The message warned the French to leave land claimed by the English. The refusal of the French helped to bring on the French and Indian War that lasted from 1754 to 1763. In that conflict, Washington served first as a lieutenant colonel and then as a colonel in command of troops from Virginia.

In the meantime Lawrence had died and Colonel Washington became the master of Mount Vernon. He married a beautiful and wealthy widow, Martha Custis, and took her and her two young children to Mount Vernon to live. Washington be-

FIRST PRESIDENT APRIL 30, 1789—MARCH 4, 1797

GEORGE WASHINGTON

Born: February 22, 1732, Pope's Creek (later called Wakefield), Westmoreland County, Virginia
Parents: Augustine and Mary Ball Washington
Education: Attended local country schools at intervals, then studied surveying
Religion: Episcopalian
Occupation: Surveyor, farmer, army officer
Political Party: Did not join a political party
Married: 1759 to Mrs. Martha Dandridge Custis (1731-1802)
Children: One stepson and one stepdaughter
Died: December 14, 1799, Mount Vernon, Virginia
Buried: Mount Vernon, Virginia

came a successful farmer, but this happy, peaceful life was not to last. When the American Revolution broke out in 1775, Washington was asked by the Continental Congress to command the colonial army. Few generals ever faced greater difficulties. Washington served without pay. It was often hard to get food for his troops, and the soldiers were without adequate clothing. At Valley Forge, Washington's army spent a terrible winter suffering from hunger and freezing cold. But General Washington managed to keep an army together until the colonies won their freedom. In 1783, a treaty was signed with Great Britain recognizing the independence of the United States. Washington then returned to Mount Vernon, expecting to spend the rest of his life there. But his country still needed him.

As chairman of the Constitutional Convention that met in Philadelphia in 1787, he helped to draft the Constitution of the United States. The Constitution stated that the head of the government should be a President. Washington was the man everyone trusted to get the new government started. On the first election day, every vote was cast for General Washington.

On April 30, 1789, Washington walked out on the balcony of Federal Hall in New York, the city that had been chosen as a temporary capital. Beside him stood Robert R. Livingston, Chancellor of New York State, holding an open Bible. George Washington repeated the oath of office in which every President since has promised to "preserve, protect, and defend the Constitution of the United States."

In 1790, the capital was moved to Philadelphia, Pennsylvania, where the business of government was carried on during the next ten years. In the meantime President Washington was helping to plan a new capital city (which one day would be named "Washington" in his honor). Washington himself laid the cornerstone for the present Capitol building in the new city.

▼*George Washington* (at right of the two standing) *and the Marquis de Lafayette inspect the encampment at Valley Forge during the American Revolution.*

▶A View of Mount Vernon *(George Washington's home in northern Virginia), a painting by an unknown artist. National Gallery of Art, Washington D.C., Gift of Edgar William and Bernice Chrysler Garbisch.*

After serving as President for a term of four years, he was elected to a second term and continued to try to give the nation a strong central government. Some political leaders did not want a strong central government, and the American people were divided in their opinions about some of the important problems of the time. When France and England went to war, President Washington issued a Proclamation of Neutrality in 1793. The Proclamation stated that the United States would not take sides. Washington believed that it would be neither wise nor safe for a new nation that was still weak to become involved in another war. The President was criticized by those who favored France. Most citizens hoped that Washington would run for a third term, but he refused. He had been serving his country for 45 years, and he was anxious to retire to Mount Vernon.

Two years after retirement, George Washington died and was buried at Mount Vernon. In the funeral oration delivered before Congress, General Henry ("Lighthorse Harry") Lee paid tribute to his former commander in these words: "He was first in war, first in peace, and first in the hearts of his countrymen."

ALSO READ: AMERICAN REVOLUTION; CONSTITUTION, UNITED STATES; CONTINENTAL CONGRESS; DISTRICT OF COLUMBIA; FRENCH AND INDIAN WAR; PRESIDENCY.

WASPS AND HORNETS Wasps are usually thought of as large insects that sting. Some wasps live in communities, and are called *social wasps,* or *hornets.* All wasps have slim bodies with a narrow connection between the front and back parts. Two transparent wings (called *membranous* wings) with veins in them are attached to each side of the front part of the body. Two smaller wings are fastened to the back edge of the front pair. The stinger is at the rear tip of the wasp. Only queen and other female wasps have stingers. The males have none.

Bees, not wasps, are usually the honey-makers. But in the South American tropics, there are wasps that store honey made from nectar. The honey is stored in their paper (wood pulp) nests, which hang from trees.

A community of hornets may include hundreds, or even thousands, of hornets. The colony is made up of a queen, a few males, or drones, and a large number of female workers. The hornets' communities are in nests made of paper. The hornets make paper by chewing bits of woody plant material until the fibers that make up the wood are broken apart and thoroughly mixed with the hornets' saliva. Some nests are built hanging from tree limbs, some are attached under eaves of roofs, and some are in the ground. One kind of wasp, the *yellow jacket,* often burrows into the ground to make a nest.

Unlike hive bees, hornets die when cold weather arrives. Only the queen survives, if she finds a well-sheltered place. When warm weather returns, the queen builds a number of small containers or cells. She lays an egg in each cell, puts food in, and seals the cell. In about 14 days, female worker hornets come out of the cells. The workers build more cells and hunt for food. The queen's main task is to lay eggs.

Solitary wasps do not live in communities, but a few may make small nests close together. Some solitary wasps are larger than hornets, while others are only one-fourth of an inch long. One kind of solitary wasp is the *mud dauber,* which builds small nests by sticking mud to beams in barns or under eaves. *Digger wasps* hollow out holes in the ground for nests. The *potter wasps,* or *mason wasps,* make nests of clay.

Among solitary wasps, the female feeds her young by stinging an insect and sealing it into a chamber with one or more eggs. The insect is paralyzed and lives until the egg hatches into larvae. The larvae then eat the insect. Almost each kind of solitary wasp hunts a different kind of insect.

ALSO READ: BEE, INSECT, SPIDER.

WATCH see CLOCKS AND WATCHES.

▲*Hornets may give painful stings to anyone who disturbs them.*

▼*Social wasps build their nests from chewed wood and saliva. The nests are shaped into a series of cells.*

WATER Water is one of the most important and peculiar substances on Earth. Its importance is obvious—without it, nothing could live. Three-fourths of the Earth's surface is covered with water. The human body is 70 per cent water. All living organisms are at least half water. Its peculiarity is less obvious, but is one reason for its importance.

Water is peculiar in two important ways. One is that it can absorb (soak up) and hold a tremendous amount of heat. More heat is needed to raise the temperature of water one degree than is needed to raise the temperature of any other substance. But once water has absorbed heat, it loses it very slowly. The water in seas, lakes, and rivers changes temperature more slowly than does the land around it, and this affects climate. The Gulf Stream carries warm water from the Gulf of Mexico through the North Atlantic and keeps Europe warm in the winter.

Water is also peculiar because it expands (swells up) when it freezes. Most substances shrink when they freeze. Because water expands when it freezes, ice is less dense (lighter) than liquid water. Because ice is less dense, it rises to the surface, or floats, while the denser warm water stays near the bottom of the seas, lakes, and rivers. If the ice didn't float, the warm water

▲*This fountain* (left) *in the gardens of the Royal Palace in Caserta, Italy, shows how man has used water with sculpture to create beauty. The constant pounding of the ocean's waves can cause coastlines to erode. This rocky arch* (right) *was carved by the action of water over thousands of years.*

would flow to the top, give off its heat, and freeze. The oceans could freeze completely, and the plants and animals in them would die. An example of this idea is that fish do not freeze in very cold weather. This peculiar expansion of freezing water has made life in the ocean possible, and thus it has made all life possible.

Pure water is a clear, colorless, odorless, tasteless liquid at ordinary pressures and temperatures. It freezes at 32 degrees Fahrenheit, and it boils at 212 degrees Fahrenheit.

Pure water contains only the elements hydrogen and oxygen. Each water molecule has two hydrogen atoms joined to one oxygen atom, so the chemical formula for water is H_2O. But water is rarely pure. Water is called the "universal solvent" because it will dissolve so many different substances. Drinking water, for example, often has a definite odor, taste, or color because of the substances dissolved in it. The beverages we drink are mostly water. Other substances dissolved in the water add color and flavor.

"Hard water" is water which has dissolved large amounts of certain minerals. "Soft water" contains few minerals. It is difficult to wash with hard water because it doesn't readily form soapsuds. Water softeners can be used to remove the minerals and make hard water softer.

Heavy water is heavy not because of any substances it has dissolved but because it contains atoms of an unusually heavy form of hydrogen, called *deuterium*. Heavy water is used in scientific research and the production of nuclear energy.

The early centers of civilization were built near water. Recently, land has become more scarce and people have had to move farther from natural sources of water. To do so, they have had to take water with them. Rivers have been dredged and widened so that ships can move far inland. Irrigation (transporting water from wet to dry areas) has greatly increased the amount of usable farm land. Today, men not only use water

▼*Water is necessary to life. Sable antelopes get their fill at a water hole in Africa.*

▲*Water dripping over rocks has frozen into a beautiful cascade of ice* (left). *Water is essential to the growth of crops to provide food. A rice paddy* (right) *is an example of how man uses one method of irrigation for a particular crop.*

for farming, they actually farm the water. Water plants, especially algae, may soon be an important source of food.

For further information on:

Bodies of Water, *see* LAKE, OCEAN, RIVER, WELLS AND SPRINGS.

Properties, Forms, and Effects of Water, *see* BUOYANCY, CHEMISTRY, CLIMATE, CLOUD, CONSERVATION, DISTILLATION, EARTH HISTORY, ECOLOGY, FLOOD, FROST, GEYSER, GLACIER, GULF STREAM, HURRICANE, HYDROGEN, ICE AGE, ICEBERG, LIQUID, OXYGEN, QUICKSAND, RAIN AND SNOW, RAINBOW, SEACOAST, SURFACE TENSION, TIDE, WATER CYCLE, WATER POLLUTION, WAVE, WEATHER.

Uses of Water, *see* BOATS AND BOATING, DIVING, ELECTRIC POWER, FIRE FIGHTING, FISHING INDUSTRY, HARBORS AND PORTS, IRRIGATION, NAVIGATION, NAVY, OCEAN LINER, PLUMBING, SAILING, SHIPS AND SHIPPING, SKIN DIVING, SUBMARINE, SURFING, SWIMMING, WATER SKIING, WATER SUPPLY.

WATER BIRDS More than 600 different species of birds live in streams, ponds, and marshes, and along the banks of rivers and the shores of oceans. These water birds spend much of their time swimming or wading. They eat plants and animals that grow in and near the water. They often build nests on or near the water.

SWIMMING WATER BIRDS. Ducks, geese, and swans are the best-known swimming birds. They have webbed feet and wide, flat "duck bills." Oil from special glands waterproofs their feathers. A typical duck is about two feet long and has a short neck. A goose is larger and has a longer neck. A swan is even larger and has an even longer neck.

A loon looks like a large duck with a sharp bill. Loons have solid, heavy bones, which prevent them from floating well. A loon often swims with only its head and neck above water. It dives below the surface to catch fish. Grebes are similar to loons, but are smaller and have longer necks. Grebes are excellent divers but poor fliers. Both loons and grebes are awkward on land and rarely go ashore. Grebes even build floating nests.

Cormorants are large, dark diving birds with webbed feet and hooked bills. Cormorants swim low in the water like loons, but cormorants are more likely to be seen perched on rocks and buoys. The anhinga, or snakebird, is similar to the cormorant, but has a long, snake-like neck. The anhinga is not properly a

▲*A spoonbill watches over its nestful of chicks. This mother bird is not yet fully mature. At a later age, her feathers will be more distinctly pink.*

swimming bird, because it rarely swims. However, it lives near water and eats by diving and spearing fish with its sharp, pointed bill.

WADING WATER BIRDS. Herons, ibises, storks, and cranes are some of over 100 species of wading birds. These birds often have long legs and long necks. Their long legs are useful in wading in deep water and their long necks for scooping food from under water. They eat fish, frogs, shellfish, insects, and plants.

Herons, egrets, and bitterns are all members of the heron family. The largest heron is the *great white heron,* a pure white bird four feet tall with a yellow beak and yellow legs. The *great blue heron* is slightly smaller and is blue-gray in color. The *American egret* and the *snowy egret* are white herons with black legs. The white feathers of egrets were once used to decorate hats. So many egrets were killed for their feathers that they almost became extinct. It is now illegal to kill them. *Night herons* and *bitterns* are smaller and shorter-necked than other herons. The *least bittern* is only about a foot tall.

The only American stork is the *wood ibis,* a large, white wading bird with a dark, featherless head, black feathers under the wings, and a long, curved bill. The *white ibis* is much smaller, has a feathered head, and has black only at the wing tips. The *roseate spoonbill* is related to the ibis but is pink and has a curious, spoon-shaped bill.

Another remarkable pink wading bird is the *flamingo.* The flamingo has very long, slender, stilt-like legs, a long neck, and a hooked bill. Flamingos nest in large groups in the marshes of southern Florida.

Shore birds are small wading birds that feed along the shore, catching sand fleas, worms, and small crabs. The *plover* is a plump shore bird with a short bill. Sandpipers, curlews, and godwits have long, slender bills. The curlew's bill curves downward, the godwit's curves upward.

Today, water birds are disappearing because their marshes have been drained to get land for farming and building, and shorelands have been taken to provide sites for homes and factories. Birds are driven from their homes and crowded together in areas too small to support them. Those birds that do survive run the risk of being shot by hunters.

ALSO READ: BIRD, CRANE, DUCKS AND GEESE, SEABIRDS, STORK.

▼*Flamingos are beautiful water birds whose long legs and webbed feet make wading easy for them.*

WATER CYCLE Water is continuously moving among the oceans, the air, and the land. This movement is called the water cycle. The water cycle is made up of three natural processes: *evaporation, condensation,* and *precipitation.*

There is always some water in the air. The water is in a gaseous form called *water vapor.* Water vapor is made up of water molecules that have separated from the surface of water. This separation process is called *evaporation.*

Warm water evaporates faster than cold water. You can prove this by putting a quarter-inch of water into each of two pie tins. Place one pie tin on a sunny window sill or on a radiator. Set the second pie tin in a cool place indoors—but not in a refrigerator. Examine both pie tins after several hours. Which pie tin has less water—the warm one or the cool one?

Water evaporates from the surfaces of oceans, lakes, ponds, rivers, streams, and puddles. More water evaporates in warm weather and warm climates than in cold. Water also evaporates or *transpires* from the leaves of plants. Roots take up water from the soil. The water rises through the plant to the leaves. It evaporates through tiny holes in the undersides of the leaves.

Condensation is the opposite of evaporation. In condensation, a gas changes to a liquid. For example, water vapor changes to water. When the water vapor at the mouth of a teakettle spout comes into contact with cooler air, the water vapor condenses to form a visible cloud of water droplets. Blow your breath on a mirror. The water vapor in your warm breath condenses on the cool surface of the mirror, making the mirror cloudy.

Cool air cannot hold so much water vapor as warm air. Therefore, when warm air cools, some water vapor must leave the cooling air. The water vapor condenses. When condensation takes place high above the earth, clouds form.

The tiny droplets of water that make up a cloud bump into each other as air currents move through the cloud. The bumping droplets join and form larger droplets. Finally, after about a million tiny droplets have joined, a *raindrop* has formed. The raindrop is heavy enough to overcome the upward push of the air currents, and it falls out of the clouds. If the air is cold enough, snowflakes, sleet, or hailstones are formed. The forming and falling of raindrops, snowflakes, sleet, and hailstones is *precipitation.*

Rain falling on the earth runs into streams or soaks into the ground. The streams may flow into lakes and ponds, or join and form rivers. The rivers flow into the oceans or lakes. Water va-

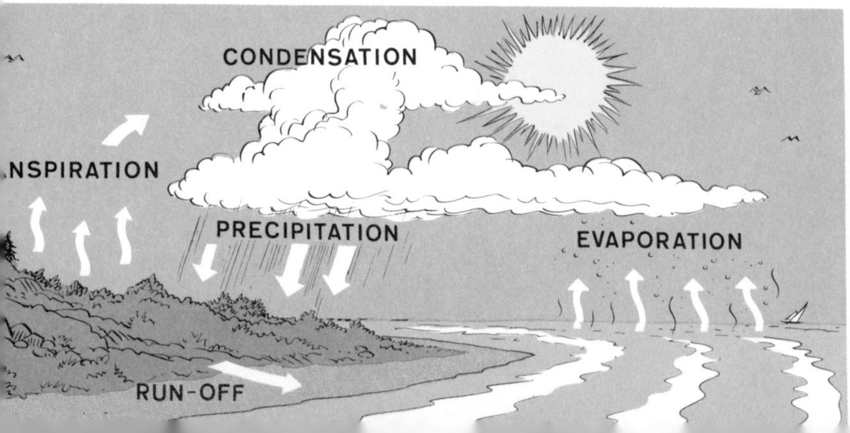

▲*Some waterfalls cascade in a series of drops.*

por evaporates from all these bodies of water. Some of the water that soaks into the ground is taken up by plants. The plants transpire to give off more water vapor. The water vapor condenses and forms clouds. Precipitation falls from the clouds. This circular, never-ending process is the water cycle.

ALSO READ: CLOUD, DISTILLATION, FOG, HUMIDITY, RAIN AND SNOW, WEATHER.

WATERFALL When a stream or a river plunges over a cliff, it forms a waterfall. A waterfall often occurs where a stream bed passes from hard rock into soft rock. The running water *erodes,* or wears away, the soft rock faster than the hard rock. As a result, the channel in the soft rock becomes lower than the channel in the hard rock. A cliff and a waterfall are formed.

As water continues to pour over the waterfall, it may cut under the cliff. After a while, the cliff breaks off and tumbles into the stream, and the waterfall moves upstream a short distance. This is happening at Niagara Falls where the Horseshoe Falls have been moving upstream four or five feet a year. The smaller American Falls have moved upstream two or three feet a year. After a long time—thousands of years—falls may wear down to become *cataracts* or *rapids,* a series of low falls.

Yosemite Falls in California (which is actually made up of 2 falls) is the highest waterfall in North America. The upper falls is 1,430 feet high, the lower falls 320 feet. The water plunges into the valley of the Yosemite River. Yosemite is a *hanging valley* waterfall. During the last ice age, glaciers cut the valley of the river. A small glacier cut a shallower valley that joined the Yosemite Valley. When the glaciers melted, they left behind the small "hanging valley" opening into the deep valley of the Yosemite River. When water from the stream in the small valley

▶*Bridal Veil Falls, a lacy cascade near Provo, Utah, falls in one steep drop.*

plunged down into the deeper valley, a waterfall was formed.

The highest waterfall on Earth is Angel Falls in Venezuela. It is 3,212 feet high, with one long drop of 2,648 feet—over one-half mile! The waterfall with the most water passing over it is the Guaira Falls between Brazil and Paraguay. Its average flow is 470,000 cubic feet a second.

Many old towns are built near waterfalls, because the falling water was once used to turn water wheels. The water wheels provided the power to turn the grindstones of flour mills and run other machinery. Today, water power is used in hydroelectric plants to produce electricity.

ALSO READ: DAM, EROSION, GLACIER, ICE AGE, NIAGARA FALLS.

▲ *A sculptured lion on top of a hill commemorates the victory of the Allies over Napoleon at Waterloo.*

WATERLOO Waterloo is the name of a small town in Belgium. The French emperor Napoleon Bonaparte was defeated near there at the Battle of Waterloo, on June 18, 1815.

The battle was fought after Napoleon escaped from the island of Elba, where he had been imprisoned since 1814. On June 16, 1815, Napoleon attacked a Prussian (German) army under General Gebhard von Blücher near the Belgian town of Charleroi. Believing that he had crushed the Prussians, Napoleon then marched northward with about 125,000 men. At Waterloo, on June 17, he met British and Dutch armies, commanded by the British general, the duke of Wellington. These armies together numbered about 93,000 men. Heavy rains prevented Napoleon from moving his big guns, and he did not attack that day. The following morning the French cavalry charged again and again but they could not break the line.

Meanwhile the Prussians had recovered from the attack at Charleroi and were marching toward Waterloo. Wellington's troops were just beginning to weaken when Blücher arrived. The Prussians attacked fiercely from the right, and the French were routed. Napoleon escaped from the battlefield, but later surrendered to the British. During the battle, the French lost about 40,000 men. Allied losses numbered about 22,000.

ALSO READ: ENGLISH HISTORY; FRENCH HISTORY; NAPOLEON BONAPARTE; WELLINGTON, DUKE OF.

WATER PLANT see ALGAE, MARINE LIFE, POND LIFE.

▼ *Two scientific researchers check aquatic life in a stream into which warm water has been discharged by the factory in the background. The scientists are finding out the degree of water pollution caused by this discharge.*

WATER POLLUTION Small amounts of natural wastes are present in almost all water. These wastes include silt washed out of the soil, the waste products of plants and animals, and the remains of dead plants and animals. Water can cleanse itself of most natural wastes through the action of oxygen and bacteria. However, when humans add large amounts of man-made wastes, the water becomes overloaded and can no longer cleanse itself thoroughly. The wastes pile up and the water becomes polluted.

Millions of tons of acid from coal mines run into the rivers of the eastern United States. Paper mills, chemical plants, and other factories empty wastes into streams. Power plants use huge quantities of fresh water to cool and condense steam. This water becomes hot, and if hot water is dumped into streams or lakes, it kills fish and plants.

Many cities are growing so fast that they cannot give their sewage proper treatment. As a result, harmful sewage is poured into the rivers. Some laundry detergents contain *phosphates,* which cannot be eliminated by sewage treatment. Phosphates act as fertilizers. When phosphates get into rivers or lakes, they increase the growth of certain water plants, and this robs the water of oxygen for fish and other water life.

Lake Erie is a good example of what pollution can do to a body of water. This lake is dying because millions of tons of sediment, sewage, and chemical wastes are poured into the lake every year. Some parts of Lake Erie have so little oxygen that very little life can exist there.

With increasing population, there is a growing demand for clean water for drinking, cooking, bathing, irrigation, fishing, and other uses. An increased population can also cause increased pollution. To have enough clean water, the dumping of industrial wastes and untreated sewage will have to be stopped. Although some businesses and cities are making efforts to halt water pollution, too many of them are not. It takes money to clean up pollution. But water is essential to life and health.

ALSO READ: AIR POLLUTION, LAKE, MARINE LIFE, SOAPS AND DETERGENTS, WATER, WATER SUPPLY.

▼*Water skiing is a popular sport at DeSoto Bend on the Missouri River in Nebraska. All water skiers should wear life preservers in case of accident.*

WATER SKIING Water skiing is the art of skimming over the water on skis while being pulled by a rope attached to a motorboat. The first skis designed especially for water skiing were wooden planks.

Modern water skis are made of fiber glass, aluminum, or wood. They are usually about 5 to 7 inches wide and 5 to 6½ feet long. The skis are not connected to the boat. Instead, the water skier grips a wooden tow bar, which is attached to a rope going to the boat. The skier's feet are inserted into rubber binders mounted on the skis. Many water skiers use only a single ski, with two rubber binders for the feet.

One of the best-known water skiing areas is Cypress Gardens, Florida. Water skiers entertain tourists there daily with many spectacular tricks. Water skiing events can be divided into three main categories—trick riding, slalom, and jumping. Trick riding includes such things as turning around on skis and skiing sideways or backward. In the *slalom,* the water skier weaves in and out between a series of markers, riding on one or two skis. Ski racing is also becoming popular. A number of people have skied non-stop for 200 miles from Nassau in the Bahamas, to Miami, Florida. Jumping involves skiing upward over a waxed, wooden platform. Some skiers attach themselves to kites and use the ski jump to get them high enough into the air for flying. *Aquaplaning*, a sport similar to water skiing, is also performed at water shows. Aquaplaners ride on a broad platform which is attached to a boat by ropes. They stand on the platform and support themselves by hanging onto the ropes.

Most of the boats used in water skiing have motors of 40 horsepower or more. They should be capable of speeds of 20 miles an hour. In addition to the operator of the boat, there should be at least one other person aboard. This person faces to the rear and watches the skier, for safety purposes.

A water skier starts by bending his knees and holding his arms straight ahead with his hands gripping the tow bar. As the boat begins to pick up speed, the water skier rises to a standing position. Because even the best water skiers can become tired or have accidents, all skiers should wear life jackets.

ALSO READ: SPORTS, SWIMMING.

WATER SUPPLY There are about 364 billion billion gallons of water on the Earth. Less than three per cent is fresh water. The rest is the salt water of the oceans. Of the small amount of fresh water, much is frozen as ice, and some is too deep underground to be easily obtainable. Only about one-tenth of the fresh water is available for human use.

About 1,200 billion gallons of water are available in the U.S. each day. Over 300 billion gallons a day are used.

◀*The Grand Coulee Dam in Washington State supplies irrigation water to a large number of farms in the area by controlling the waters of the Columbia River. The reservoir created by the dam will eventually supply water to more than a million acres.*

▲*Electrically-powered aerators are used in special treatment plants to purify water for drinking.*

Ocean water can be converted to fresh water by *desalinization*—removing the salt. This is most often done by *distillation*—evaporating and condensing the liquid so that the salt and water are separated. Brackish (slightly salty) water can be desalinated by electrodialysis—using an electric current to separate the salt. Freezing methods may eventually provide the cheapest way of desalinating salt water. When salt water is frozen, the salt does not become part of the ice. If the ice and salt could be easily separated, fresh water could be obtained.

A farmhouse or a small town can be supplied by nearby sources of water, such as lakes, ponds, or wells. A large town or a city usually needs more water than is available from nearby sources, so water must be brought from far away. Often a river is dammed to form a lake or *reservoir.* An aqueduct is a pipeline, canal, or tunnel that carries water from a reservoir to a town or to farmland for irrigation.

Water Treatment

Although many rivers and lakes are sources of water supply, they also are used for dumping sewage and industrial wastes. This dumping pollutes the water and makes it unfit for human use. Polluted water can be made clean and pure through several processes.

In a typical treatment plant, the water is first *aerated*—sprayed into the air. The aeration improves the taste and helps in the removal of certain minerals through the purifying action of air and sunlight. Then the water is *coagulated*—chemicals are added that cause small particles to lump together. The water passes into a *sedimentation* tank where the particles are allowed to settle to the bottom. The water is then filtered and chemicals are added. Almost all water is *chlorinated* (chlorine is added in very small amounts) to kill bacteria.

In most parts of the United States, water is *fluoridated.* This means that the chemical fluorine is put into the water. Fluorine helps prevent tooth decay.

ALSO READ: WATER, WATER CYCLE, WELLS AND SPRINGS.

▼*James Watt, Scottish engineer and inventor.*

WATT, JAMES (1736–1819) James Watt was a Scottish inventor and engineer. The electric unit of power, the watt, was named in his honor.

Watt was born in Greenock, a fishing village in Scotland. His father was a merchant. When he was 18 years old, Watt went to London to learn how to be an instrument maker. When he returned to Scotland, he became the instrument maker for the University of Glasgow. In 1764, Watt was asked to repair a small model of the Newcomen steam engine, a machine used to pump water out of mines. While repairing the engine, Watt began to experiment with the steam engine. In 1769, he patented a steam engine that could work faster and do more varied work than the Newcomen steam engine.

In 1775, Watt went into business manufacturing steam engines, and he became very wealthy and successful. His steam engines were used in many factories in Europe and the United States.

Watt spent the rest of his life inventing and improving machines. He developed a new type of propeller for boats, an improved copying press, a machine for reproducing statues, and many other mechanical devices. He is credited with introducing the word *horsepower* as a unit of power, a way of measuring power.

ALSO READ: ENGINE, ENGINEERING, INVENTION.

◀*It's great fun to dip in the ocean when big waves are coming in. These two swimmers are using the "buddy system" for safety's sake.*

WAVE When a stone falls into a pond of water, it pushes molecules of water away from it. The molecules push against surrounding molecules and bounce back. The pushed molecules in turn push against more molecules. In this way a wave moves across the surface of the water. The wave carries no water with it. If a piece of paper is dropped in the water as the wave moves past, the piece of paper moves only up and down. The piece of paper does not move across the water at all.

A water wave is a *transverse* wave—the molecules move up and down and at right angles to the direction that the wave is

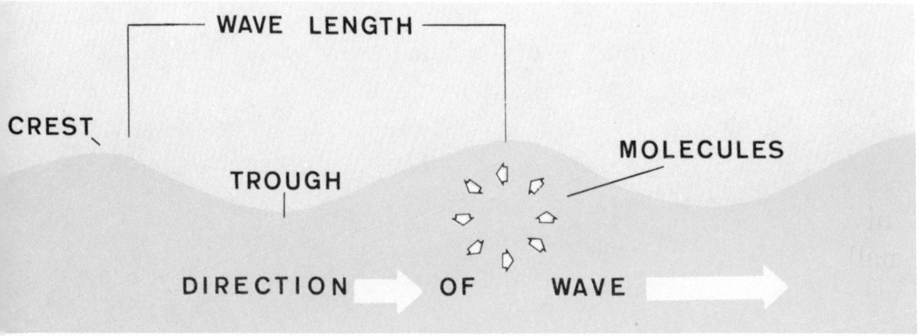

moving. Sound waves are *longitudinal* waves—the molecules move in the same direction as the wave, squeezing tightly together and then spreading apart. These are the two basic types of waves.

What makes waves? Energy. When a stone is thrown into the water, the stone has energy. That is, the stone has force and some power to do work. If a stone is thrown at a piece of fragile glass, for example, the glass breaks when the stone hits it. This is because of the energy the stone has as it moves through the air. When a stone hits water, the energy in the stone is transferred to the water in the form of waves.

A wind blowing across a body of water also has energy. Some of the energy in the wind is transferred to the water. The energy of the wind is changed into waves. These waves travel in the same direction as the wind. The stronger the wind blows, the larger the waves. A hurricane has a great deal of energy in its winds and can make giant waves 50 feet high. The *tsunamis,* or tidal waves formed by earthquakes, are often even larger.

When a person speaks, the sound waves carry the energy produced by the vibrations of his vocal cords. The tremendous energy of thunder produces very powerful sound waves. The sound of the explosion can have so much energy that it will damage ear drums. The energy in a loud sound wave can even smash windows far away from the source of the sound.

Light and radio waves are forms of electromagnetic energy produced by electric and magnetic fields. These electromagnetic waves, such as X-rays, do not have to move in matter as water and sound waves do. Because of this, they can travel for billions of miles through empty space.

ALSO READ: LIGHT, MATTER, OCEAN, RADIATION, RADIO, RADIO ASTRONOMY, SOUND, SPECTRUM, WATER.

▼*Honeybees produce beeswax which they use to build combs to hold honey and eggs.*

WAX Wax is a soft, solid substance that has a dull luster. It has a somewhat greasy texture and softens gradually when heated.

Wax is produced both naturally and artificially. It comes from animal, vegetable, and mineral sources. Beeswax is perhaps the best-known type of animal wax. It comes from the abdomen of the worker bee and is used to construct the honeycomb. Spermaceti is a type of animal wax taken from the sperm oil of the whale. Lanolin, used in polishes, is a wax taken from the fat that coats the wool of sheep.

Vegetable waxes cover the leaves, nuts, and berries of many plants. The berries of the wax myrtle tree provided America's early colonists with wax for candle-making.

Mineral waxes are produced in the petroleum refining process. They include paraffin and ozocerite. Most commercial waxes are made from paraffin.

◀*Mark Twain, the great American author, is shown here in wax with two of his most famous literary creations, Tom Sawyer* (left) *and Huckleberry Finn* (right). *The exhibit is in the National Historical Wax Museum in Washington, D.C.*

Waxes come in a variety of textures and strengths and are used for many different purposes. Candles, matches, polishes, carbon paper, crayons, and cosmetics all contain wax. Wax is also used in the production of food containers and electrical insulations, and as a leather dressing and a textile finish.

People have made faces, figures, and other objects out of wax since earliest times. They discovered that wax can easily be molded when it is soft, and can be tinted by adding coloring. The ancient Egyptians made wax images of their gods, and Greek children played with wax dolls. During the Middle Ages, European kings, queens, and saints were modeled in wax.

The most famous name in waxworks is that of Madame Tussaud. She operated a waxworks museum in Paris during the French Revolution. In 1802, she went to England, and opened a waxworks in London. It is still visited by thousands of people every year.

Today, there are many waxworks exhibits throughout the world. They often include a Chamber of Horrors, where visitors can see a life-like wax figure posed in the act of strangling a victim, or some other frightening scene. Models of historical figures, movie stars, sports figures, or astronauts may also be displayed. Most of the figures look startlingly real.

ALSO READ: BEE, CANDLE, COSMETICS, MATCH, PLANT, SOLID, WHALES AND WHALING.

WAYNE, ANTHONY (1745–1796) Anthony Wayne was a general in the Continental Army during the Revolutionary War. He gained the nickname "Mad Anthony" Wayne for his daring and valor in combat.

Anthony Wayne was born at Waynesboro, Pennsylvania. He was trained to be a surveyor. His father owned a prosperous leather tannery, which Wayne managed after his father died.

When the Revolutionary War began, Wayne became a colonel in the Continental Army. He fought in a battle at Three Rivers in Canada. He was a brigadier general in the battles of Brandywine, Germantown, and Stony Point. His leadership in

▲*"Mad" Anthony Wayne and his officers talk with defeated Indian leaders near Greenville. The discussions resulted in the Treaty of Greenville in 1795.*

the battle of Stony Point won him a medal from Congress. Wayne was at Valley Forge with George Washington. He also defeated the British in Georgia.

After the war, Wayne retired from the army. In 1783, he was given a plantation in Georgia, but he could not make a success of it. He represented Pennsylvania in Congress in 1791.

In 1791, President Washington appointed Wayne major general in command of troops on the old northwest frontier. This land was east of the Mississippi River, north of the Ohio River, and west of Pennsylvania. Other generals had already tried to defeat the Indians tribes of the Wabash and Maumee Rivers. They had failed. Wayne used careful military planning and strategy and trained his troops well before he sent them into combat. On August 20, 1794, he met and defeated a confederation of Shawnee, Ottawa, Chippewa, and Potawatomi Indians in the Battle of Fallen Timbers in the Ohio territory. This battle, followed by the Treaty of Greenville, brought peace to the Ohio territory and opened it to white settlement.

ALSO READ: AMERICAN REVOLUTION.

WEAPONS Our earliest ancestors, wandering across the plains of Africa, must have looked very weak and defenseless. All around were animals with "natural weapons," such as great teeth, claws, or tusks. Other animals could run very fast to escape from their enemies or climb up to the highest branches of a tree. Man, in comparison, was a tiny creature with weak hands and small teeth, who could seldom outrun his enemies. But he had a better brain than any of the other animals, and he survived because he was able to make weapons. From the beginning these weapons were as important to man as claws to a tiger or speed to a gazelle. In the course of a few thousand years, man's weapons have developed from the battle-ax to the hydrogen bomb. Weapons used to attack an enemy have become known as *offensive* weapons. Those used to ward off an enemy or destroy his weapons are called *defensive* weapons.

The Stone Age hunters quickly learned that they could throw a weapon much farther if they fastened it to the end of a long wooden shaft, to make a spear. They also invented the bow, which could hurl a weapon farther than a man could throw. The early hunters used their weapons mainly to kill animals for food and to defend their territory against other bands of hunters. After the first farmers learned how to domesticate (tame) animals, weapons were used more and more against other people, to defend or seize territory. People began to build *fortifications,* or walls, around their settlements. *Siege* weapons, such as battering rams and catapults, were developed for attacking, or *besieging,* fortifications. Defenders on the walls often hurled down rocks or poured boiling oil onto the attackers. The

◀*The bow and arrow was one of man's earliest weapons. This figure of a Greek soldier* (left) *was made over 2,500 years ago. Big guns* (right) *that fire shells capable of hitting distant targets are among the weapons used in modern warfare.*

invention of metal working, first in copper and bronze, and then in iron, meant that much sharper and stronger weapons could be made. A deadly weapon called the *crossbow* was also invented. The crossbow was heavier than a hunting bow and fired an arrow with great force and accuracy.

The invention of gunpowder brought about great changes in the history of weapons and warfare. Guns were first used in Europe in the 1300s. They rapidly became the major weapons of war. In the late 1700s an American manufacturer, Eli Whitney, invented the method of "interchangeable parts," which meant that guns could be mass-produced.

By the time of World War I (1914–1918), new types of explosives, made with chemicals, had been invented. Chemical explosives were used in new weapons, such as bombs, mines, hand grenades, and torpedoes. Special types of vehicles were designed to carry weapons. These included bomber airplanes, battleships, armored tanks, and submarines. During World War II (1939-1945), scientists developed the first atomic bombs (A-bombs). An even more deadly weapon, the thermonuclear or hydrogen bomb (H-bomb) has since been invented. Warfare is no longer limited to hand-to-hand fighting on the battlefield. Soldiers using modern weapons are often miles away from one another. Rockets carrying nuclear missiles can be fired at targets thousands of miles away and guided by remote control.

ALSO READ: AIR FORCE; ARMOR; ARMY; BOW AND ARROW; EXPLOSIVES; FORTIFICATIONS; GUNS AND RIFLES; NAVY; ROCKET; SUBMARINE; SWORDS AND KNIVES; TANK; WAR; WHITNEY, ELI.

▼*The weasel has a long, slim body and sharp teeth.*

WEASEL The weasel is a small, meat-eating mammal. It lives in parts of Europe, Asia, and the Americas. In Europe, these animals are called stoats. The weasel has a slender body from six inches to two feet long, and short legs.

Weasels are very fast, active animals. They kill by biting

their prey at the base of the skull. Weasels are fierce fighters and have been known to kill animals many times larger than themselves. Their food usually consists of small mammals, such as rabbits and mice. Weasels are helpful because they eat rodents that attack many crops.

A weasel has soft underfur with stiff, shiny guard hairs. The fur is usually reddish brown on its back and head, and white on its belly, throat, and feet.

Weasels that live in cold regions turn white when winter comes. Their white fur serves as protective coloring in the snow. One species that has white fur in the winter is called the *ermine.* People hunt the ermine for its beautiful fur.

▲*The badger, a member of the weasel family, has powerful claws with which it can dig a burrow very quickly.*

Weasels nest in rocks, trees, or in burrows in the ground. The female may have as many as five to ten young in one litter. Young weasels are able to hunt when they are about eight weeks old.

Minks, martens, ferrets, and polecats are closely related to weasels and are similar in appearance and behavior. Badgers, wolverines, and skunks are also related to weasels but are less similar. Badgers have heavy bodies, thick skin, short legs, and short tails. They have strong front claws and use them to dig elaborate, comfortable burrows. Badgers sleep in their burrows during the day and hunt at night. Wolverines are larger and darker than badgers. A large wolverine weighs about 50 pounds and a badger about 25 pounds. Both animals are very strong for their size and are almost fearless.

Skunks are small, gentle animals with attractive black and white coats. The skunk is noted for the foul-smelling liquid produced by scent glands under its tail. If a skunk is threatened, it first stamps its feet and lifts its tail. If the enemy does not back off, the skunk turns and sprays.

ALSO READ: MAMMAL, PROTECTIVE COLORING.

WEATHER Weather is the condition of the air above a particular place on Earth at a particular time. It varies from place to place and from time to time. Climate is the weather pattern at a particular place over a long period of time. If it rains tomorrow, that affects the weather, but not the climate.

Weather is essentially a product of sunlight, air, and water. The sunlight heats the Earth, the water wets the Earth, and the air moves the heat and water around.

The Sun

The sun shines for a few hours every day on most places on Earth. The Earth receives heat and light from the sun. The amount of heat and light each place receives depends on the angle of the sun's rays and how long the sun shines. The equator becomes very hot because the sun's rays hit it directly. The

North Pole is always cold, because even when the sun's rays strike the pole, they strike it at an angle.

With two pieces of black paper you can test the effect of the angle of the sun's rays. Place one piece of paper in direct sunlight, and one so that the sun's rays hit it at an angle. Which of the two pieces becomes hotter when left in sunlight for a period of time? What causes this result?

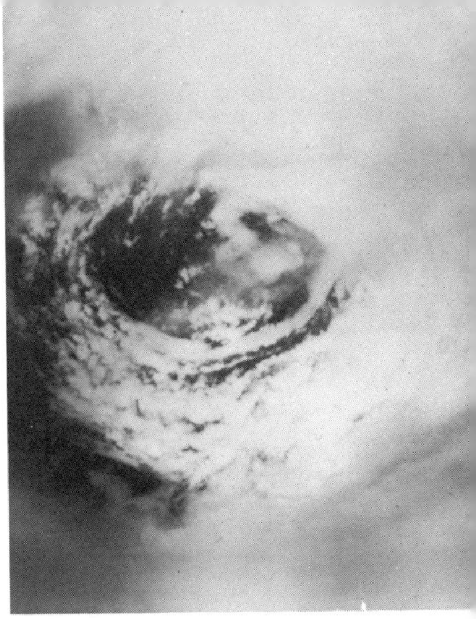

▲*A picture of the eye of Hurricane Betsy taken on September 2, 1965, from a U.S. Air Force plane flying high above this destructive storm.*

Air

The air around the Earth is constantly moving. The movement of the air is caused primarily by heat. When air becomes warmer, it expands. The molecules move farther apart, the air becomes lighter, and the air pressure falls. When air becomes cooler, the molecules move closer together, the air becomes heavier, and the air pressure rises. The light, warm air rises, and the heavy, cool air falls. When warm air rises from a place, cool air moves in. This movement of warm and cool air is *wind.* Winds usually blow from cool places to warm places.

Wind results whenever one place on Earth becomes hotter than another. Sea breezes usually blow in from the ocean during the day because the land is hotter than the water. Land absorbs heat more quickly than water and gives it off more quickly. So, during the day, the air above the land heats up more than the air above the water. The warm land air rises and the cool sea air blows in. In the nighttime the land cools off more quickly than the water, so a breeze blows from the land out to sea.

These air movements also occur on a large scale. The equator receives much more heat than the poles. As the warm air above the equator rises, the cool air from the poles moves toward the equator. The path of these large-scale air movements is affected by the rotation of the Earth. The rotation causes winds in the Northern Hemisphere to bend to the right and winds in the Southern Hemisphere to bend to the left.

▼*Sailors release a weather balloon from the deck of a ship. The instruments hang below the balloon.*

The air rising from the equator begins to sink back toward the Earth at about 30 degrees latitude. Part of this sinking air mass moves back towards the equator. Another part continues toward the poles. The Earth's rotation bends the path of the air mass moves back toward the equator. Another part continues These winds blow almost constantly from below 30 degrees latitude to near the equator. In the Northern Hemisphere the trade winds blow from the northeast, and in the Southern Hemisphere they blow from the southeast. The path of the air mass that continues moving towards the poles is also bent by the Earth's rotation. This air mass forms the prevailing winds called *westerlies.* In the Northern Hemisphere the westerlies blow from the southwest. In the Southern Hemisphere they blow from the northwest.

Water

Three-fourths of the Earth's surface is covered with water. This water is in constant motion. Water from the oceans evaporates to form water vapor in the air. The water vapor collects to form clouds. The wind blows the clouds around. Some of the clouds dump their water on the land. The water soaks into the land, or runs through streams and rivers to the ocean. Some of the water that has soaked into the land is taken up by plants. The plants give off water vapor that collects with water that has evaporated from streets and ground pools to form new clouds. These clouds are blown around by the wind until they drop their water back onto the land or into the ocean. The process continues.

Weather Patterns

The movement of heat, air, and water across the Earth's surface produces certain characteristic weather patterns.

Near the equator the air is always warm and is therefore always rising. At about 30 degrees latitude, the warm air that rose from the equator begins to sink back to Earth. So at this latitude the air is always falling. These two areas have very calm weather. The area around the equator, called the *doldrums,* has calm, wet weather because of all the water vapor condensing from the rising warm air. The area around 30 degrees latitude has calm, dry weather. This area is called the *horse latitudes,* supposedly because so many horses died there on sailing ships stranded by the lack of wind.

The temperate zones of the Earth are the areas between 23½ degrees latitude and 66½ degrees latitude, north or south. The weather in these areas ordinarily forms at the *polar fronts*—the lines where the prevailing westerlies collide with the cold air moving from the poles. These air masses move alongside each other for a while. But then the cold air mass begins to cut under the side of the warm air mass. This movement of the cold air forms a *cold front.* At the same time the front edge of

▼*The Nimbus weather satellite* (below) *takes pictures of the Earth's cloud cover. Its automatic picture transmission system sends the pictures back to Earth where they are printed out on maps* (right).

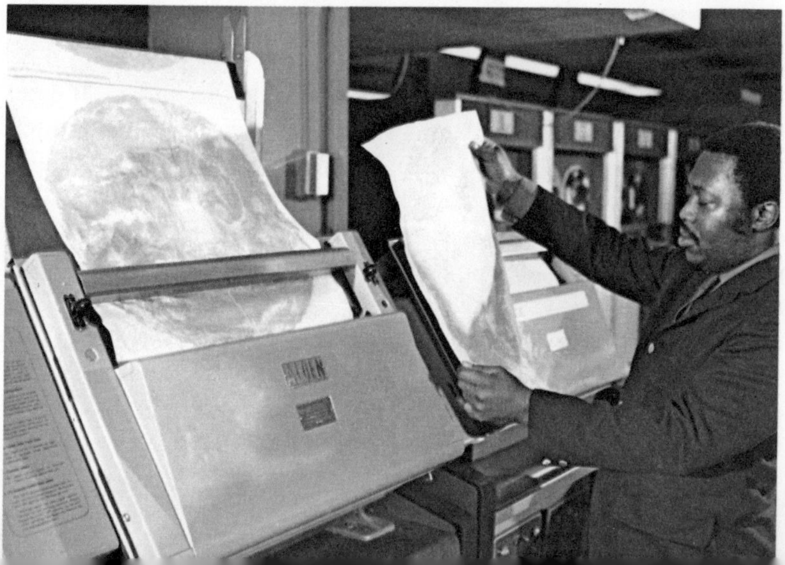

the warm air mass rises over the cold air, forming a *warm front.*

This movement of the warm and cold fronts forms a *cyclone,* a circular movement of air around a low pressure area. In the Northern Hemisphere cyclones move counter-clockwise, and in the Southern Hemisphere they move clockwise.

Air also moves around high pressure areas. This movement is called an *anti-cyclone.* In the Northern Hemisphere anti-cyclones move clockwise. In the Southern Hemisphere they move counter-clockwise.

Cyclones and anti-cyclones result from the effects of large-scale air movements between high and low pressure areas, and the effect of the Earth's rotation, called the *Coriolis effect.* Air tends to move from high pressure areas to low pressure areas, and the Earth's rotation causes the air to move in curves rather than straight lines.

In a low pressure area the wind blows towards the center and the air rises, forming clouds and rain. The weather can change suddenly and unpredictably. In a high pressure area the weather is usually calm, with light winds and little rain.

▼The greatest wind velocity ever recorded anywhere in the world—231 miles an hour—was registered at this U.S. Weather Bureau station on top of Mount Washington in New Hampshire in 1931.

Local Conditions

Even with the same large-scale air movements, different places can have different weather because of local conditions. Mountains, forests, and large bodies of water can affect the weather.

Air masses moving in from the ocean carry a great deal of water vapor. In order to pass over mountains, the air masses have to rise. If the mountains are high enough, the rising air becomes so cool that its load of water vapor condenses to form clouds and rain. The rain falls on the ocean side of the mountains. The wind that passes over the mountains has given off all its moisture and is dry, so the land on the other side of the mountains receives little rain. This is why the western part of the state of Washington is wetter than the eastern part.

Plants hold heat and release it gradually. Because of the lack of plant growth, deserts absorb heat rapidly and give it off rapidly. They cool off very quickly at night. Forested areas have more even temperatures.

Meteorology

Meteorology is the study of the atmosphere and of weather. Meteorologists use various instruments to study and forecast the weather. A *barometer* is used to measure the air pressure, a *hygrometer* to measure the humidity (amount of moisture in the air), a *wind vane* to measure wind direction, and an *anemometer* to measure wind speed. A *radiosonde* carried aloft by a balloon measures the weather conditions at high altitudes. Today, weather satellites orbit the Earth, sending back pictures of clouds and weather disturbances across the Earth's surface.

To know what the weather is going to be like in one place, a meteorologist must have weather reports from many different places. The United States Weather Bureau receives reports from every major station every hour. Smaller stations report every three to six hours. These reports are combined on large charts and maps that show weather conditions at high altitudes. Meteorologists at individual stations can use this information in an effort to forecast the weather in their particular areas.

For further information on:

Climate, *see* ARCTIC, AUTUMN, CLIMATE, DESERT, GULF STREAM, JUNGLE, LATITUDE AND LONGITUDE, SEASON, SPRING, SUMMER, TUNDRA, WINTER.

Meteorology, *see* ATMOSPHERE, BAROMETER, EARTH, PHYSICS, SATELLITE, SCIENCE, SPACE RESEARCH, TEMPERATURE SCALE.

Weather Conditions, *see* AURORA, CLOUD, DROUGHT, FLOOD, FOG, FROST, HAIL, HURRICANE, LIGHTNING AND THUNDER, MONSOON, RAIN AND SNOW, TORNADO, WIND.

Weather Features, *see* AIR, AIR PRESSURE, HEAT AND COLD, HUMIDITY, LIGHT, SKY, SUN, WATER CYCLE.

WEAVING see SPINNING AND WEAVING.

▲*Daniel Webster, American statesman.*

WEBSTER, DANIEL (1782–1852) Daniel Webster was a great American statesman who served his country as a U.S. senator and as secretary of state during the first half of the 1800s. He was a fine public speaker whose speeches helped hold the Union together before the Civil War.

Webster was born in Salisbury, New Hampshire, on January 18, 1782. He was educated at Dartmouth College and became a lawyer. A member of the Federalist Party, he was elected to Congress in 1812. In 1816, he moved to Boston, Massachusetts, and was appointed to the U.S. Senate in 1827.

In speaking in the Senate and in arguing cases before the Supreme Court, Webster spoke eloquently for a strong Constitution and strong national government. He had an impressive physical appearance with massive body, large head, and piercing eyes, in addition to his fine speaking voice.

John C. Calhoun and other Southerners said that state governments had the right to nullify federal laws. In a debate with Senator Robert Y. Hayne of South Carolina in 1830, Webster attacked this idea. The words, "Liberty *and* Union, now and forever, one and inseparable," are often quoted from his speech.

"The Devil and Daniel Webster" is a story by Stephen Vincent Benet. The story tells how Daniel Webster was such a clever speaker and lawyer that he saved a man's soul from the Devil.

In 1840, Webster became secretary of state under President William Henry Harrison. He completed the agreement with Great Britain known as the Webster-Ashburton Treaty (1842), which settled the northeast boundary dispute between the U.S. and Canada. He returned to the Senate in 1845 and in a famous speech supported the Compromise of 1850. Webster's argument for conciliation and compromise between the North and the

South probably put off the Civil War for ten years. In 1850, he became secretary of state under Millard Fillmore.

Webster wanted the Whig nomination for the Presidency in 1852, but he did not receive it. He died on October 24 of that year at his home in Marshfield, Massachusetts.

ALSO READ: CALHOUN, JOHN C.; FILLMORE, MILLARD.

▲*Noah Webster, who compiled the first American dictionary.*

WEBSTER, NOAH (1758–1843) Noah Webster was an American educator and writer. He wrote the first American dictionary, which became known as "Webster's Dictionary." Besides the usual English words, it included some words which had come into use in the U.S. from American Indian languages, from African tongues, and from several European countries.

Webster was born in West Hartford, Connecticut. He was educated at Yale College and later studied law. He supported himself while a student by teaching school. Webster found that few American textbooks were being used in the schools. The American people had only recently won their independence, and teachers were still using British books. Webster wrote three textbooks using American words and stories. The most successful of these was Webster's *Elementary Spelling Book,* which was used for many years in the United States.

Webster practiced law for several years, and later worked as editor of two newspapers. He was knowledgeable about many subjects, including science, medicine, and history. Webster published his first dictionary in 1806, after working on it for three years. He then made a more detailed study of the English language and traveled to England and France to consult other scholars. In 1828, he published his greatest work, *An American Dictionary of the English Language.* This dictionary established set forms of spelling and pronunciation in the United States. It included words that were particularly American. Webster's dictionary has since been revised many times.

ALSO READ: DICTIONARY.

WEDDING CUSTOMS see MARRIAGE.

▼*Edward H. White, the first astronaut to walk in space, floats in a state of weightlessness outside his Gemini 4 spacecraft.*

WEIGHT Every object pulls every other object towards it, even two pencils at rest on a desk. This pull is called the gravitational force. The size of the gravitational force depends on two things—the mass (quantity of matter) of each object, and the distance between the two objects.

Unless an object is unusually massive, its gravitational pull is not very large. Only the Earth itself, and no object on it, is massive enough to have a noticeable gravitational pull. The gravitational pull of the Earth on an object is called the object's *weight.*

The weight of an object can change in three ways. If the object gains mass it becomes heavier, and if it loses mass it be-

▲*A weightlifter hoisting heavy barbell weights. He must stand upright, and his arms must be fully extended when he completes the lift.*

comes lighter. If the object moves closer to the center of the Earth it becomes heavier, and if it moves away from the Earth it becomes lighter. If an object is moved from the Earth to a more massive planet, such as Saturn or Jupiter, it becomes heavier. If it is moved to a less massive planet, such as Venus or Mercury, it becomes lighter. But in all cases the *mass* remains the same.

In outer space, far enough from other objects so that their gravitational pull is very slight, an object becomes almost weightless. Astronauts traveling from Earth to moon experience this weightlessness. As they near the moon, the gravitational pull on the moon affects them, and they become weighty again. The moon is less massive than the Earth, so the astronauts never become as heavy as they were on Earth.

ALSO READ: GRAVITY AND GRAVITATION, MATTER.

WEIGHTLIFTING Weightlifting is a sport in which men, and sometimes women, lift heavy weights according to certain rules. Many people lift weights for exercise. Serious weightlifters compete in contests to see who can lift the heaviest weights. Weightlifting has been an Olympic sport since 1920.

The standard equipment for weightlifting is a *barbell* and *weights.* A barbell is a straight steel rod, and a weight is a metal disk with a hole through the center. Weights of different sizes are slipped onto the barbell and attached with clamps. A *dumbbell* is a short metal bar with a weight permanently attached at each end. Dumbbells are used for exercise but not in competition. For competition, weightlifters are divided into seven classes based on their body weights. The winner of a competition is the lifter who has the highest total of weights lifted for three differents kinds of lifts.

ALSO READ: EXERCISE, MUSCLE, SPORTS.

WELLINGTON, DUKE OF (1769–1852) Arthur Wellesley, first duke of Wellington, was one of Britain's greatest military generals. He is best remembered for his victory over the French emperor Napoleon at the Battle of Waterloo in 1815.

▼*The Duke of Wellington, British soldier and prime minister.*

Arthur Wellesley was born in Dublin, Ireland. He was sent to school in England and later attended a military academy in France. At the age of 18, he became an officer in the British army. From 1796 to 1805, Wellesley served in India, where he defeated several local princes and was made a general. On his return from India, he found that Napoleon had conquered much of Europe and was threatening to invade England. In 1808, Wellesley was sent with an army to attack Napoleon's forces in Spain and Portugal. By 1814, the British had driven the French out of these regions. As a reward for this victory, Wellesley was made duke of Wellington.

In 1815, Napoleon escaped from the island of Elba, where he

had been imprisoned, and raised another army. Wellington was put in command of the British and Dutch armies in Belgium. With the help of a Prussian (German) army under General Gebhard von Blücher, Wellington finally defeated Napoleon at Waterloo. Wellington served as prime minister of Britain from 1828 to 1830. He was later made commander in chief of the British army for the rest of his life.

ALSO READ: NAPOLEON BONAPARTE, WATERLOO.

▼*H. G. Wells, English author and historian.*

WELLS, H. G. (1866–1946) Herbert George Wells was a British writer of science fiction and history. He was born in Bromley, England, and studied science at the University of London. Wells taught school for several years before becoming a writer.

Wells is probably best known for his science fiction novels, many of which have been made into motion pictures. His book *The Time Machine* is about a scientist who invents a marvelous machine that takes him into the future. *The War of the Worlds* is a frightening story of an attack on Earth by Martians, creatures from the planet Mars.

Wells's scientific studies helped him to write about many ideas and inventions not known in his day. Wells also wrote a popular historical book, *The Outline of History,* which many people consider to be his greatest work. With his son Geoffrey and British biologist Julian Huxley, Wells wrote a book on biology, *The Science of Life.*

ALSO READ: SCIENCE FICTION.

WELLS AND SPRINGS A hole dug for the purpose of finding water is a well. In some places, water flows freely from a small opening in the earth. This natural flow of water is called a spring.

The water that flows from wells and springs comes from the ground water held beneath the Earth's surface. Rainwater soaks into the ground and sinks until it hits rock. If the rock is cracked, the water will continue to sink until it reaches a level where the rock is unbroken. If the rock is *porous*—has many small holes in it, like sandstone—water will sink through these holes until it reaches a layer of rock that is not porous. The non-porous layer holds the water in an area called the *saturated zone.* The upper level of water in the saturated zone is called the *water table.* In order to provide water, a well must be dug down to the water table.

The distance from the Earth's surface down to the water table depends not only on how deep the non-porous layer of rock is, but also on the height of the water table. After heavy rains or after snow melts in the spring, there will be more ground water, and the water table will be higher. In dry periods, the water table will be lower, or it will disappear altogether, because no

▼*This farm pond, which is spring-fed, is used mainly for irrigation. It also makes an excellent swimming pool.*

▲*An old well in the Italian countryside still supplies water.*

water is soaking into the ground. When the water table gets too low, the well runs dry.

In some places, a layer of porous rock is sandwiched between two layers of non-porous rock. If these layers of rock follow the shape of a hill, then there are two water tables. One is on top of the upper non-porous layer, the other is between the two non-porous layers. If you dig a well through the upper layer and into the sandwiched porous layer, water will flow out of the top of the well. If the rainwater enters the porous layer near the top of a high hill, and if the well is dug at the bottom of the hill, the water may shoot from the well high into the air. The weight of the water flowing downhill produces the pressure that makes the water shoot out. This kind of well is an *artesian well.*

A *hot spring* is usually formed when water is heated by rocks deep in the earth. If the water becomes hot enough, it boils and forms steam, and the water can shoot into the air. This is called a *geyser.* One such geyser is Old Faithful, in Yellowstone National Park.

A river cutting a valley may cut through a water table and the non-porous rock beneath it. The part of the water table left behind is called a *perched water table.* Rainwater flows down to the non-porous layer of rock, and then it flows sideways to where the river cuts through the rock layers. The water then flows out of the side of the valley to form a spring. Springs may dry up during periods of little rain.

Wells can be drilled, dug, or driven, depending on the soil and rock and the height of the water table. The bottom of the well, below the water table, is lined with porous material so the water can seep through. The upper part of the well is lined with non-porous material to keep out soil and surface water that might be contaminated.

ALSO READ: GEYSER, WATER, WATER SUPPLY.

WEREWOLF see ANIMALS OF MYTH AND LEGEND.

▼*John Wesley spent three years in Georgia. He is shown preaching to a group of Indians there.*

WESLEY, JOHN AND CHARLES The Wesley brothers were British religious leaders. John Wesley (1703–1791) was the founder of the Methodist Church, one of the largest Protestant churches. Charles (1707–1788) is best known for his hymns. The Wesleys were the sons of Samuel Wesley, a minister of the Church of England.

The brothers were born in Lincolnshire, England, and attended Oxford University. While at Oxford, Charles Wesley and some of his friends formed a religious society called the Holy Club. John returned to Oxford to teach in 1729 and became a member of the club. Its members studied the Bible and did good works. They practiced religion in such an orderly and methodical way that other students mocked them, calling them "Methodists."

In 1738, within a few days of one another, the Wesley brothers had religious "awakenings" that changed their lives. They both became *evangelists,* or traveling preachers. Charles's hymns include "Jesus, Lover of My Soul," and the popular Christmas carol "Hark, the Herald Angels Sing." John Wesley traveled widely throughout England, Ireland, and Scotland, riding on horseback over 5,000 miles a year. He taught that man can be saved through faith in Jesus Christ. Wesley formed many Methodist societies in the places he visited. He did not intend to start a new church. He wanted to renew people's interest in the Church of England. But the Church opposed Wesley's emotional way of preaching. The Methodists began to train their own preachers and gradually formed their own church.

▲*Charles Wesley, one of the founders of the Methodist Church.*

ALSO READ: EVANGELIST, PROTESTANT CHURCHES.

WEST GERMANY see GERMANY.

WEST INDIES The West Indies are a long chain of islands stretching about 2,000 miles from Mexico and Florida to South America. The islands separate the Atlantic Ocean from the Caribbean Sea and extend a little into the Gulf of Mexico. Their total land area is about 91,000 square miles, the size of Oregon, but their population approaches 30 million people.

When Columbus discovered the Americas in 1492, he came first to the West Indies. He thought he had found islands just east of India, so he called them the Indies Islands. They were later referred to as the West Indies to distinguish them from the East Indies, which lie between Asia and Australia.

Early mapmakers often marked on maps imaginary islands called Antilia. Some people thought the new islands found by Columbus might be Antilia, so they named them the Antilles. Today, they are called both the West Indies and the Antilles.

The "Greater" Antilles are the four large westernmost islands of the West Indies–Cuba, Jamaica, Hispaniola (shared by Haiti and the Dominican Republic), and Puerto Rico. The "Lesser"

▼*The island of St. Thomas in the Virgin Islands is surrounded by water for swimming, but drinking water is scarce. The white square on the hill in the background is covered with concrete. Rainwater, flowing down the smooth surface of the concrete, is collected at the bottom of the hill.*

WEST INDIES NATIONS

Barbados

Capital: Bridgetown
Population: 254,000
Area: 166 square miles

Dominican Republic

Capital: Santo Domingo
Population: 4,174,000
Area: 19,129 square miles

Haiti

Capital: Port-au-Prince
Population: 4,768,000
Area: 10,714 square miles

Jamaica

Capital: Kingston
Population: 1,959,000
Area: 4,411 square miles

Trinidad and Tobago

Capital: Port-of-Spain
Population: 1,040,000
Area: 1,864 square miles

See also the articles on CUBA and PUERTO RICO.

Antilles are the smaller islands curving south from Puerto Rico. They are sometimes divided into the Leeward Islands and the Windward Islands. The French and the Dutch share one of the Leeward Islands, which the French call St. Martin and the Dutch call St. Maarten.

Alexander Hamilton, an American statesman, was born on the island of Nevis in the West Indies. He worked while a young boy in the town of Christiansted, on St. Croix in the Virgin Islands.

Northeast of the Windward Islands are the Leeward Islands. "Leeward" means away from the wind. The Netherlands Antilles are Dutch islands just north of Venezuela in the southern Caribbean, where huge refineries process most of Venezuela's oil. Curaçao, Aruba, and Bonaire are the largest Dutch islands. Willemstad is the capital of the Netherlands Antilles.

The Bahamas are a scattering of islands between Florida and Hispaniola. Much farther north, and not really a part of the West Indies, are the islands of Bermuda.

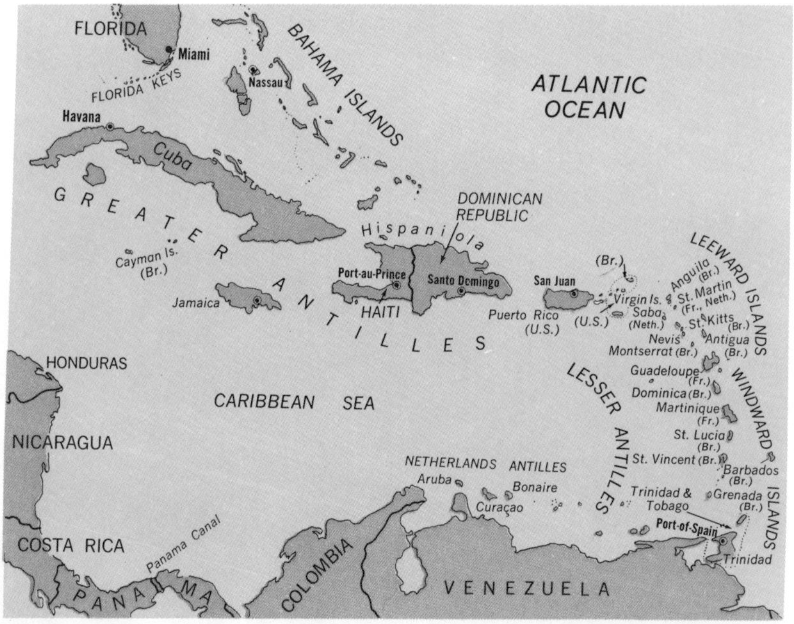

▲*Boys dressed as "tin men" parade down a city street in St. Thomas, one of the Virgin Islands in the West Indies.*

Climate and Resources

The West Indies are in the hot tropics. But because they are surrounded by the sea, the ocean breezes help to cool them. Hurricanes often occur between July and October.

The crops best suited to these islands are sugar, tropical fruits such as bananas and oranges, tobacco, cacao for chocolate, coffee, cotton, and sisal for rope. Offshore fishing is a common occupation. Textile mills, furniture making, and handicrafts provide some employment. Industry has grown in Puerto Rico because of tax benefits given to manufacturers and the development of electric power.

The islands are not rich in minerals but there is nickel in Cuba, bauxite for aluminum in Jamaica, and oil and natural asphalt in Trinidad. Tourism is an important industry in many of the islands. Airplanes bring in thousands of visitors from the chilly parts of North America during the winter months. In general, however, the West Indies are poor. Wages are low and luxuries few. Without major industries or large farms there cannot be the profits and savings of mass production. Unemployment is widespread.

The People

Most West Indians are black or of mixed ancestry, the descendants of Negro slaves brought over from Africa in earlier days to work on the plantations and in the mines. Cuba, Puerto Rico, and the Dominican Republic have a high proportion of people of European descent. Many people in Trinidad are descendants of workers brought originally from India.

Virtually no descendants survive of the first inhabitants of the islands, the Arawak and Carib Indians. Their forefathers were almost entirely wiped out by diseases brought by Europeans or mistreatment by early colonizers.

▼*The entrance to the market at Port-au-Prince in Haiti, on the island of Hispaniola in the West Indies.*

Nations of the West Indies

There are now six independent nations in the West Indies. Six islands or groups of islands are "associated" with Britain. Five other groups are British possessions, two are part of the United States, seven of France, and six of the Netherlands.

Haiti occupies the western third of the island of Hispaniola. The name Haiti is an Arawak Indian word meaning "many mountains." Haiti was the first West Indian nation to become independent. In the late 1700s, a daring black named Toussaint l'Ouverture led a revolt of Haitian slaves against the French. He was tricked and captured, but his follower Jean-Jacques Dessalines continued the struggle. At last, in 1804, Haiti declared its independence, the first black republic in the world.

Unfortunately Haitians, as slaves, had never been educated nor had the chance to learn the art of government. After their

▲*A woman balances a basket of bananas on her head while walking with her son in Kingston, the capital of Jamaica, in the eastern West Indies.*

first strong leaders died, the country was plagued by civil war and banditry. United States Marines occupied Haiti from 1915 to 1934 to try to maintain order. In 1957 François Duvalier was elected president. He organized a cruel secret police service called the *Tonton Macoute,* and made himself dictator. When he died in 1971, his young son Jean succeeded him.

The Dominican Republic occupies the other two-thirds of Hispaniola. Columbus's brother Bartholomew founded the capital city of Santo Domingo as early as 1496. The country became independent in 1844. It, too, suffered from political turmoil. When the Dominicans refused an American demand to establish a stable government in 1916, U.S. troops occupied the country and remained until 1924. A military leader named Rafael Trujillo Molina was elected president in 1930 and ruled until he was killed in 1961.

In 1962, a Dominican politician with supposed Communist sympathies, Juan Bosch, was elected president. The following year a small group of military officers seized power. In 1965 a revolt began with the object of putting Bosch back in power. To protect American citizens in the country and to prevent a Communist take-over, the United States sent troops to occupy the country. Later that year, an Inter-American Peace Force replaced U.S. troops. In 1966 Dominicans elected Joaquin Balaguer president, and foreign troops left the country.

Jamaica is an Indian word meaning "island of springs." Now an independent country, Jamaica was a Spanish colony from 1494 until the British captured it in the 1600s. It became a British pirate base and the main slave market of the Caribbean.

Most of the British colonies in the Antilles joined to form a West Indies Federation in 1958. But a union of such scattered islands proved unworkable. Jamaica, Barbados, and Trinidad and Tobago decided to become separate, independent countries in 1962. Kingston, the capital, is Jamaica's only big city. It is also a major Caribbean port.

Jamaican farmers grow sugar, bananas, oranges, and grapefruit. Jamaica produces excellent ginger and most of the world's allspice. The island is a leading source of the aluminum ore called bauxite. But the chief source of income is tourism.

Port Royal in Jamaica was a headquarters city for pirates who raided other cities around the Caribbean Sea or attacked Spanish treasure ships. In 1692, the city was destroyed by an earthquake. Kingston replaced it as the capital.

Barbados, which means "bearded," was named by the Portuguese for the long wisps of fiber hanging from the island's fig trees. It is the most densely populated of the West Indies, with an average of 1,500 people living on each square mile. The most eastern of the West Indies is Barbados.

Trinidad and Tobago are two islands, but one country. Trinidad is best known for its colorful capital, Port-of-Spain, and for a huge lake of liquid asphalt almost two miles around. The calypso (story-telling) music of Trinidad developed from African and Spanish rhythms. The two islands lie near the coast of Venezuela. Tobago, the smaller island, has a neighboring small island known as Bird of Paradise Island. It is the home of these unusual birds.

The Bahamas, off the Florida coast, consist of some 700 islands and more than 2,000 reefs and keys of rock or coral. The Bahamas now have control over their internal affairs and leave to Britain the direction of their foreign relations and defense.

The Associated States of the West Indies are former British colonies now semi-independent. They are Antigua, Dominica, Grenada, St. Lucia, St. Vincent, and St. Christopher-Nevis-Anguilla—three islands also referred to as St. Kitts. Nutmegs, cloves, and cocoa grow on the "spice island" of Grenada. The harbor city of Castries on St. Lucia is one of the most attractive harbors in the islands.

The U.S. Virgin Islands in the lesser Antilles once belonged to Denmark. The United States bought them in 1917 for 25 million dollars. St. Croix, St. Thomas, and St. John are the three main islands. The sunny climate and lovely beaches bring many tourists to the Virgin Islands National Park on St. John and to the other islands. Charlotte Amalie, on St. Thomas, is the capital and chief port of the U.S. Virgin Islands.

Bermuda is a group of some 300 coral islands, of which 20 are inhabited. The coral formed on the peaks of huge underwater mountains that almost reach the surface of the sea. Bermuda is about 800 miles southeast of New York City.

Heavy rainfall helps the growth of trees and flowering plants in Bermuda. Easter lilies are raised for export. The beautiful scenery and beaches and the moderate climate attract thousands of tourists.

Bermuda was discovered by a Spanish sea captain, Juan de Bermudez, but settled by the British. Its parliament dates from 1620. Hamilton is the capital and main port.

Guadeloupe and *Martinique* are French possessions in the West Indies. Guadeloupe consists of two main islands connected by a bridge. A volcanic eruption from Mt. Pelee in 1902 wiped out Martinique's capital city of St. Pierre in minutes. The present capital is Fort-de-France.

ALSO READ: CARIBBEAN SEA, CUBA, PUERTO RICO.

WESTMINSTER ABBEY Westminster Abbey is the national church of the English people. It stands on the banks of the River Thames, in the borough of Westminster, London. The kings and queens of England have been crowned in Westminster Abbey since 1066.

Westminster Abbey was founded in 1050 by King Edward the Confessor. It was called an abbey because earlier churches on the same site had been part of a monastery. The main part of the abbey was built between the 1200s and the 1500s. The

The "steel bands" of Trinidad have unusual drums. Tops are cut off oil drums so that drums of different sizes will have different pitches. Trinidad is noted for the music of the *calypso* singers and the steel band musicians.

▼*A quiet beach along the Caribbean Sea in Trinidad, at the southern tip of the West Indies.*

▲*Westminster Abbey is one of the historic landmarks of London, England.*

church is shaped like a giant cross. The nave, or main hall, is 531 feet long. The southern part of the transept is known as Poet's Corner. Many great British poets are buried there, including Geoffrey Chaucer and Alfred, Lord Tennyson.

At the very eastern end of the nave are several chapels where many of England's monarchs are buried. The burial chapel of King Henry VII is hung with colorful banners. In the chapel of Edward the Confessor stands the ancient coronation chair of the British monarchs. In the center of the nave is the Tomb of the Unknown Soldier of World War I.

ALSO READ: CATHEDRAL, LONDON, RELIGION.

WEST POINT see UNITED STATES SERVICE ACADEMIES.

WEST VIRGINIA Most of West Virginia lies in a vast coal region that stretches from Alabama to Pennsylvania. No other state produces so much coal as does West Virginia.

Coal brings West Virginia hundreds of millions of dollars every year. It also presents problems that are hard to solve. There are two kinds of coal mines in West Virginia. One is the underground mine. The other is the strip mine, or surface mine.

The Land and Climate

The shape of West Virginia might make you think of a strange, thick-bodied animal. Look at the map of the state. The pointed nose is pushed between Pennsylvania and Maryland. One foreleg is between Ohio and Pennsylvania. The other is between Maryland and Virginia. Notice the floppy paw at the end of it.

West Virginia is in the great Appalachian Highland. The eastern part of the state is in the Appalachian Mountains. But most of it is in the western part of the highland, or the Allegheny Plateau. The plateau is made up of long ridges. Westward from the mountains, the ridges become lower.

Because West Virginia is very mountainous, its river valleys are unusually important. All of the state's main roads and railroads follow rivers. The larger rivers are used for water transportation. Towboats pull heavy barges up and down the Kanawha, the Ohio, and other rivers. Most of the level farmland is in the river valleys. Good cropland and good transportation made people want to live and work in the valleys. So most of West Virginia's towns grew up there.

West Virginian weather depends upon how high you are. The climate of Spruce Knob, the highest point, is very different from that of Harpers Ferry, the lowest. In general, West Virginia has hot summers with plenty of rain. The higher parts have less heat and more rain than the lower areas. Winters are rather cold. In the lowlands, however, snow is likely to stay only three or four days before melting. High in the mountains, it may last through most of the winter.

▼*Horseback riders pause near an observation tower in Pipestem State Park, West Virginia.*

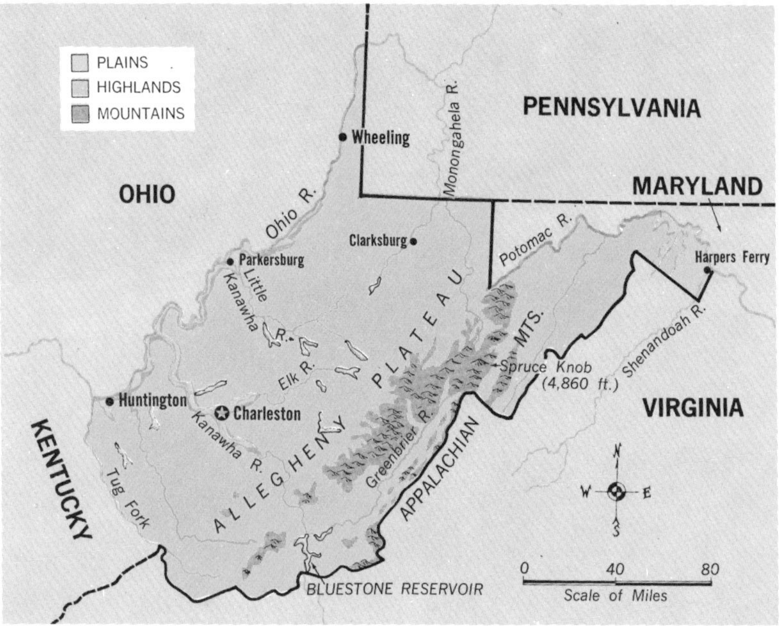

WEST VIRGINIA

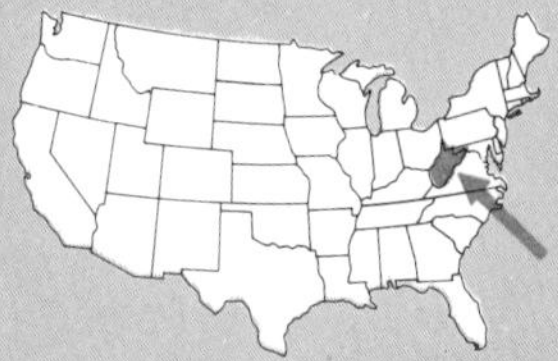

State flower
Great laurel or rhododendron

State bird
Cardinal

State tree
Sugar maple

Capital
Charleston
(71,505 people)

Area
24,181 square miles
(ranks 41st)

Population
1,744,237 people
(ranks 34th)

Statehood
June 20, 1863
(35th state admitted)

Principal river
Kanawha River

Highest point
Spruce Knob, near the eastern border
(4,860 ft.)

Largest city
Huntington
(74,315 people)

History

Not many Indians lived in what is now West Virginia. Some Tuscaroras, Shawnees, and Delawares had villages on the edges of the area. But most Indians came only to hunt and fish in the wooded mountains. Many got salt from salty springs.

West Virginia's written history begins with the coming of Europeans. But until the Civil War, that history is part of Virginia's. West Virginia lay within the boundaries of Virginia. In the 1700s, this section was frontier country. It was settled after 1731 by frontiersmen from Pennsylvania and Maryland.

This northwestern part of Virginia was different from eastern Virginia. The northwestern farms were small. Farming was done by the owner and his family. The large and rich eastern plantations were worked by slaves. Easterners played a bigger part in governing Virginia. In western Virginia, therefore, people were discontented. The Civil War gave such people the chance they wanted. In 1861, Virginia decided to leave the Union. The northwestern counties were strongly against the move. They separated themselves from the rest of the state.

Virginian troops tried to hold West Virginia. Union forces fought on West Virginia's side, and they won. In 1863, West Virginia became the thirty-fifth state. Wheeling was the first capital. Charleston has been the capital since 1885.

West Virginians at Work

Before the Civil War, nearly all the people of northwestern Virginia were farmers. But there were other occupations. Some men took salt from the waters of salty springs. Others mined coal. Some people ran small mills that wove woolen cloth.

▲*A good way to see some of the beautiful countryside of West Virginia is to climb aboard the Ridge Runner Railroad* (left), *a miniature train powered by a steam locomotive. Plays are staged outdoors* (right) *in Grandview State Park, West Virginia.*

But it was hard to carry such products to the east, where most Virginians lived. At first there was only a rough wagon road over the mountains. By the 1850s, goods were moving eastward by rail. At last they could be shipped cheaply and easily.

Today manufacturing is the big industry of West Virginia. The leading manufacture is chemical products. Both salt and coal are used in manufacturing them. Next in importance are iron and steel. West Virginian coal provides fuel for the furnaces. The state is also known for its beautiful glassware and pottery. Mining coal is the state's second-biggest business.

Milk, beef, chickens, and eggs are the main livestock products. Hay and apples are the leading crops.

West Virginia's resources and industry have not made it a rich state. Oil and gas have replaced coal as a fuel in many places, so not so much coal is needed. The region called Appalachia, of which West Virginia is a part, is one of the poorest areas in the nation. Unemployment is a serious problem.

The state is doing its best to improve business. Among other things, it is building up the tourist industry. The state's forested mountains offer pleasant places for recreation. Hunting and fishing are good. One of the historical spots to visit is Harpers Ferry, where John Brown's raid took place in 1859.

ALSO READ: APPALACHIAN MOUNTAINS; BROWN, JOHN; CONFEDERATE STATES OF AMERICA; JACKSON, THOMAS JONATHAN ("STONEWALL"); LEE, ROBERT E.; VIRGINIA.

Radio signals from the outer edge of the universe are received and studied at the National Radio Astronomy Observatory in Green Bank, West Virginia. The world's largest movable radio telescope, with a 300-foot dish, is one of eight telescopes at the observatory.

WESTWARD MOVEMENT In 1775, at the outbreak of the American Revolution, the United States was made up of 13 sparsely populated colonies strung along the eastern seaboard from New England to Georgia. During the next 75 years, thousands of people traveled westward from those colonies, settling areas of wilderness land from the Appalachian Mountains to the Pacific coast. In 1775, Spain and France held most of the territory west of what is now Ohio. French land in the Middle West became part of the United States through the Louisiana Purchase of 1803. Lands in the far West extending to the Pacific Ocean were ceded to the United States through the Treaty of Guadalupe-Hidalgo after the Mexican War. By 1850, the land area of the U.S. was 35 times larger than it had been in 1775.

In the early 1700s, people in the colonies were already venturing westward. Recent immigrants and former indentured servants who had little money settled along the frontier (then at the eastern foothills of the Appalachian Mountains).

Most settlers were totally unprepared for wilderness living. Few had any knowledge of the American Indians, and they did not know how to deal with them. For years, they suffered attacks from wild animals and raids from Indians.

Finally, these backwoodsmen began fighting back against the danger of the wilderness. By 1775, strong leaders were beginning to emerge among the backwoodsmen—people who were not afraid of the frontier and its dangers, but considered it an exciting challenge. These leaders were hunters and trappers who liked the loneliness of the wilderness. They ventured westward into ever more distant areas to seek animals for food and for trade. Others followed to settle the lands these men had explored. These early westward pioneers became known as "frontiersmen." One of the best known was Daniel Boone, who blazed a trail—called the Wilderness Road—through the Cumberland Gap in the Appalachian Mountains.

During the American Revolution, George Rogers Clark, a frontiersman and army general, led the fight against the British to put the Northwest Territory under American control. Indians in the Northwest Territory went on the warpath and in 1789 attacked and burned hundreds of pioneer settlements. These Indian raids were put down by General Anthony Wayne.

▲*Wagon trains formed at Independence, Missouri, for the long journey westward on the Sante Fe Trail. The wagons were repaired here, and supplies for the trip were unloaded from river boats.*

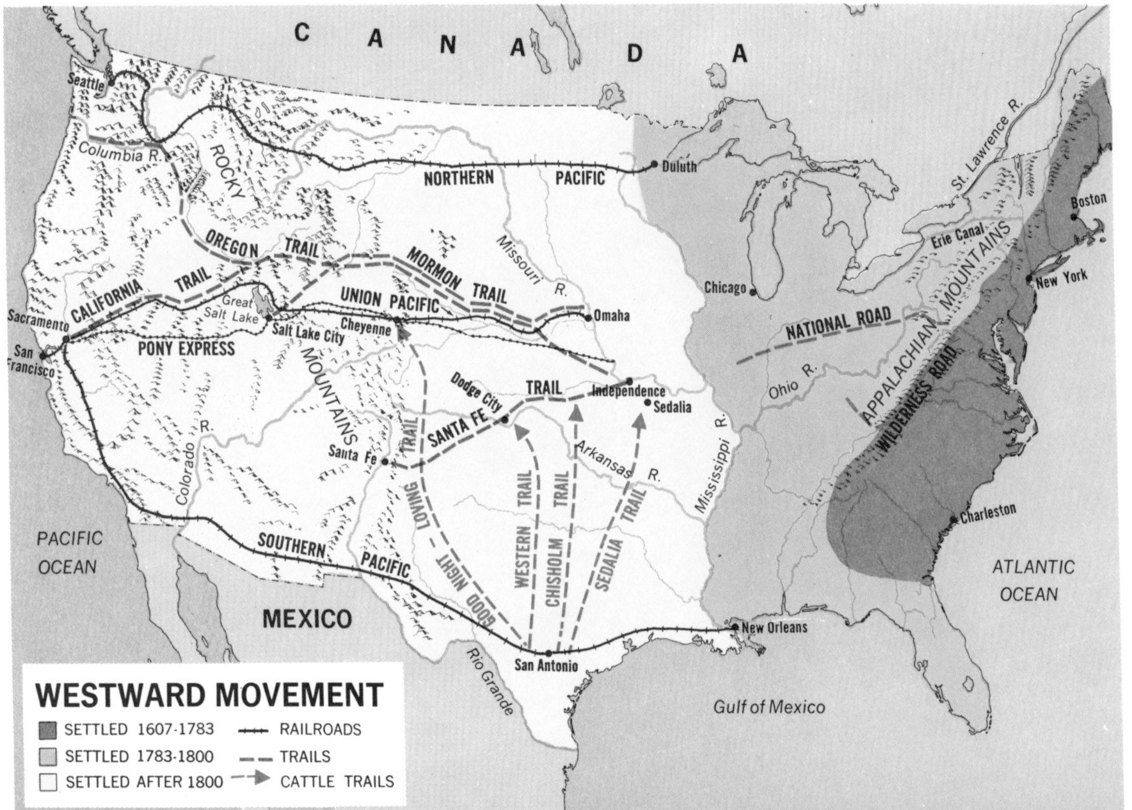

▶*A wagon train is pictured crossing the North Platte River. An encampment for the night is prepared across the river with the wagons parked in a circle as a defense against Indian attacks.*

In 1803, President Thomas Jefferson purchased the Louisiana Territory and the city of New Orleans from France. He assigned Meriwether Lewis and William Clark to explore the Louisiana Territory between the Missouri River and the Pacific Ocean. They returned with tales about great forests, fertile plains, wild animals and birds, rivers, lakes, and giant mountains in the West.

The Far West was a rugged, unknown land. The idea of crossing mountains and deserts to find homes in a dangerous wilderness appealed to men and women who were seeking adventure. Whole families piled their belongings into Conestoga (covered) wagons and began the hard journey westward.

These pioneers often came into conflict with the Indian inhabitants who saw their lands being taken away from them. Foreign powers who owned land on which the pioneers settled tried to prevent their passage. The Spanish in Mexico owned Texas and California and the British claimed Oregon. Americans settled in these areas and later won control of them. The Santa Fe Trail from Missouri to New Mexico opened the West to trade with the Spanish. Texas became independent after a revolt by American settlers against Mexico in 1836. Farmers in the Northwest found the Oregon country to be fertile land, and in the 1840s thousands of people took their covered wagons over the Oregon Trail to settle there. Settlers began crossing the Sierra Nevadas into California in the 1840s. By 1848, the treaty ending the Mexican War added California to U.S. territory.

After the Civil War ended in 1865, thousands of veterans went west where they were given free lands, called *homesteads,* on which to settle. In California, the Central Pacific Railroad Company began laying railroad track toward the East. In Nebraska, The Union Pacific Railroad began laying track westward. On May 10, 1869, the two sets of track were joined together at Promontory Point, Utah.

ALSO READ: AMERICAN HISTORY; APPALACHIAN MOUNTAINS; BADLANDS; BOONE, DANIEL; CLARK, GEORGE ROGERS; CROCKETT, DAVY; FUR TRADER; GOLD RUSH; GREAT LAKES; GREAT PLAINS; INDIANS, AMERICAN; LEWIS AND CLARK EXPEDITION; LOUISIANA PURCHASE; OREGON TRAIL; PIONEER LIFE; SANTA FE TRAIL.